Robert Emmet: The Making of a Legend

Robert Emmet, miniature by John Comerford, commissioned by the Emmet family after Emmet's death and sent to his brother in New York.

Robert Emmet:
The Making of a Legend

Marianne Elliott

P

PROFILE BOOKS

First published in Great Britain in 2003 by
Profile Books Ltd
58A Hatton Garden
London EC1N 8LX
www.profilebooks.co.uk

Typeset in Lapidary 333 by MacGuru
info@macguru.org.uk

Printed and bound in Great Britain by
Clays, Bungay, Suffolk

A CIP catalogue record for this book is available from the British Library.

ISBN 1 86197 643 7

Contents

For Roy Foster

List of illustrations

14 Sarah Curran, by Edward Corballis.

15 'The ordeal of Anne Devlin' by W. C. Miles, from *Weekly Freeman*, 12 December 1903.

16 'Anne Devlin is put to the Test', from 1969 school textbook *The Birth of Modern Ireland* by Margaret MacCurtain and Mark Tierney

17 Robert Emmet, by Edmond Fitzpatrick, *c.*1850s.

18 The execution of Robert Emmet, 20 September 1803, depicted by F. W. Byrne, 1877.

19 The execution of Robert Emmet , from the *Irish Emerald*, 2 December 1899.

20 'Heroines of Irish History, IV: Sarah Curran at Bully's Acre', from the *Irish Fireside* colour supplement, 12 August 1885.

21 Statue of Robert Emmet (St. Stephen's Green, Dublin) by Jerome Connor.

22 'Shade of Robert Emmet: "Not Yet!"', *Dublin Opinion*, its very first cartoon, March 1922.

23 1898 centennial poster.

24 The search for Emmet's grave: St. Michan's, from *J. J. Reynolds, In the Footprints of Emmet*.

25 The search for Emmet's grave: Old Glasnevin, courtesy Belfast Central Library.

26 Portrait of Emmet, by John Mulvany 1897.

27 Robert Emmet on Stage: Brandon Tynan as Robert Emmet, 1902, from *The Irish Patriot* by George Morehead.

28 Robert Emmet on Stage: Terence Burns as Leonard MacNally and Louis Rolston as Robert Emmet in Seamus McKearney's 1957 play, staged in Belfast.

Credits: National Library of Ireland: 1, 2, 3, 4, 5, 6, 8, 9, 10, 11, 12, 13, 14, 17, 18, 19, 21, 23; courtesy Belfast Public Libraries: 7, 8, 25; Whytes Fine Art, Dublin: 15; courtesy of the author: 16, 20, 21, 22, 24, 26, 27, 28.

Acknowledgements

Second only to completion of a major project is the satisfaction of thanking those who have helped along the way. Here my debts are huge. First let me thank the many librarians and archivists who make the task of a professional historian possible. All the libraries and archives cited in the bibliography were staffed with people who could not have been more helpful. Dawn Bowen of the Hampshire Record Office, Gerry Healey of the Linenhall Library, Martin Smith of the Public Record Office of Northern Ireland, Orna Somerville of University College Dublin's Archives, Louise Morgan of the National Gallery of Ireland, Jane Maxwell and Felicity O'Mahony of Trinity College, Dublin, Siobhán O'Rafferty and Petra Schnabel of the Royal Irish Academy and Helen Hall of Liverpool University's library were particularly helpful. In the Folklore Department of University College Dublin, the National Library of Ireland and Belfast Central Library, I received help that went far beyond what I would normally expect. To Séamus Ó Catháin (most of all), Bairbre ní Fhloinn and Daíthí Ó hÓgáin of the Department of Irish Folklore, Sara Smyth, Joanna Finegan, Avice-Claire McGovern, Sandra McDermott and Ciaran McInerney of the National Library of Ireland and Nick Silvester and Darren Topping of Belfast Central Library, I owe more than I can easily repay. Their generosity and expertise lightened many a burden. My sisters, Geraldine Walsh and Eleanor Dent, Helen Kokelarr of Liverpool University and in particular my mother, Sheila (O'Neill) Burns, never complained when asked to help at short notice.

Patrick Long, Christopher Farrington, Catherine O'Donnell and Caoimhe ní Ghormáin gave invaluable research assistance and Gillian O'Brien picked up the pieces on many an occasion with good humour and characteristic judgement and efficiency. Colin Graham, Patrick Geoghegan, Frank Harte, Nicholas Carolan, Norman Vance, Vincent Morley, Tom Bartlett, David Wilson, Don Akenson, Pierre Joannen, Joanna Bourke, Kevin Bean, Ian Kemp, Richard Haslam, James Quinn, Bill Doyle and Brian Walker have all responded to my many questions with generosity. Richard English's expertise and wealth of knowledge were a particular source of inspiration and a regular corrective to my errors. Owen Dudley Edwards, Ian McBride and George Watson read significant sections of the book in manuscript. Christopher Woods was as generous and constructively critical as in the past and patiently read the entire work in draft. I owe a particular debt to them all and can only apologise for any errors that have remained after their scrutiny.

Research was financed throughout by the British Academy and written up during tenure of a British Academy Readership. To it and its ever-patient staff, most notably Dr Ken Edmond, I owe a particular debt. Diane Urquhart, Pat Nugent, Dorothy Lynch, David McGuinness, Ian McKeane and most of all Linda Christiansen, my colleagues at the Institute of Irish Studies of Liverpool University, were endlessly supportive and always generous with their time and ideas, and there are significant sections of the book which could not have been written without the advice and insight of Frank Shovlin.

I owe a considerable debt to the publishing team at Profile Books (Andrew Franklin, Mark Handsley, Penny Daniel, Josine Meijer, Oula Jones, Claire Beaumont), and most of all Jennifer Munka and Ruth Killick, who continued to have faith in me, undeterred by their experience in editing and publicising my last book. I am also grateful to Dáithí O'Ceallaigh and Cormac Kinsella for agreeing so readily to launch the book. For permission to quote from Austin Clarke, I wish to thank his son Professor Aidan Clarke; from Valentin Iremonger, his daughter Dr Susan Iremonger; from Robin Skelton, his daughters Alison Skelton Faulkner and Brigid Skelton; from Denis Johnston, his publisher Colin Smythe; and Professor Eavan Boland for permission to quote her *Object Lessons*, and my thanks to Michael Kinneally and Anne Saddlemyer for advice along the way.

The book is dedicated to Roy Foster for his friendship and support over many years, and it could never have been written without the patience and support of my long-suffering family, my husband Trevor Elliott and my son Marc.

'The man dies, but his memory lives: that mine may not perish, that it may live in the respect of my countrymen'

Robert Emmet at his trial, 19 September 1803

'A nation's history is made for it by circumstances and the irresistible progress of events; but the legends they make for themselves ... they are the kind of history which a nation desires to possess'

Standish O'Grady, History of Ireland. The Heroic Period
(London, 1878), 22.

Introduction

And those who here are laid at rest,
  Oh! hallowed be each name;
Their memories are for ever blest –
  Consigned to endless fame.

Thus did Robert Emmet write of those who had been executed after the 1798 rebellion.[1] Of course, he was wrong; very few attained such apotheosis. But *he* did, and this book traces the process. Robert Emmet (1778–1803) was a young idealist, a university-educated Protestant, a member of the Anglo-Irish elite. However, after leading an unsuccessful rising in 1803, he was tried for high treason, and suffered the penalty: public hanging and beheading. At the end of his trial he delivered an impressive and lengthy vindicatory speech, which became one of the most influential examples of Irish oratory. There was already sufficient here for legend making. But this was a story that was also a tragic romance in reality, for Emmet had been conducting a love affair with the youngest daughter of Ireland's most celebrated barrister, and her early death completed the tale of youth, romance and tragedy. The failed rebellion, and the tragic deaths it had occasioned, was largely ignored in the legend as it developed and the power of the legend would deter any serious analysis of the ideology that it came to underpin.

There has been much written on the emergence of national identities in the nineteenth century, and the processes of 'invention', 'imagination', 'memory', 'forgetfulness' and 'myth-making'.[2] The story of Robert Emmet is neither an invention nor a myth, though it does fall into the selective-memory and historical-error element in the making of a nation, so famously discussed by Ernest Renan over a century ago.[3] It is a legend in its historical origin, its simplicity and its pervasiveness. There are few Irish people who have not heard of him, or for whom the name does not conjure up an image, however garbled. He was the central figure in what later nationalist writings liked to call 'the romantic drama of Irish history'.[4] In this he became the most iconic of Ireland's many national icons, his youthfulness, good breeding, tragic romance, untimely and dramatic end and memorable trial speech forming a narrative of noble victim against the foul oppressor. The sentimental detail is remembered, the uncomfortable forgotten. It is a story entirely of high points, which are told and retold and passed down from parent to child, from teacher to pupil, and simplified in song, verse and picture. The low points, the incongruities and contradictions of reality, would have detracted from it. Thus the *Irish Weekly Independent* for 9 March 1895:

> Year after year as the anniversary of Emmet's birth, or
> that of his sad but glorious death, passes by us, we take
> down the story of his life and wander through its pages,
> until every incident has burned its memory into the mind
> of both young and old Ireland, and the task of mere
> biographical writing has become useless, or, at least,
> unnecessary.

However, icons by definition are static images and there is a plaster-cast quality about Emmet in a legend perpetually recycled. A pamphlet or newspaper article about Emmet from the 1840s or 1860s could be interchanged for those in the 1900s, without the reader noticing much difference. Perhaps this is why his story has been largely overtaken by that of his young housekeeper, Anne Devlin, who has an altogether more earthy quality – although hers too has become a legend, awaiting analysis.

Of course, Emmet's real life lent itself to this process in a way that others did not. Only parts of Theobald Wolfe Tone's life have entered legend, for this was a gregarious and convivial man, and a compulsive talker and writer. He left behind far too much detailed self-analysis to be easily simplified as legend. Emmet, in contrast, was something of a recluse. His writings were few, and recollections of things he had said focus almost exclusively on his formal speeches in a student debating society and that uttered during the drama of his trial. These few high points were perfect for processing as legend. That Robert Emmet acted stoically during his trial and execution is not disputed, nor that he had the talent and intellect to wrest posthumous victory from defeat. However, the holy picture image of Robert Emmet is partly based on fiction and largely on the guilt-induced recollections of other young men who had known him in Dublin as a student of Trinity College. Such sanctification has clouded an understanding of the man's real talents, though these did not extend to military leadership. Thirty years ago, as a postgraduate student in Paris, I came to know a different Robert Emmet through the archives of the Consulate (Napoleon Bonaparte's introduction to political power). From these I built an image of a single-minded negotiator with talents as a military tactician, at least on paper, and a young man who commanded the respect of a number of hardened senior figures in the French government and military command. Then I wrote an account of Emmet that challenged the romantic image of the legend.[5] Now I know that the two are not mutually exclusive. Nor do we necessarily need to jettison the image of the gentle youth as his college companions remembered him.

The ever-perceptive and compassionate Dervla Murphy recalled an incident from her Waterford childhood that has resonances here. Her parents had given shelter to a very young man who befriended her, taught her about endangered wildlife and showed endless patience and good humour – a 'magic sort of person', an intelligent adult who had retained the enthusiasm and wonderment of childhood. But Charles Kerrins was an IRA man on the run. He had killed a Dublin detective and was condemned to be executed by the Irish government in December 1944. He had innocence, selfless dedication, heroism, fanaticism and ruthlessness all rolled into one. And he too laughed at death, as Emmet was said to have done. Robert Emmet, like Kerrins, was zealous and single-minded in his pursuit of armed resistance, even without popular support. Of course, we know so little about Robert Emmet's thinking that this cannot be proved in its entirety. But neither can the pure victim image that has commanded such veneration for so long.

For such a popular hero there is curiously little about Robert Emmet in the rich manuscript sources of the Irish Folklore Commission. This is partly because the guidelines for the collectors, compiled in the 1930s when it was first set up, contain only a brief mention of Emmet, and most of the references in its Schools Collection are recycled from printed accounts or later ballads.[6] Rather the legend of Robert Emmet originated with the educated elite of Dublin: surviving United Irishmen who printed versions of his speech; writers and poets who were graduates of Trinity. His name features regularly in printed works that began to appear almost immediately after his death. By 1825 his reputation with the literate elite was such that a new periodical, *The Dublin and London Magazine*, ran a lengthy and entirely fictional series on him, knowing that the name of Emmet would both sell and establish the new title.[7] These (including the fictional essays) were the sources from which the Emmet legend developed, particularly as they were used by Dr Richard Madden for his influential biography of Emmet, published in 1846, and endlessly serialised thereafter. The expansion of nationalist newspapers and illustrated weeklies in the second half of the nineteenth century did the rest, illustrations in turn further simplifying the image. This was 'booklore' informing folk memory and 'print culture' defining national identity, much as Thomas Carlyle had foreseen.[8] Above all, it was the Romantic movement – on which the manner of Emmet's death exercised a dark fascination, far beyond the confines of Ireland – that produced the texts on which the Emmet legend was based.

I cannot recall when I first encountered the Emmet legend. I do not remember it at school. Indeed, I remember very little Irish history having been taught at my north Belfast schools in the 1950s and 1960s. Rather, I seem to have grown up with the Emmet legend in my home, largely through the songs of Thomas Moore, sung by my father and used in childhood piano lessons. This would have been most Irish people's introduction to the name of Robert Emmet. Moore's songs about Emmet, issued from as early as 1808, are melancholy, wistful and sentimental laments, rather than rousing rebel songs. And so generations of Irish people differentiated the romantic legend from the militant nationalism of the men of violence. In fact the same legend served for both. The Emmet commemorative ceremonies that inspired the generation of the 1916 rising always included Moore's songs in their programmes. By then it was Emmet as the epitome of heroic sacrifice that was being emphasised, but even that had been a part of the romantic legend.

The Emmet legend also gave to Irish nationalism the archetypal 'informer' – a word of utmost infamy in Irish nationalist tradition. This was Leonard MacNally. His role as one of Emmet's defence counsel at his trial and 'friend' in his final hours, was central to the picture of Robert Emmet as victim and gave rise to a belief that Emmet was entrapped into his role as rebel leader. The progression of Emmet from hero to victim to martyr was facilitated by the presence of Leonard MacNally. His notoriety was enhanced by the preservation of his anonymity for so long, his progressive unmasking coinciding with and contributing to the development of the central themes of the legend. He too was part of my childhood lore of heroes and villains, not least because of my actor-father's casting as MacNally, and a home often filled with other actors, all consumed by the story of Robert Emmet in

Seamus McKearney's nationalist play *Robert Emmet*. This reproduced the traditional legend, long after it was being reassessed elsewhere in Ireland. In the north, nationalists have not had the comfort of re-assessing their identity in a way that independence gave to fellow na-tionalists south of the border. In 1911, during a famous battle in the Westminster parliament, the Irish MPs became embroiled in an inter-nal squabble over name calling. 'What ruffian said "McNally?"', screamed one MP. '"McNally", it appeared', remarked George Dan-gerfield, who reported the incident in his classic *The Strange Death of Liberal England*, 'was a name you could not mention among Irishmen'.[9]

This is a book about how one young man who had organised a rebel-lion in 1803, and suffered the consequences, came to be the most popular of Irish historical heroes, at a time when modern national consciousness was taking shape. That he also became the symbol of blood sacrifice and the triumph of failure — at least until Patrick Pearse, himself profoundly influenced by the Emmet legend, replaced him — is also analysed and explained. He had died for Ireland with a smile on his lips. At least that is what all the poems and songs said, and in the very many Irish ballads to appear over the next two cen-turies about 'The Dead Who Died for Ireland',[10] the name of Robert Emmet invariably appeared. Who he actually was and what he actu-ally did no longer mattered. He had been reduced to the most basic of forms, a talisman for nationalist hopes, and *Moore's Melodies* had given way to the simplest of messages in 'Bold Robert Emmet', the most popular of all the media through which Irish people remem-bered Robert Emmet after 1900.

> Bold Robert Emmet, the darling of Erin,
>   Bold Robert Emmet will die with a smile;
> Farewell! companions both loyal and daring,
>   I will lay down my life for the Emerald Isle.

1 Early life and political apprenticeship

The Irish are very unjustly accused of being bad subjects;
but it may be fairly said, they are the worst rebels. The
most remarkable of these men were the family of the
Emmetts, three sons of Dr Emmett, a physician of some
note ... [who] infused into their minds an extravagant
sort of patriotism ... The youngest brother, Robert, was a
very clever man, but devoid of prudence and of
judgement. His objects were quite visionary; yet he was
an honourable enthusiast ... He possessed the powers of
eloquence in a surprising degree.

Memoirs of ... Henry Grattan, by his son Henry Grattan[1]

On 19 April 1798 the fellows and students of Trinity College Dublin
were summoned to appear before the ultimate board of discipline,
presided over by the formidable Lord Chancellor of Ireland, John
Fitzgibbon, Earl of Clare and Vice-Chancellor of the university, and
Dr Patrick Duigenan. They were both arch anti-papists, notwithstanding their Catholic parentage, and were noted for their vicious
rhetoric in the Irish parliament. The Catholic students at Trinity – the
first generation of such, since they were only officially admitted in
1793 – would have been particularly apprehensive. The dining hall
where the visitation took place was completely filled, for expulsion
had been threatened to those who failed to attend, and the visitors
and members of the board took their places on the raised platform
behind iron railings. One of the students takes up the story:

On the day of the visitation we all assembled in the hall. Lord Clare, as vice-chancellor of the university, sat as acting visitor, with Dr. Duigenan as his assessor, on an elevated platform at the end of the dining-hall. Then followed in order the provost, senior and junior fellows, and scholars, as members of the corporation; then the graduate and undergraduate students; and lastly, the inferior officers and porters of the college. The great door was closed with a portentous sound, and shut in many an anxious heart.' [2]

It was the progress of militant republicanism in the college that was the immediate cause of the inquisition. At least four United Irish societies were suspected to be recruiting among the students, two of whom had already been expelled. The Society of United Irishmen, founded in 1791 as an advanced, though constitutional political reform movement, was by the spring of 1798 a revolutionary one, actively seeking French military aid and planning for rebellion. By now government intelligence networks were good and the Lord Chancellor was the main recipient of the highly confidential reports. He knew of the United Irishmen's negotiations with the French government to secure an invasion of Ireland, negotiations initiated by a former Trinity student, Theobald Wolfe Tone. He also knew about intensified preparations for a rebellion in Ireland, with 279,896 armed men reputedly ready to take the field.[3] Only the previous month the main Leinster leaders had been arrested in Dublin, at a meeting that was to have named the date for the rising. A number were Trinity graduates, including Thomas Addis Emmet, whose younger brother Robert was now among the 19 students expelled at the end of the visitation.[4] The political activism of the student body – a thorn in Dublin Castle's side for the past two decades – had been extinguished.

Although even his critics – of whom there were many – credited Fitzgibbon with talent and fair-mindedness in the courts over which he presided, he was vengeful and relentless in his pursuit of those who tried to undermine the two pillars of his political gospel: the connection with England and the Protestant Ascendancy. Renegades from within the golden circle were guaranteed a particularly intense vigilance, bordering on what Fitzgibbon's biographer calls 'childish sadism'.[5] Trinity was the finishing school for those entitled to enter that golden circle and Fitzgibbon made much of this during his visitation. Let those of you who flirt with treason, he warned the assembled students, 'look to the great situations of this country all filled by persons educated here', and reflect on how their prospects would be blasted by expulsion. 'Those who have seen Lord Clare in his visitorial capacity', the anonymous student continued, ' will never forget him – the hatchet sharpness of his countenance, the oblique glance of his eye, which seemed to read what was passing in the mind of him to whom it was directed.'[6]

The first students called were already suspected of being United Irishmen. John Egan and Thomas Robinson had entered College as sizars in 1792 and 1794 respectively. Sizars formed the lowest social category at Trinity. They were bursary students, paying no fees, wearing a gown 'as plain as a parish sexton's' and required to perform certain menial duties. The patronising tone used in his memoirs by a future Deputy Grand Master of the Orange Order in Ireland, William Blacker, is typical of the scorn sizars had to endure, for though by then Egan was a scholar (the coveted scholarship being awarded only to the best students), he was described by Blacker as 'a low vulgar wretch … [who] had been a sizar and probably a Papist'. [7] Blacker had arrived at Trinity from Ulster in October 1795, a foppish country buck, enrolled as a fellow commoner – the second highest category after that of 'nobleman'. As such he would have been entitled to dine at the Fellows' table and wear a gown 'as full of tassels as a livery servant's'. Throughout his life he was noted for ultra-loyalism. He was present at the famous Battle of the Diamond (21 September 1795) that prompted the formation of the Orange Order. It was in his rooms in college that Trinity's first Orange society met in 1796. He tells of mounting conflict between loyalist and republican students thereafter. That summer he was granted a commission to raise a corps of yeomanry in his home county and by October 1797 he counted as many as 400 students in college yeomanry corps.[8]

The only other student remembered by Blacker was the seventeen-year-old future poet, Thomas Moore, whose mother's ambition was to raise her talented son out of the Catholic shopkeeping class via his college education. Moore, as a Catholic of relatively humble circumstances, was particularly intimidated by the proceedings. Like all the other students interrogated, he was called upon to take an oath that would have involved giving information against fellow students. At first he demurred like most of the others. At less than five feet in height, Moore looked younger than his years and the normally terrifying Lord Chancellor showed an almost paternalistic indulgence towards youths such as he. 'The scene was amusing', recalled the student witness. 'The book was presented to him. He shook his head and declined to take it. It was thrust into his right hand. He hastily withdrew the hand, as if he was afraid of its being infected by the touch, and placed it out of the way behind his back. It was then presented to his left hand, which he also withdrew, and held behind his back with his right. Still the persevering book was thrust upon him, and still he refused, bowing and retreating, with his hands behind him, till he was stopped by the wall.' It is an account endorsed by Moore's own recollections of appearing before this 'terrific tribunal'. On the second day the visitors had to accept that few of the students would take such an oath incriminating others, and they were allowed to take one that permitted them to give information 'in a general way, without compromising individuals'.[9]

The same indulgence was not extended to the fellows and Fitzgibbon accused Whitley Stokes of sedition, wrongly as it turned out. Stokes, friend to Tone and several United Irishmen now in prison, had not taken an active part in the United Irish Society since he was admitted a member in 1792, but had continued his friendship with other members. Many students and one of the fellows, Dr Graves, Robert Emmet's tutor, spoke in support of Stokes. This shuffling, forgetful intellectual was not made of revolutionary stuff and exclusion from College emoluments for three years was his punishment for past associations.

However, the evidence against the secretaries of the four United Irish cells in College seemed overwhelming. William Corbet – the nineteen-year-old son of a Co. Cork farmer – along with his elder brother Thomas, defiantly challenged the authority of the visitation and refused to take the oath. Thomas Flinn from Dublin did not appear at all. The fifteen-year-old Cornelius Keogh refused to take the oath, but already was damned because of his parentage. His father, John Keogh, was leader of the Catholic Committee, which had engineered the 1793 Catholic Relief Act forced by London on the furious Irish Ascendancy – not least John Fitzgibbon. And then there was Robert Emmet.

Robert Emmet was born in Dublin on 4 March 1778, the youngest son of Dr Robert Emmet (1729–1802), and his wife Elizabeth Mason (1740–1803). There were three other children, Christopher Temple (b.1761), Thomas Addis (b.1764), and a daughter, Mary Anne (b.1773). But Elizabeth Emmet had had sixteen pregnancies before Robert was born, and there had been four Roberts before him, all of whom died in infancy. The Emmets were a well-established Protestant family from Tipperary, and latterly Cork; the Masons came from Kerry. The couple had moved to Dublin where Dr Emmet became physician and governor of St Patrick's hospital for the insane and later, in 1783, state physician. It was thought some string-pulling had helped him along the way, for, through his mother, Rebecca Temple, he was related to George Nugent Temple Grenville, 1st Marquis of Buckingham (Lord Lieutenant of Ireland, 1782–3 and 1787–9).[10] Theirs was a well-connected and comfortably off family, with a town house in St Stephen's Green and a country residence, 'Casino', on the southern outskirts of Dublin near Milltown. Robert junior's childhood coincided with the pinnacle of Georgian Dublin's most splendid and confident years. With the recently refurbished Irish parliament building but a few paces from Trinity College, the seat of government in Dublin Castle located at the top of the same street, and the magnificent town houses of the Irish Ascendancy dotted around the streets and squares nearby, there was a sense of being at the very centre of power in these confident years of Anglo-Irish rule. The main political expressions of such confidence were the Volunteers and the 'patriot' movement in the Irish Parliament. Though established first to protect Ireland during the American War of Independence, the Volunteers came to embody the parliamentary patriots' campaign for greater legislative independence from England, of which Henry Grattan became the leading champion. Their military reviews (almost a weekly occurrence in St Stephen's Green) were hugely popular civic occasions.

But there was another aspect of Dublin not represented in such decorous scenes and one much commented upon by visitors to the capital: the proximity of rich and poor, splendour and squalor. After dark the poorly lit St Stephen's Green was transformed from a favourite haunt of the fashionable to one infested with robbers, footpads and prostitutes, and, unlike London, the poor and destitute lived cheek by jowl with the affluent. Whitley Stokes wrote in 1799 of his experiences as a physician among the poor in the streets adjacent to Trinity, where fever was perennial, sanitation non-existent and as many as ten in a family shared a single room. Living conditions were even worse in the so-called Liberties, just west of the Castle. In July 1798 the Revd James Whitelaw, rector of St Catherine's in Thomas Street, conducted a census of Dublin. In the area incorporating the Liberties he found decay, disease and severe overcrowding. Here was the centre of Ireland's textile industry, most notably the now-declining silk industry. Its artisans and manufacturers had a long history of fighting against foreign (largely English) imports and unsurprisingly supplied a significant number of United Irishmen. Here lived a population of weavers, small shopkeepers, labouring poor and beggars, crowded into its crooked lanes and alleyways. The 'degree of filth and stench [is] inconceivable', wrote Whitelaw. The 'deleterious effects' of the 'brothels, soap manufactories, slaughter-houses, glass-houses, lime-kilns, distilleries, etc.' in the midst of such populousness were all too obvious. He also commented on the excessive numbers of dram-shops licensed to sell spirits and the prevalence of drunkenness in the city – nearly a third of the houses in Thomas Street alone so licensed. Little wonder that Lord Edward Fitzgerald – colonel-in-chief of the United Irishmen – was able to evade arrest here for over two months in the spring of 1798, though by then he was the most wanted man in Ireland. This sector of Dublin society was traditionally disaffected and easily mobilised by charismatic leaders of a higher class: James Napper Tandy in the 1780s, Lord Edward in the 1790s, and Robert Emmet a decade later, for it was in these streets that 'Emmet's rebellion' took place.[11]

The wealthier classes were not oblivious to the poverty around them and the last two decades of the Irish Parliament witnessed a growing interest in reform. The rising status of the medical profession was part of this, as was the increase in charitable giving. The Emmet family was well known for charitable work among the Dublin poor and Mrs Emmet was often accompanied by young Robert. He seems to have been close to his mother and had few companions of his own age. It is likely that his mother was over-protective, given the appalling rate of fatalities among her offspring.[12] At the time of Robert's birth, the eldest son, Temple, was completing his training as a barrister, while Thomas, at the age of fourteen, was about to enter Trinity College. Thomas later transferred to Edinburgh University to study medicine and was elected president of a number of its student societies.[13] Temple appears to have been exceptionally talented by the standards of the day. By the age of twenty he had been called to the Irish bar. In a profession that valued oratory and turned those so gifted into popular idols, Temple Emmet, the darling of the College Historical Society, arrived with a reputation already made. But he died prematurely in 1788 – of smallpox, it was said – leaving a baby daughter, Catherine or Kitty (his wife having predeceased him), who was cared for by her grandparents and after their deaths by Mary Anne and her husband Robert Holmes.[14] On his brother's death, Thomas abandoned his medical studies and took up his brother's profession as a barrister. He was admitted to the Irish bar in 1790 and was a formative influence on his younger brother thereafter, for although he married Jane Patten (daughter of a dissenting minister at Clonmel) in 1791, they moved into a house adjoining the family home in St Stephen's Green.

Though a popular figure in Dublin society, Dr Emmet was later criticised by some for having filled his sons' heads with 'an extravagant sort of patriotism'.[15] The Emmet family was also noted for its support of Catholic emancipation. Robert grew up in an environment where the early leaders of the United Irishmen (Thomas included) discussed their views openly. The advanced thinkers of the day were regularly invited to Dr Emmet's dinner parties and on one of these occasions Dr William Drennan was flattered when parts of his radical *Letters of Orellanea* were recited by the twelve-year-old Robert Emmet.[16] This had called for an end to religious discord and championed the right of extra-parliamentary agitation in favour of parliamentary reform. Predictably reforming lawyers figured prominently on the guest list. Robert's elder brother Thomas had formed a close friendship with Tone and Tone's particular friend Thomas Russell. By 1792 their informal political club had developed into the Society of United Irishmen, which championed the cause of Catholic emancipation and challenged the whole concept of Protestant ascendancy. But just as young Robert was preparing to follow his brothers to Trinity, the atmosphere of optimistic reformism in which he had been nurtured was falling apart. The outbreak of war with revolutionary France (1793) ushered in a raft of repressive legislation and made seditious the kind of radical ideas so openly discussed until then.

After private education at a number of schools in Dublin, Robert Emmet entered Trinity College on 7 October 1793 as a pensioner, 'persons of moderate income', the largest category of student. He was fifteen. He proved himself an able student, and was also destined for a legal career, having been entered at the King's Inns in Dublin on 2 November 1795.[17] The core syllabus at Trinity consisted of classics, mathematics, natural philosophy, logic and ethics and exams were 'strenuous *viva voce* affairs', lasting eight days, four times a year, and conducted in Latin before the entire college body, fellows and students alike. They were competitive in the extreme and one had to be diligent as well as clever to shine. Trinity students were considered the hardest worked of all the university students in eighteenth-century Britain and Ireland. Emmet displayed a particular talent for mathematics and science; a much-repeated anecdote from this time tells of him having worked out a successful antidote for a poisonous substance that he had accidentally swallowed because of his nail-biting habit.[18] Indeed, the Castle was warned to keep an eye on the students expelled in 1798 because of their particular aptitude for mathematics and military manoeuvres.[19] In this he was fortunate to have among the fellows the Revd Matthew Young, a mathematician of some repute, Professor of Physics (since 1786) and an extremely popular teacher. It was this passion for mathematics that was the bond of friendship between Emmet and Dacre Hamilton, remembered by Moore as very clever and very 'innocent', son of a widow of slender means and expelled for his refusal to incriminate others at the April visitation.[20] However, the syllabus was not as dry as it sounds. The ethos of the college had been one of liberal whiggery for much of the century and the key texts that had inspired the Enlightenment were central to the curriculum. John Locke's *Two Treatises of Government* were such favourites with the students that one of the fellows brought out a new edition in 1798 to refute the belief that they had prefigured Paine's *Rights of Man*.[21] A page from Emmet's personal copy of Locke's *Second Treatise*, reproduced by Thomas Addis's grandson in his *Memoir* of 1915, is heavily annotated and underlined.[22]

It was, however, for his oratorical skills that he was largely remembered, first in an informal debating society that met in the rooms of the student members, then in the more formal Historical Society. In both he always took the 'popular', anti-government side. In December 1797 he was admitted as a member of the College Historical Society, the first college debating society in the British Isles, where most of Ireland's political class received their early experience of public speaking. It was no longer the political powerhouse of his brothers' days – when opposition politicians had used it as a kind of alter-parliament. In 1794 it was actually expelled from College premises for continuing to admit non-college members and banned from discussing contemporary political issues when it returned a year later.[23] In the 1790s the records of the society were not as well kept as in the 1780s and there was a pettiness about its proceedings that Tone, in a blistering speech as auditor of the society in July 1789, had already drawn attention to.

It is difficult to assess Robert Emmet's contribution to the society because of the poor record keeping. Indeed, the absence of evidence about his college career may tell us as much about his character as its presence. He appears to have been a rather serious and quiet young man, 'wholly free from the follies and frailties of youth', according to his friend Tom Moore, 'the pursuit of science, in which he eminently distinguished himself, seemed at this time the only object which at all divided his thoughts'.[24] Moore recalled finding Emmet 'in full fame' when he became a member of the debating society, 'not only for his learning and eloquence, but also for the blamelessness of his life, and the grave suavity of his manners'.[25] Although the description given of him in 1803 by his former mathematics tutor, the Revd Thomas Elrington, may have been coloured by distaste for his treasonable activities, it is unlikely to have been entirely fabricated. 'In 1798 he was near twenty years of age, of an ugly sour countenance; small eyes, but not near-sighted; a dirty-brownish complexion; at a distance looks as if somewhat marked with small-pox; about five feet six inches high, rather thin than fat, but not of an emaciated figure; on the contrary, somewhat broad-made; walks briskly, but does not swing his arms.' Another described him as 'slender made, about 5'7", very swarthy and rather ill looking, dark brown hair, thin visage and small eyes'.[26] John Patten, Jane Emmet's brother, later spoke of Dr Emmet's anxieties about his younger son. 'He had not the gravity or sedateness of Temple and Thomas Addis Emmet; his boyishness of air, and apparent unfitness for society, or unwillingness to engage in active intercourse with men of the world, made the poor old doctor uneasy of Robert's destiny.' Patten attributed this to the 'extreme diffidence of Robert – he was so modest, reserved and retiring … You might live with him for five years – aye, for ten years – in the same house – in the same room even and never discover that he thought about himself at all.' When his mind *was* made up', however, Dr Emmet told Patten, 'he had no diffidence – no distrust – no fear of himself', and he thought that 'his taste for the reading of military tactics' would see him assume the command of an army with no hesitation or misgivings.[27] Thomas Moore also recalled Robert's enthusiasm, when he was moved by Moore's playing of a traditional air to exclaim: 'Oh that I were at the head of twenty thousand men marching to that air.'[28]

Robert Emmet appears to have lived at home during his four years at Trinity, uninvolved in student pranks or riotous behaviour. Unlike Tone and even his brother Thomas, his name is absent from the books of censures and cautions.[29] This might explain why contemporaries were so impressed by his performances at the Historical Society, standing as they did in such stark contrast to his normal demeanour. The Society's records reveal Emmet as a valued member, but one who was already looking elsewhere, for he was regularly fined in early 1798 for late attendance. His last attendance was on 28 February 1798, when he spoke on behalf of the motion that a soldier ought 'consider the motives of war'. He was remembered as a powerful speaker. A contemporary later told Dr Madden of Emmet's debut at the society on 7 February 1798. The topic was political – at a time when the society had been banned from discussing modern politics: 'Is unlimited freedom of discussion the best means of stopping the progress of erroneous opinions?' He thought that it had been 'got up expressly' for Emmet's début. Emmet spoke in favour of the motion, arguing the necessity and advantages of liberty of discussion in all communities, its encouragement a mark of good government, its suppression the consequence of despotism and tyranny. He was opposed by a future Lord Chief Justice of Ireland, Thomas Lefroy, then aged 22, but was able to answer all his objections. 'If a government were vicious enough to put down the freedom of discussion, it would be the duty of the people to deliberate on the errors of their rulers, to consider well the wrongs they inflicted, and what the right course would be for their subjects to take, and having done so, *it then would be their duty to draw practical conclusions.*'[30]

Thomas Moore, Emmet's contemporary though two years younger, idolised him and has left the fullest account of the transformation from introspective youth to impassioned orator.

> Were I to number, indeed, the men among all I have ever known, who appeared to me to combine, in the greatest degree pure moral worth, with intellectual power, I should, among the highest of the few, place Robert Emmet. Wholly free from the follies and frailties of youth … the pursuit of science, in which he eminently distinguished himself, seemed, at this time, the only object that at all divided his thoughts with that enthusiasm for Irish freedom which, in him, was an hereditary as well as national feeling … Simple in all his habits, and with a repose of look and manner indicating but little movement within, it was only when the spring was touched that set his feelings, and – through them – his intellect in motion, that he, at all, rose above the level of ordinary men. On no occasion was this more

particularly striking than in those displays of oratory with which, both in the Debating, and the Historical, Society, he so often enchained the attention and sympathy of his young audience. No two individuals, indeed, could be much more unlike to each other, than was the same youth to himself, *before* rising to speak, and *after*; – the brow that had appeared inanimate, and almost drooping at once elevating itself to all the consciousness of power, and the whole countenance and figure of the speaker assuming a change as of one suddenly inspired.'[31]

Though fairly typical of Moore's exaggerated style, his testimony finds endorsement in Catherine Wilmot's Paris diary of 1802, in which she also refers to contemporary perceptions of Emmet as somewhat effeminate in appearance, largely it seems from a tendency to blush.

> We have lately become acquainted with Robert Emmett, who I dare say you have heard of as being amongst the politically distinguish'd in Dublin College. His face is uncommonly expressive of everything youthful, and everything enthusiastic, and his colour comes and goes so rapidly, accompanied by such a nervousness of agitated sensibility, that in his society I feel in a perpetual apprehension lest any passing idle word should wound the delicacy of his feelings. For tho' his reserve prevents one's hearing many of his opinions, yet one would swear to their style of exaltation, from their flitting shadows blushing across his countenance in everlasting succession. His understanding they tell me is very bright.[32]

Not for Emmet then the frivolities and indiscretions of student life, which had seen others as gifted suffering spells of exclusion. It seems too that Emmet tried to turn the younger student from a fashionable flirtation with treason, for Moore had published an anonymous article in the United Irishmen's soon-to-be-suppressed newspaper the *Press*. 'With that almost feminine gentleness of manner which he possessed ... he owned to me that on reading the letter, though pleased with its contents, he could not help regretting that the public attention had been thus drawn to the politics of the University, as it might have the effect of awakening the vigilance of the college authorities, and frustrate the progress of the good work ... which was going on there so quietly.' Emmet never tried to involve his young friend in the societies that he was now helping to organise within the college, for which, in retrospect, Moore was grateful. Shortly after their conversation his parents were warned by his college tutor that his intimacy with Emmet was bringing him to the hostile attention of the college authorities. Certainly Moore was shocked at the revelations he heard during the college visitation.

Emmet had sought to remove his name from the college books – which would have made it impossible for the visitors to call him to account – but was dissuaded by his tutor, seemingly on the instructions of the Vice-Chancellor. 'I have been for some time in possession of everything that has been going forward in the College', Fitzgibbon told the assembled members when Emmet's name was called out on 19 April, 'and I know that Emmett is one of the most active and wicked members of [the] society of U[nited] I[rishmen] – and I did desire [the] Provost not to suffer any person whatever to take his name off the College Books, that I might bring him and others of his association to punishment – We will now call Mr Emmett – and if he does not appear, we will expel him.' He did not appear, and, with eighteen others, he was expelled. The heads of the other Universities in England and Scotland were written to and asked not to admit any of them. With this, their chance of a professional career in either Britain or Ireland was effectively removed.[33] The commercial concerns on which many of them now embarked would provide the networks through which what became known as 'Emmet's rebellion' was organised.

Moore is rather disingenuous in his account of his Trinity days; his effusiveness about the United Irishmen with whom he was on terms of friendship may well reflect a recognition of how near he himself had come to the flame before retreating – a common reaction in Britain's and Ireland's recovering radicals. In fact, the Trinity students were deeply implicated in United Irish preparations for a rebellion and French invasion. A number of the expellees, notably Robert Emmet, Michael Farrell, Thomas Flinn and William Corbet, had indeed been actively recruiting within the college and meeting regularly with the United Irish executive in Dublin.[34] The security crisis in Ireland – a major attempt at French invasion in 1796, increasing revolutionary activity, military suppression and sectarian atrocities – was the background to the March arrests of Thomas Emmet and the other leaders, as well as the purge of Trinity students.

By May there were military searches for arms in the suspect parts of inner Dublin. On Friday 18 May a smith was caught in the act of making pike-heads at his forge in Thomas Street. The following day Lord Edward Fitzgerald was captured nearby. On Monday the 21st more pikes were discovered at Rattigan's timber yard in Dirty Lane, and in reprisal the military emptied his house of furniture and burnt it in the street. Searches intensified over the following days; suspects were taken up and flogged to extract information. On 23 May the long-feared rebellion began. As rebels assembled they were confronted by massed yeomanry, 'drumbeat to arms' at midnight and assembled at their various 'alarm posts', one in St Stephen's Green. By now Dr Emmet had boarded up his town house and moved the family to Casino. On the outskirts of the city large groups of rebels stopped the northern and western mail coaches and engaged the crown forces in a number of areas just to the south of the city. At Crumlin and Tallaght they forced the first body of yeomanry to retreat, but were overcome by reinforcements. The bodies of the killed were displayed in the lower yard of Dublin Castle. Outside the capital, insurgents in the rest of Ireland responded to the signals from

Dublin with varying degrees of success. Counties Meath, Kildare and Carlow succumbed early to crown forces. Wexford held out for over a fortnight, the ferocity of its resistance shaking the confidence of the governing class and finally convincing the British prime minister that their demand for military reinforcement was more than perennial whingeing. Ulster turned out late (7–9 June) and was easily overcome. By mid-June Lord Lieutenant Camden believed the worst was over. But a sizeable rebel force continued to operate in the Wicklow Mountains under Michael Dwyer and Joseph Holt, and the ferocity of the victors helped ensure that an undercurrent of popular disaffection was developing a life of its own.

Camden was warned to restrain the vengefulness of his supporters by the London government, which was responding to the complaints of military officers about the loyalist frenzy among the irregular forces that had largely quelled the rebellion. The acting Chief Secretary, Lord Castlereagh, had, with difficulty, restrained the members of the Irish Parliament from demanding the retrospective application of the summary justice meted out to rebels under new martial law procedures introduced in late May. Besides being unconstitutional, such would draw upon the administration accusations of cruelty and vengeance and undermine its duties of 'justice and mercy' in attempting to win back the 'deluded inhabitants of Ireland, disposed to return to their allegiance'. Upon which one member pointed out the incongruity of the same 'deluded' paying with their lives, while the 'prime movers' who had seduced them had the protection of the constitution.[35]

And so it was to prove. Most of the principal United Irish leaders – imprisoned before the outbreak of the rebellion and the imposition of martial law – were to live to old age, despite the outcry of loyalists baying for their blood. It was all part of the misguided leniency of the new Lord Lieutenant, Lord Cornwallis, who arrived at the end of June and whom the loyalists came to loathe – a sentiment that he soon returned, his despatches to London full of complaints about their vengeful sectarianism. By then the government believed the worst was over and something needed to be done to stop the vendettas in the countryside and to induce the 'deluded wretches' still in arms to surrender. In return for surrendering and taking an oath of allegiance, they would be permitted to return home – though the other side of the coin was the full implementation of summary punishment under martial law for those who failed to surrender. But how to deal with the crisis in the overflowing prisons, particularly when the imprisoned leaders continued to provide inspiration to those still in arms?

The problem was that there was insufficient information to bring them to trial and it is one of the incongruities of the 1798 crisis that while torture was used to extract information from the lower rank of rebel, it was never used on the top leaders. These, after all, were gentlemen and were largely treated as such. So what of those informers and betrayers who figure so prominently in the popular tales of 1798 and 1803, largely informed by the spy-detector *par excellence*, W. J. Fitzpatrick, whose sensational works inspired the primacy accorded the villains in the Emmet legend.[36] Of those singled out by Fitzpatrick, Leonard MacNally (1752–1820) became the most infamous. MacNally was a barrister of radical sympathies, a friend to prominent patriot lawyer John Philpot Curran, and though not as talented, was nevertheless a successful advocate to a number of United Irishmen. His change of heart occurred in 1794. An old acquaintance from his days at the Inns of Court in London, John Cockayne, came to Dublin and contacted him. Cockayne was accompanied by William Jackson, a gregarious English clergyman lately come from France. MacNally himself was a *bon viveur*, comic playwright and composer. In April 1794 he hosted a dinner for Jackson and Cockayne, and provided their entrée to the leading United Irishmen in the city. But Jackson was a French agent and Cockayne had been sent by Pitt's government to spy on him. At the dinner Jackson had sounded out United Irish opinion about a possible French invasion. MacNally dismissed the idea. But others did not and were badly compromised when Jackson was arrested shortly afterwards. These were frightening times and many original members of the United Irish Society retreated as the war crisis deepened. One of these was MacNally, terrified in the knowledge of his own vulnerability after his association with Jackson. He was ripe for recruitment by the government's spy-makers, and for the next six years MacNally's reports were the fullest and most reliable of any agent in Ireland. Surprisingly they are devoid of the obsequiousness ascribed to him by legend and they very often contained severe critiques of government policy.[37]

Intelligence-gathering should have been a top priority with the powers allied against the French revolutionary regimes after 1793, for secret warfare was a recognised feature of France's war strategy. But it was many years before Britain mastered it, and then it was largely through the work of the Alien Office under the direction of William Wickham. By 1798 he was responsible for co-ordinating secret service reports from Ireland. Most of the Irish intelligence was processed at the Castle by under-secretary Edward Cooke. However, since he was also handling the early stages of the campaign to 'persuade' Irish politicians to a Union and a multitude of other issues, he was often overwhelmed. Nor was it always easy to act on good information, for Ireland still lacked a police force or a paid magistracy and much of the success in Dublin relied on the legendary energy of Town-Major Henry Sirr. Moreover, it was not always easy to gain convictions of those taken up on secret evidence, for producing such evidence in court destroyed the source thereafter.

On 24 July the United Irish state prisoners in Dublin offered to make a full disclosure of their activities in return for an end to the bloodshed, a stay in the executions of the leaders under sentence of death, and their own exile. Three had already been executed – Henry and John Sheares and John McCann – and Oliver Bond and William Byrne were next. Thomas Addis Emmet, William James MacNeven and Arthur O'Connor were delegated to conduct negotiations with government. Cornwallis, Castlereagh, and, surprisingly, Lord Chancellor Clare wanted to accept the offer. In the months before the outbreak of the rebellion, a serious rift had developed in the national leadership. The 'moderates' (middle-class men like Thomas Emmet and Dr William James MacNeven) had opposed a rising before the French came; the 'extremists' like Lord Edward and Arthur O'Connor had wanted to proceed, with or without the French. Now it was the 'moderates' who were more enthusiastic about what became known as the 'Kilmainham treaty', for it gave them a chance to parade their original aims as reasonable and distance themselves from the bloodshed of past months. The London government also thought the 'treaty' something of an apologia for past actions and preferred to publish an amended version. This was deemed by the prisoners a breach of faith since it seemed to suggest that they had given names, when they had entered into the agreement on the explicit understanding that they would not be required to do so, and they published a disclaimer in the Dublin press on 27 August. Statements in the London press, claiming that they had acknowledged their 'crimes' and 'implored pardon', the state prisoners considered an attack on their honour and a number of blistering letters were sent to the press and the Castle in consequence. The prisoners were disingenuous in their belief that they were treating with the government on equal terms. They also showed little understanding of the real difficulties Cornwallis's government was experiencing in implementing a general policy of clemency. So enraged were government supporters in the Irish Parliament at the state prisoners' statement to the press 'that it was with difficulty they were restrained from taking ... revenge', as Castlereagh reported to Pitt on 7 September.[38]

But the various agreements had been worked out in haste – the prisoners trying to stop the executions, the government trying to find evidence that could be used in justification of the actions recently taken to put down the rebellion. Indeed, given that most of the communications were oral, London asked the Irish government to provide a statement of what actually *had* been agreed. The main point in the statement sent to London, which differed substantially from the recollections of the prisoners, was that concerning their voluntary banishment: 'On the part of Government, a full discretion was reserved of retaining any or all of the prisoners in custody so long as the war should last, provided their liberation was deemed inconsistent with the public safety.' [39]

However, the prisoners believed that they would be allowed to exile themselves to a neutral country and questioned their continued detention. Some too were demanding to be brought to trial and the government had already admitted that it was not confident of convicting them. What to do with the ninety who had signed up to the Kilmainham treaty and several hundred other United Irish prisoners became one of the major problems of that autumn and winter – particularly since information showed that their very presence in the country was proving an inspiration to continuing disaffection. The Irish government would have been happy to let them go to America, but the American minister in London, Rufus King, objected. The antirepublican Federalist administration in Washington had a particular dislike of the Irish in America, who tended to support their opponents. The state prisoners were bitter and were to wreak their revenge on King some years later when they had, after all, made their way to America.[40] Castlereagh was disdainful of the American decision.

> It is perfectly natural that America should be very jealous
> of receiving Irish convicts; but, unless she prohibits
> emigration from this country altogether, she will infallibly
> receive United Irishmen, and the majority of our
> prisoners are not more dangerous than the general class
> of American settlers. Were it not that the loyal would be
> disgusted and indignant at their being at large in this
> kingdom, the greater part of them might be discharged
> on bail without much danger to the State.[41]

Although the confinement of the prisoners had been relaxed in the aftermath of the Kilmainham treaty, it was tightened up again after the publication of their advertisement and further public disclaimers were prevented by Cooke's threat that in such an event the agreement would be considered voided and the executions recommenced. The 'indignation and resentment' at what they considered a breach of the 'compact' made with government was accordingly bottled up for nearly four years, because most were only finally released in 1802.[42] As time went on, disaffection in the country showed little sign of abating and the state prisoners were known to be continuing to organise it from within the gaols. Accordingly, it was decided in March 1799 to remove the leading prisoners to Fort George in north-east Scotland, several hundred of those Castlereagh thought bailable being sent into military service.

At a day's notice the state prisoners were moved from Dublin, via Belfast, to Scotland. They were not told where they were going and for the first year there were tight restrictions on their correspondence. Visitors could only be seen in the presence of a third person. Thomas Emmet was indignant and wrote in September to deter his wife from making the journey to Scotland. Ultimately conditions were relaxed sufficiently for Mrs Emmet and three of their children to join him. But for men as proud as Thomas Emmet and his particular friends, Russell and MacNeven, these years of confinement and isolation left them bitter and vengeful.

2 United Irishman

I am charged with being an emissary of France! ...
Connexion with France was indeed intended – but only
as ... auxiliaries in war, and allies in peace. Were the
French to come as invaders or enemies ... I should
oppose them to the utmost of my strength.

Robert Emmet's speech at his trial, 19 September 1803

The brother of one of the Fort George prisoners, who had been petitioning for his release, was surprised by government anxiety about the
powers of these men. 'I was astonished to find him so extremely formidable to the Government', he wrote in April 1800, 'they consider
him a person of the first abilities, and from conviction decidedly hostile to it ... they conceive him capable of wielding the strength of the
country, and directing his animosity against themselves.'[1] This was
quite a change of tone from communications at the time of the Kilmainham treaty. The reason was that in those months when the two
governments wrestled with the prisoner problem, intelligence started
coming through of the reorganisation of the United Irishmen under
secondary leaders who were taking their orders from the state prisoners; one of those new leaders was Robert Emmet.

I

Robert Emmet falls out of official intelligence for most of 1798, even
though those with whom he was shortly to be associated in recon-

structing the United Irish movement were already being watched.[2] He was living at Casino – the house in St Stephen's Green having been shut up – and negotiating entering the tanning business of his sister-in-law's brother, John Patten. But a number of poems written in these months show no diminution of his republicanism and anger at the continuing bloodshed. They are in the style of the romantics, dark, gothic pieces, impassioned laments for the 'martyred dead' and the bloodshed of 1798. 'Arbour Hill' was where a number of the executions had taken place in 1798. (I quote from it extensively in Chapter 6, as its words prefigure much of what Emmet was to say in his famous speech of 1803.) In the context of the events of 1798 it is a lament for the horrific bloodshed and reflects the feelings of his brother and the 'moderates' on the United Irish executive. The events of 1798 had reinforced the view of the 'moderate' leaders that a rising should never have taken place without a French landing.

> O sacred Justice! free this land
>   From tyranny abhorred;
> Resume thy balance and thy seat,
>   Resume, but sheath thy sword.
> No retribution should we seek –
>   Too long has horror reigned;
> By mercy marked may Freedom rise,
>   By cruelty unstained.

However, as the Kilmainham treaty fell apart during the autumn and winter months of 1798–9, a new strategy was being developed by some of the state prisoners and implemented by those United Irishmen like Robert Emmet who still remained at large. Emmet's poetry becomes angrier and calls for renewed action.

> Genius of Erin, tune thy harp
>   To freedom, let its sound awake

Thy prostrate sons, and nerve their hearts
   Oppression's iron bonds to break.
   . . .

Show her fields with blood ensanguined,
   With her children's blood bedewed –
Show her desolated plains,
   With their murdered bodies strewed.
   . . .

Erin's sons awake! – awake!
   Oh! too long, too long, you sleep;
Awake! arise! your fetters break,
   Nor let your country bleed and weep.[3]

By 1798 Leonard MacNally was losing favour with the United Irish-men and his information was becoming less abundant. Several other key informants defected that summer and there was a sudden vacuum in secret information reaching the government, a vacuum that was never quite remedied before the 1803 rebellion. Indeed, it was not until the information from a new source started to come through early in 1799 that Robert Emmet's new role began to be revealed. The informant was another member of the legal fraternity, James McGucken, a Catholic attorney from Belfast and former member of the Ulster provincial directory of the United Irishmen. He had acted as legal aid to a number of Ulster United men, not least James Coigley, who had been arrested in England after having carried out a secret mission to Ireland. McGucken was returning from his trial when he was arrested in Liverpool along with William Dowdall, pro-prietor of the United Irishmen's recently suppressed newspaper the *Press*. After the guilty sentence and execution of Coigley, McGucken would have required little reminding of the perilous situation in which he found himself and even W. J. Fitzpatrick admitted that he only 'turned' when the rope, metaphorically, was round his neck.[4]

It was through McGucken that information on Robert Emmet

began reaching the Castle early in January 1799. By then he was heavily involved in restructuring the United Irish organisation, only this time it consisted solely of a military command with detailed instructions of how to bring the people into the field when the French arrived. The recent failed insurrection had shown that whereas there was no shortage of foot soldiers, they lacked discipline and commanders. Moreover, although the group associated with Thomas Addis Emmet had doubts about the wisdom of giving the French any excuse to take over Ireland, their horror of popular disorder was even greater, 'the worst government on earth' being 'preferable to anarchy'.[5] The plan was to establish a military command, each level knowing only the name of the immediate superior. Communication would then cease until the French arrived. For they would do the fighting, the Irish rank and file being recruited and organised at the final moment and confined to diversionary duties. A report presented to the French government some months later described this 'new military structure'.[6] The country was divided into baronies. Some were left under the old system to confuse the government. In the others three colonels appointed would each choose four captains, who would choose three lieutenants and so on down the grades – the emphasis always on personal knowledge of those so recruited. The best-organised counties were Dublin, Wicklow, Kildare, Wexford, Tipperary, Cork, Meath, Down and Antrim, and the capture of Dublin would be the preliminary to securing the east of the country where they were strongest. Three military booklets, containing instructions for the officers, plans of attack and details for the discipline of the men, had been printed and distributed. But there would be no committee meetings as before, nothing put in writing, all instructions issued orally to one colonel in each county. 'In Dublin no committees are held, no watchword is yet given out, but there is a general whisper running through the United Irishmen that they are to be ready at a moment's warning.'[7]

It is likely that Robert Emmet was heavily involved in the military planning and he was credited 'with considerable talent' by Surgeon Thomas Wright, the only leading United Irishman that government managed to arrest in these months. McGucken encountered Emmet on a number of occasions as he was visiting the state prisoners. Emmet told him about their efforts to establish the new organisation, spoke of Wright as one of the key men in Dublin and mentioned others elsewhere in the country. McGucken also discovered that he was one of the colonels for Dublin and was responsible for receiving communications from Connacht. Others mentioned by McGucken as liaising with the state prisoners included Hugh O'Hanlon, who had seen service in Spain's Irish brigade, James Farrell, a printer, and William Putnam McCabe, son of one of the original Belfast United Irishmen.[8]

The new organisation was to lie dormant until the French arrived and in the early months of 1799 the United Irish representatives in France were led to believe that such an invasion was imminent. Ireland had remained disturbed since the suppression of the previous year's rebellion and the government's policy of abolishing the Irish parliament had so alienated loyalism that the United Irishmen were even trying to woo the Orangemen and the yeomanry. Though not all United Irishmen opposed the Union, Robert Emmet and the prisoners in Kilmainham did. Emmet is known to have attended the parliamentary debates on the Union and the many friends of the United Irishmen among the legal fraternity were urged to vote against it. [9]

McGucken appealed to the government not to arrest these new leaders, since his channels of information would then disappear. But ministers visibly relaxed after the departure of the state prisoners for Scotland, and at the beginning of April warrants were issued for the arrests of Emmet, Wright, O'Hanlon, Farrell and those named as having come to Dublin to be given the new instructions for the other counties. O'Hanlon was taken but escaped and warned Emmet, who went into hiding, creating false panels and trap doors at Casino – devices that he would use again in 1803. In the end Wright was the only significant leader taken up and questioned. Emmet's great-nephew later claimed that Robert visited his brother in Fort George. There is no contemporary evidence for this and it would have been impossible after September/October 1799, when the London government introduced new restrictions on visits and communications with the Fort George prisoners.[10] The next definite information we have on his whereabouts is in August 1800, when news reached Dublin Castle that he was in Hamburg with Malachy Delaney, one of the Kildare leaders in the 1798 rebellion.[11] The information had come from the British representative in this neutral city, for the government's domestic intelligence system appears to have entirely broken down. In this respect at least the cessation of communication by the new organisation had proved entirely successful.

The way the disaffected were responding to any report of a French invasion attempt, real or imagined, seemed to endorse the leaders' belief that the formal organisation could be left in cold storage until such an eventuality. Castlereagh agreed: 'The organisation is much broken', he wrote to Home Secretary Portland in June 1799, 'but still enough of it remains … to render a formidable insurrection inevitable, should the enemy land in force.'[12] It was to secure such an invasion that Emmet and Delaney were sent to the continent. Over the next few months they, and a number of other leaders, made their way to France. Among them were McCabe, Emmet's first cousin William St John Mason, Michael Farrell, a fellow Trinity College expellee, and William Henry Hamilton, another lawyer and one of the most talented of the group. Some of these had travelled via London to help mobilise a diversion within existing disaffection, particularly among the very large numbers of Irish who had arrived after participating in the 1798 rebellion.[13]

II

In France Napoleon Bonaparte had come to power in November

1799. Bonaparte was anti-republican and at first was anxious to sue for peace with England. But his overtures in January 1800 were contemptuously dismissed by the British Foreign Secretary, Lord Grenville. Thereafter he fought successfully to turn the tide of war in France's favour and his successes raised expectations of another French invasion that summer. The invasion scare was real enough for Cornwallis to review Ireland's defence capability, and what he found did not inspire confidence. It was exactly the situation that the re-vamped United Irish organisation had looked to and was the immediate background to Emmet and Delaney's mission. At a meeting in Dublin, twenty backers agreed to supply 20 guineas a year each to support the mission.[14] In Hamburg they met the double-agent Samuel Turner, who reported their mission to the Dublin Government. In his correspondence he talked of 'young Emmet' and in contrast to Delaney – with a career behind him in the Austrian army and active service in the 1798 rebellion – he must have appeared somewhat lightweight. Certainly Turner viewed Delaney as the senior member of the delegation. But Emmet was a talented military tactician and the memorandum, drawn up by them and which so impressed Bonaparte, bears his hallmark. Indeed, Turner stated as much: 'Several memorials were prepared by E, drawn up in the usual language of the party here.'[15]

It was through Delaney's Austrian experience that they were able to cut through the usual red tape in securing permission to enter France, for in Austria he had known General Augereau, now French commander in Holland. Turner takes up the account: 'After communicating with them he (Augereau) considered the mission of so much consequence as to induce him to quit his command and escort them to Paris where he introduced them to the First Consul.'[16] No evidence has been found of their having formally met Bonaparte – although such a meeting became part of the Emmet legend – but he was sufficiently impressed by their first memorial to personally approve and finance their onward journey to Paris. The document that opened such doors was forwarded to the French Foreign Minister, Charles Talleyrand, on 5 September 1800. This former bishop under the *ancien régime* was one of the great survivors of the revolutionary era. He had embraced the revolution at the outset, survived the Terror and served every regime thereafter. Few came as tough and wily. However, he was well disposed towards the Irish, having been Foreign Minister in 1797–8 and negotiated with Tone. Indeed his continued support of Tone's widow and children, after Tone's death in 1798, saved them from destitution.

Emmet and Delaney's statement spoke at length of the discontent in Ireland caused by the Act of Union, but nevertheless did not minimise the difficulties in the way of a successful campaign – not least the large number of government forces in the country, which were detailed. The new organisation (which could put 500,000 in the field) had been organised solely to assist such an invasion and communication was kept to a minimum – even their compatriots in France being kept unaware of their mission. But a force of considerable size (25–30,000 men, with arms for a further 75,000) was essential to minimise bloodshed, and France would be compensated for this expedition, along with those undertaken in the past. This was 'the last time' they would look for assistance from France, the two men told Talleyrand when they met with him in Paris on 6 January. They presented him with another memorial further elaborating on points raised in that of August. He thought it 'extremely well done, clear, precise and nobly written', and asked for Bonaparte's instructions. These were issued on the same day in Bonaparte's marginal notes to Talleyrand's report: 'Citizen Talleyrand should pass this project to General Bernadotte and ask the two Irishmen to engage in talks with this general to whom the government would entrust any expedition that might be sent against Ireland.' The following day Talleyrand wrote to Bernadotte to this effect, enclosing Emmet and Delaney's document.[17]

The expectation of a French attempt on Ireland ran high in both

France and Ireland in the first months of 1801, and even though the Brest fleet, which was thought to have been preparing for Ireland, sailed instead for Santo Domingo, Bonaparte had juggled with a number of options that spring, including Ireland. But the United Irishmen would not have known this. They became progressively disenchanted with France's new leader, particularly after his signing of peace preliminaries with England that August. For some years Bonaparte had had the status of a mythic deliverer among the Irish peasantry. 'Some yet of the peasantry don't credit the news', McGucken reported, 'others exclaim much against him … others declare that from thence forward they never will again embark on politics … the scene is certainly changed and French treachery is the order of the day.'[18]

Certainly the ending of a war, which had lasted for nearly a decade and had dictated recent events in Ireland, would have brought to a close the United Irishmen's plans and many in France thought that the First Consul should be asked to negotiate terms for them as part of the peace negotiations. Ironically the chief British negotiator was Lord Cornwallis, who arrived in Paris on 7 November.[19] Robert Emmet called on Talleyrand to ask whether the position of the United Irishmen in France was to be discussed in the negotiations. In a series of letters to a family friend – the Marquise de Fontenay, who, with her husband, had escaped to Ireland during the French Revolution – he gave an account of the meeting:

> Dec. 19th 1801. I had some time ago formed the
> resolution of not soliciting the interference of this
> Government, but of simply asking whether they had yet
> made any stipulation for us or not. This I did, and having
> received an evasive answer, I left the place without
> making any demand, telling them at the same time, that
> we merited their intervention at least as much as the
> patriots of Naples. I first learned by letter from London,
> that the principal motive that influenced the British

Government in making the peace, was the declaration of
Lord Cornwallis, that if ten thousand men landed in
Ireland, the country would be infallibly lost. I have also
been informed by a gentleman coming from London, that
it is the intention of the British Government to proclaim
a general amnesty, and to provide a system of conciliation
in Ireland. So that, if we have not found friends to
acknowledge or appreciate our services, we found
enemies at least capable of estimating our importance.[20]

The disillusionment expressed in this letter was further increased by
press reports that Bonaparte offered to trade the United Irish exiles
in France for the French Royalists given refuge in England – and he
told his brother some months later of 'the willingness of [the French]
government to deliver up the United Irishmen, tied neck and heels,
to England'.[21]

At the time of the October letter to the Marquise de Fontenay,
Robert Emmet was staying with Michael Gallagher in the rue d'Am-
boise, and he seems to have consorted chiefly with old companions
like Delaney, Gallagher and Gallagher's former tutor at Trinity College, William (Surgeon) Lawless. Indeed, he attributed the prolonga-
tion of an eye complaint at the end of 1801 to the absence of his
doctor-friend, who had gone to Amiens to observe the peace negotiations between Britain and France.[22] Although he spoke perfect
French, Emmet did not mix in French society in these years – apart
from attending the anti-Bonapartist salon of the still young and brilliant Madame de Staël – who he seemed to impress, judging from the
later account of him by her granddaughter, the Baroness d'Haussonville.[23] Besides, republicans were out of favour in the Paris of the
Consulate, and Emmet, who had much in his character of the pure
(and prudish) republican, must have been rather shocked by the aristocratic excesses and décolleté fashions of its people. He preferred
the society of the English (as well as the Irish and Americans), as

noted by Catherine Wilmot, who had arrived in France at the end of 1801, one of a flood of English and Irish gentry to take advantage of the opening up of travel after the peace preliminaries were signed. On 13 March 1802 she wrote to her brother, a barrister in Ireland, of her meeting Robert Emmet. 'His understanding they tell me is very bright. But I am not likely to know much about it. For his extreme prejudice against French society will prevent our meeting him any-where except at the house of an English gentleman, who is soon re-turning to London.'[24]

In a letter written to John Patten from Amsterdam the following Au-gust, Emmet himself tells of good relations with 'the most respectable persons' in Paris, including the scientist Louis-Nicholas Vauquelin (who had offered to introduce him to 'one of the first chemists of Europe'), the American ambassador Robert Livingston, writer and diplomat, Joel Barlow, and honorary American and legendary Polish patriot, Tadeusz Kosciuszko. Evidence emerging after the 1803 rebel-lion suggested that Livingston, a wealthy man in his own right, had of-fered to fund the purchase of arms by Emmet.[25] Emmet's passion for chemistry and military tactics was undiminished. He took part in ex-periments conducted by the American–Irish engineer and inventor, Robert Fulton, experiments that he was to adapt to his military plans in Ireland in 1803. At some stage between October 1801 and April 1802 he had moved to the rue de la Loi, near the Bibliothèque Nationale and the Palais Royal, where the Irish in the city tended to congregate.[26]

There were large numbers of United Irishmen and refugees from the 1798 rebellion petitioning for relief in these years. General Hum-bert, who had commanded the French force that landed in Ireland in 1798, estimated some 1,000–1,200 such in France in October 1800.[27] Among them we find the names of Lawless, Gallagher, St John Mason, Thomas Corbet, Cornelius Keogh and Hamilton, who was president of the society of United Irish refugees in Paris. But Emmet's name never appears. He was provided for by his father, he explained to the Marquise de Fontenay when she offered help. And so he was, £517 15s. 8$^{1/2}$d. being transmitted to him through John Patten's merchant house between his departure for France and June 1802.[28] It all speaks of a very proud young man, disdainful of going cap in hand to the French.

III

In December 1801 Robert Emmet learnt of the liberation of some of the Fort George prisoners and fully expected that of the others to follow. His father had put Casino on the market and Emmet anticipated all the family being together again, apparently in America. A number of the Ulster leaders imprisoned at Fort George, as well as William Dowdall, were released after the peace preliminaries. But the fate of the others was still a worry for the British and Irish governments, for all the information demonstrated that they were as unrepentant as ever. You should 'fear and dread the principles of about ten men here', wrote Robert Hunter – one of those about to be released – on 5 November. 'The rest are broken down by confinement and ill fortunes. At the head of a faction is Emmet [Thomas] and Neilson, men of abilities and talent. They are at present crazy in consequence of peace coming on, and you are a God to Bonaparte and the French Government; but the consolation is it's only an armed truce and will last no time. At all events, it may put back their liberty for Ireland for some time, but in the end they know and are certain their union will triumph.'[29]

Fourteen out of the twenty originally sent to Fort George were detained until June 1802, when a navy frigate took them to Cuxhaven on the German coast, where they landed on 4 July. Their request to be allowed to settle their affairs in Ireland before permanent banishment had been turned down. Both Thomas Emmet and MacNeven felt their honour had been called into question by accusations made in 1798 by Arthur O'Connor that they had threatened to inform the Castle if the rebellion went ahead. Because of their prominence, the dispute had divided the prisoners at Fort George. As the frigate left Scotland, they immediately sought satisfaction, and although O'Connor had forgotten the reason for the dispute, he agreed to retract the accusation. He did and 'they bow'd to each other' but Emmet said he 'hoped it would not be construed as a renewal of intimacy'.[30]

Thomas Emmet, his wife and children (at least those from Fort George), his particular friends, among them Thomas Russell and Corkman John Swiney, travelled on to Amsterdam, where they were joined by Robert Emmet in August. Robert – in a letter to John Patten on 7 August – takes up the narrative of their first encounter in many years:

> Tom, Jane and the children and myself are at last together after many delays which have been distressing to us ... As soon as Jane is recovered from the fatigues of a voyage of 20 days across the Zuyder Zee ... we mean to set out for Bruxelles where we will establish our headquarters until the children [three sons who had remained with their grandparents in Ireland] can come to us *there*. I think it likely that Tom will remain there to practise the children in French and as it is both cheap and exceedingly pleasant we will possibly be stationary for sometime. If you come there ... I will introduce you to one of the first chemists of Europe to whom Vauquelin had offered me letters tho' I did set out too suddenly to take advantage of it. I have got in Paris letters from the most respectable persons there particularly Kosciuszko, the American Ambassador and Joel Barlow to Jefferson, most of the principal persons in New York, Pensilvania [sic] and Washington. A letter which I had written to Tom from Paris never reached him and we might both have been at a loss but that we met by accident at the P[ost] Office when we were looking for letters, and I believe the Messieurs were

a little surprised to see us run up and hug each other à
l'Irlandez without going through the previous ceremony
of taking off our hats … the post is just going out …
God bless u all. Write to me soon.[31]

He had written a large number of letters before this one, all sent
through the open post (this one bequeathed to posterity by the vigilance of Major Sirr, who seized John Patten's papers on 27 August
1803). The tone is that of great excitement at having been rejoined by
family and friends and anticipation of a lengthy stay in Brussells.

The state prisoners' bitterness at the Irish Government's failure to
honour the terms of the Kilmainham treaty had been nursed
throughout their imprisonment and they now determined on vindication. A pamphlet containing their examinations before the Irish
House of Lords Secret Committee was published in London within
months of their release. They had planned to publish in France a
more detailed paper prepared in Fort George, largely it seems by
Emmet and MacNeven. But what they learnt about France under the
Consulate persuaded them against this. 'In the propriety of this resolution', Thomas Emmet wrote to MacNeven, 'I was more convinced
by conversing with Robert, who was decided that it would be as safe
to publish it in London as in France and quoted some expressions to
me from high authority respecting the willingness of Government to
deliver up the United Irishmen, tied neck and heels, to England.'
Thomas had fully intended relocating permanently to America, the
only country that, 'with all its disadvantages, opens to me the fairest
field of honourable employment', and Mrs Emmet wanted to sail
even in the winter, so eager was she to leave Europe and start a new
life. By 25 October, however, he was less certain. 'Have you any
news', he wrote to MacNeven, now in Paris; 'we have strong rumours
of war again. If they should turn out to be well-founded, our views
would be, indeed, changed.'[32]

Whatever their jaundiced views of France, they had not altered their opinion that French military assistance would be needed to establish Irish independence. The peace between Britain and France had been fragile from the outset. Bonaparte was furious at the intrigues of the French *émigrés* in Britain and, as 1803 opened, encouraging noises were being made to the United Irish exiles in France through an unofficial channel. The nagging correspondence of the unofficial official with French ministers shows just how tentative such contacts were. But they were enough to elicit from MacNeven – with whom the contact had been made – an obsequious letter to Bonaparte on 11 January, quite at odds with his private contempt for the First Consul.[33] They needed France, but hated to admit as much, and the sufferings of most during the peace interlude, when the relief schemes ceased, further jaundiced their outlook.

The person who most reflected this ambivalence was Thomas Russell. Unlike the other released prisoners from Fort George, he travelled almost immediately to Paris. From there he wrote to James Farrell in London, signing off 'expecting to see you in free Ireland'. In a long letter to an old friend in Belfast, just before he left Fort George, he explained in detail his mix of emotions about going to France:

> You live among the people among whom I principally
> acted – to the people of Ireland I am responsible for my
> actions ... what has occasioned the temporary
> miscarriage of the cause is useless to dwell on –
> Providence orders all for the best – I am sure the *People*
> will never abandon that cause and I am equally sure it will
> succeed. But I fear that many were led so far astray, as to
> think favourable of the usurpation of Bonaparte which
> tramples on liberty in France ... it certainly was very
> fortune that no revolution took place [in Ireland] – for
> there would have been no change but a change of masters
> ... such as had the misfortune to connect the cause of

irreligion with that of Liberty ... will see that the only true basis of Liberty is morality.

Russell traced the various twists and turns of the French Revolution showing how atheists and deists had corrupted France, and now under Bonaparte 'with detestable profligacy' were bringing the French 'by the chains of superstition to the feet of tyranny'. 'I must now speak of myself ... so far from conceiving the cause of Ireland lost or being wary of its pursuit I am more than ever if possible inflexibly bent on it. For that I stay (if I can stay) in Europe. All the faculties I possess shall be excited for its advance ... [Neilson] participates in my sentiments and indeed all here who are known to you.'[34]

In Paris Russell associated with French republicans like Humbert who were both out of favour and as disenchanted as himself with Bonaparte. In London, en route back to Ireland in March 1803, he told James Farrell that all the Irish expeditions save that of Humbert had been betrayed by the corruption of Talleyrand. When asked if the renewal of war (which happened on 8 May 1803, but had been anticipated for many months) would not mean another expedition to Ireland, 'Russell said he believed not, England was the Consul's object. He hated Ireland, and would rather see it sunk in the sea, than yield the disaffected in it any assistance – but thought B. would make the attempt, since he would be defeated in England. He said the Republicans of France expected to recover their liberty thro' the medium of Ireland.'[35] An attempt on Ireland, then, was expected – but how to turn it to advantage and pre-empt it becoming a simple 'change of masters' – this was the dilemma that was to produce the event that came to be known as 'Emmet's rebellion'.[36]

on

down on Dublin town
On Sack. eet and the Coombe
It's light hung over the Liffeyside
Like a harbinger of doom.
And in the West the sun glowing red
Dissolved like a fading dream
As down the street Bob Emmet's men
Came marching in their jackets green.

Valentin Iremonger, 'Wrap up my green jacket'[1]

'I expected other resources ... but found myself
entangled with a rabble.'

NAI, 620/11/133, words spoken by Emmet to the Revd Gamble,
20 September 1803

Robert Emmet travelled back to Ireland through England in October
1802. He did not return with the intention of initiating preparations
for the rebellion that erupted the following year, although his sympathies, like his brother's, had not changed. Thomas Russell's brother,
John, spent six weeks in Paris mixing with the United Irishmen just
before Emmet's departure and heard nothing to suggest that such a
rebellion was then in contemplation. 'I did not come from France,'
Emmet claimed at his trial. 'I did not create the conspiracy – I found
it when I arrived here; – I was solicited to join it, – I took time to
consider of it, and I was told expressly, that it was no matter whether

I did join it or not – it would go on.'[2] Thomas Emmet still wanted his younger brother to accompany him to America and Robert's intention of returning to Ireland to see his parents – in an effort to make up his mind – had been postponed, first by uncertainties over his brother's terms of release, then by his arrival on the Continent.[3] Two months later his father died suddenly and was buried quietly in the family vault at St Peter's church. The family's finances were now in disarray, and Robert Holmes – appointed executor of Dr Emmet's will in Thomas's place – was beset by numerous difficulties. Casino was closed up, the furniture sold and the family moved nearer town. 'My old, revered friend Dr Emmet died a few days ago', Drennan wrote to his sister on 14 December, 'and at least £600 per annum is by his death, lost to his family … The family are about to remove immediately to a house nearer town … and they expect to set Casino in spring for which (it is said) £2,000 was offered and refused, but now I suppose it would be taken … His son Robert had come over about two months ago, but will not I suppose reside in this country.'[4]

I

It was from among the pre-1798 United Irish leaders on the Continent – most specifically those recently released from Fort George – that the first moves came for reorganisation in Ireland. The unofficial overtures from the French government sparked off a flurry of activity, bringing to a close a miserable interlude of impoverishment and aimlessness. When relief payments ceased with the outbreak of peace, most had to seek other ways of surviving. Some, like Emmet's college companion Thomas Corbet, became teachers of English, others travelled to Bordeaux in search of employment with the Irish mercantile houses. One group – which included William Putnam McCabe – attempted to establish a cotton manufacture in Rouen. It was partly financed by the Dublin merchant Phil Long (a Catholic from Waterford), and although the business concern was genuine enough, it was a perfect cover for communications between those who would organise 'Emmet's rebellion', including Long, who largely subsidised it.[5] Skilled workers like the Kildare mason Michael Quigley (imprisoned after 1798 and released when peace was declared in 1802) prospered in the building trade and were joined by large numbers of Irish workers coming to France during the peace period.[6] But most were miserably off, and the intellectuals, who had been the main leaders, particularly so.

William Henry Hamilton – in France with his wife and two children – was struggling financially. In the aftermath of 'Emmet's rebellion' he was considered by Dublin Castle to be 'a clever fellow, perhaps the most so of any engaged in Emmett's schemes'.[7] The son of a solicitor with radical sympathies, he was an officer in the army when Russell first met him in Fermanagh in 1793. A frequent companion of Russell's, he married his niece (Mary Ann, daughter of his eldest brother, John Russell) in February 1794, and, since Hamilton had resigned from the army to study for the bar, the couple left for London. There he was one of a group of Irish law students involved in organising disaffection. By early 1798 Hamilton was sitting on a combined committee of United Britons with Colonel Edward Marcus Despard, a member of the Irish landed class and former military governor of Honduras. It was this committee that Coigley had spoken to prior to his arrest in February 1798 and it was as a direct result of those arrests that Hamilton had fled to France.[8] Also implicated with Coigley was John Allen. A woollen draper in Dublin and a man of some property, Allen had been travelling to France with Coigley and Arthur O'Connor in February 1798, when he was arrested and tried, but acquitted. However, like Hamilton, he remained active and re-emerged in 1802–3 as one of the main leaders behind the 1803 rebellion.[9]

Another was William Dowdall, one of the few 'gentry' associated in 1803. He was one of the state prisoners at Fort George released back to Ireland in February 1802 and soon reactivated the old network. He had always found a patron in Henry Grattan, through the latter's friendship with the patriot politician, Walter Hussey Burgh (reputedly Dowdall's natural father). But no evidence that Grattan knew of his secret activities has been found, despite wishful thinking on the part of both the government and the United Irishmen.[10] Along with William Putnam McCabe, it was particularly with the Irish in England that Dowdall became re-involved. McCabe was the son of a radical Belfast watchmaker and a legendary recruiter for the United Irishmen. His business interests in France during the peace gave him a legitimate reason to mix with the disaffected textile workers of Lancashire and the Irish working-class community in London, recently significantly increased by refugees from the 1798 rebellion. This is the background to the so-called 'Despard Conspiracy' of November 1802 – a much misunderstood episode in British history – when Colonel Despard and a number of others were arrested in London, charged with treason and executed the following February. In fact, Despard appears to have been recruited by Dowdall to restrain the rashness of the London conspirators, for the plan was for some action in England to coincide with the movement in Ireland and both to occur only when the French arrived.[11]

Hamilton was an ally of Tone's in Paris, when Tone was fending off criticism from a newer group of United Irish exiles. Like Tone, he was on the French expedition to Lough Swilly in October 1798. Then Hamilton had narrowly escaped the fate of Tone, who had been captured and court-martialled after the defeat of the French fleet, only escaping execution by suicide. Other Irishmen, though French officers, had been executed as traitors when captured with the French forces. Recognising the dangers, the French officials in charge of prisoner exchange had expedited Hamilton's case; he was returned to France as an exchanged prisoner-of-war. Over the next four years his name appeared regularly on lists of United Irishmen in Paris; by 1800 he was President of the United Irish committee there.[12] Because Hamilton had never been arrested and was not a major figure in the United Irish organisation in Ireland, there was little intelligence about him in government agencies. In August 1798 Dublin Castle wanted to include him in the Banishment Act, but did not even have his first name, let alone sufficient evidence against him.[13] Moreover, in this pre-photography era, the identity of even well-known figures was often difficult to establish. In the summer of 1803 it was Robert Emmet's former tutor at Trinity who supplied the government with such a description, which predictably was five years out of date.

By now people like Hamilton, Lawless, Russell, MacNeven and the Emmets were semi-stateless. Those included in the Banishment Act risked execution if they returned to Ireland and even those not included felt little will to do so under the existing governing structure. Robert Emmet was one of these. They may have had little love for France, unlike the earlier generation of United Irish exiles, but there was nowhere else to go while the war continued. '"A" the Irishmen that I met in France', wrote former Trinity student George Orr, who became a double-agent after his arrest, 'always assured me that they liked the English much better than the French, and would rather be under the English Government, were they to be under any; but their heads seemed deranged with the theoretical idea of a Republic.'[14]

II

It was Hamilton's journey to Ireland at the turn of 1802/3, rather than Emmet's the previous autumn, that announced that the time was ripe for renewed action. When he left France he was in financial distress, for his wife had been unable to settle their financial affairs before she left Ireland. He borrowed money in London and made the onward journey to Liverpool as an outside passenger on the stagecoach (the cheapest fare). He told an old Fermanagh acquaintance whom he met in Liverpool that he was going to Ireland to recover some property left him by an aunt. Less than two weeks later he returned to France via London. He then had between 70 and 80 guineas and through James Farrell he took out a bill in London made payable in Paris. As a clerk in a London merchant house, Farrell had already channelled funds (largely supplied by Long) to those United Irishmen involved in organising what became known as 'Emmet's rebellion'.[15] Hamilton's return to Ireland coincided with the outbreak of serious agrarian disturbances in Munster, which he and his colleagues misinterpreted as more political than they were.[16] On his return to France preparations began in earnest for a renewed outbreak in Ireland.

Hamilton travelled to Brussels to persuade Thomas Emmet to come to Paris to replace those about to leave for Ireland.[17] He, McCabe, Thomas Russell and John Swiney then made preparations for an advance group to travel to Ireland. Michael Quigley was carrying out repairs to the Hotel Montmorency in Paris in February 1803 when he was recruited by McCabe 'to come to Ireland in order to assist in exciting another insurrection', and requested to stop at Rouen on the way. Over the winter his work during the day had prevented him entering into all the discussions among the United Irishmen in Paris, but they were clearly becoming very restless and in the evenings he heard of plans for them to join a French expedition to Louisiana, for which preparations were going forward at Le Havre. But in mid-January, Humbert – recently returned from Santo Domingo – talked to them about transforming the Le Havre preparations into an expedition to Ireland. Hamilton joined them at Rouen and they continued to Le Havre where Swiney told them about arms being amassed there for Ireland.[18] From there they travelled to Southampton, through London, Oxford, Birmingham and on to Liverpool. Hamilton had been open and talkative in the company of fellow Fermanagh-man George Kiernan when he stayed in Liverpool some weeks previously. On this occasion he said nothing about the reasons for his journey.[19]

They landed in Dublin on 5 March and met up with Robert Emmet at an inn in Capel Street. Quigley was delegated to travel to Kildare to sound out opinion among his former associates. He was typical of the bulk of those recruited in 1803 – working people, who had been 'out' in 1798 and commanded respect among like-minded people in their local communities. Many had migrated to the anonymity of Dublin city after 1798 and were key to plans to capture the capital. Miles Byrne had fought in the Wexford rebellion, but had found protection in Dublin's building trade through the agency of his stepbrother Edward Kennedy (a timber merchant). Years later Byrne recalled being recruited by Robert Emmet, through the overseer of John Patten's tannery at Dolphin's Barn, on the southern outskirts of the city. They had often discussed the patriotic reputation of the Emmet family and Byrne seized the opportunity of meeting Robert, 'a young patriot, of whom I had heard already so much'. Byrne takes up the story. 'Mr Emmet soon told me his plans. He said he wished to be acquainted with all those who had escaped in the war of '98, and who continued still to enjoy the confidence of the people ... He entered into many details of what Ireland had to expect from France in the way of assistance, now that the country was so energetically governed by the first Consul Buonaparte; but Buonaparte feared that the Irish people might be changed, and careless about their independence, in consequence of the union with England', and that this impression should be removed as soon as possible, that his brother had been consulted by members of the French government and they were all 'of opinion that a demonstration should be made by the Irish patriots to prove that they were as ready as ever to shake off the English yoke.' He said that he had been assured that the French would act as French General Rochambeau had with the American people in aiding their independence and that the methods by which the First Consul had come to be head of the French should be abhorred. Nevertheless he thought 'this great military chief' would deal fairly with the Irish as a means of getting at England; 'he therefore thought the country should be organised and prepared for those great events'. There was a good deal of embroidery in what Robert Emmet was telling potential supporters, for the United Irishmen in Paris had not yet received such assurances. 'Emmet's reason for saying the French would invade this country', Thomas Frayne was to tell the authorities, ' was only to encourage the lower order of the people as he often heard him say that bad as the English government was it was preferable to a French one, and that his object was a separation from England, to have it an independent state brought about by Irishmen only'.[20]

Byrne recalled Emmet's 'powerful, persuasive language', and he was not the only one to be won over by his reasoning. A Wicklow rebel, Matthew Doyle, was brought on board by Emmet's 'powerful and eloquent language'. He felt 'honoured and flattered' by such attention and marvelled that 'so young a man could possess such uncommon intellect'. Thomas Cloney, who had fought in the 1798 rebellion in Wexford, sought to dissuade Emmet from embarking on another rising. But he too was persuaded by Emmet's 'powers of reasoning and persuasion'. This was still the age of deference and the spell that those patriotic nobles and gentry could cast over the masses had already been shown by the legendary pull of the name of Lord Edward Fitzgerald. James Hope, the Templepatrick muslin weaver and long-standing United Irishman, was running a haberdasher's shop in the Coombe in Dublin, when he was contacted by Emmet. It was he who had introduced the new system into Antrim and Down in 1799 and, like Miles Byrne, he had been sustained by sympathetic employers after 1798.[21]

The plan remained that of 1799, with the capture of Dublin at its centre. By now, March/April 1803, Emmet was living under an assumed name, first at Harold's Cross, on the southern outskirts of Dublin, then at Butterfield Lane, Rathfarnham, further out and near the Dublin Mountains. The trusted figures among the Dublin tradesmen having been secured, these were now used to obtain a number of depots in the city, where the necessary arms were to be manufactured and stored. The main depots were in Marshalsea Lane at the back of the Bull Inn, Thomas Street, and Patrick Street, in the Liberties. Over the next four months fewer than a dozen men were to enter the main depot off Thomas Street and fewer than forty were made aware of the plan. These included just the kind of workmen and entrepreneurs whose everyday trade involved dealing with flintlocks, gunpowder and the like. Emmet took charge of the minutiae of military planning. In a letter written to his brother after the rising, he described in detail the various points of attack and defence. A surprise attack on Dublin Castle, by men assembling at the Patrick Street depot and at a number of houses secured nearby, was the centre-point of the plan. Other attacks would be made on the various barracks in the city to pin down the military. Emmet's plans show him more the inventor than the tactician and, whilst some may have been ahead of their time, the Miles Byrne-type of leader thought them fanciful and wasteful of their limited resources. Emmet suggested digging tunnels from the safe houses into the yards of the buildings to be attacked. Scaling ladders would be used to surmount surrounding walls, chains and padlocks to seal off key streets, exploding beams and iron bars with spikes laid down to block the advancing military, and hand grenades lobbed at them from upper windows. His armoury also included 'jointed' or folding pikes, intended for ease of concealment under great coats. And then there were the famous rockets that were being constructed at the Patrick Street depot.[22]

The person charged with their development had experience preparing fireworks, of which they were an elaboration. A gunsmith was employed to make several hundred sheet-iron tubes, twenty inches long, two-and-a-half inches in diameter and pointed like an arrow at one end. Emmet supplied him with detailed instructions for making the explosive filling and charges. Each would then be fastened to an eight-foot-long pole and positioned on a trestle ready for take-off. These rockets seem to have been largely intended for signalling purposes, with different emissions (sparks, stars etc.) being developed for different messages. Early in July a trial was made in fields just south of Dublin; 'it went off like a thunderbolt', Byrne recalled, 'carrying the pole along with it, and throwing fire and flames behind ... and when it fell, it went on tearing up the ground till the last of the matter with which it was filled was completely consumed.' Emmet was satisfied with its performance, subject to certain modifications of the fuse. But some of those who had been out in '98, and appreciated the need to arm the people cheaply, did not entirely approve of such expenditure on 'Robert Emmet's learned and scientific experiments'.[23] And that was not their only criticism of the main organisers, who by now also included Dowdall, Allen, Hamilton and Russell.

It was Russell's return in April that altered the pace of preparations. Hamilton had returned to France to fetch him. He was the best known of the commanders – the only one formally excluded from Ireland by the Banishment Act – and he risked drawing attention to the continuing preparations. Secret intelligence reaching government from France told of misgivings among some United Irishmen exiles about plans for another rising, 'that the moment was not yet ripe, that they would be certainly crushed'. But it was also thought 'that the secret disposition of the great majority of the Irish people was such … that when they had accredited leaders at their head, the explosion would be terrible'.[24] Government was beginning to get word of something afoot around this time, but thought those returning from France were 'not of the first order' and 'even among the Catholics the middling farmers and shopkeepers are extremely averse to a renewal of disturbance'. The Lord Lieutenant saw 'no reason to believe any system of regular disaffection in the country'.[25]

Some of the secondary leaders also complained of the expense of bringing over the leaders from France and housing them in Dublin when lack of resources dogged their preparations. The large house acquired in Butterfield Lane was nicknamed 'the Palace' and there were rumblings about unnecessary extravagance, in contrast to Emmet's previous 'simple mode of living'. Such too was Russell's reputation that too many wanted to catch a glimpse of him. Byrne recalled one evening when thirty people gathered for dinner to meet him and to hear what they might expect from the French government. 'His explanation on this point did not afford much satisfaction', for Russell believed the Irish should rise at once to free themselves and that the north to a man would rise. Both statements went counter to the principles on which they had been acting so far and it was general knowledge that the mood in the north had totally altered since 1798. But such was Russell's insistence on this point that it was decided to send two delegates to investigate, James Hope and Michael Berney, another Wexford man who had been out in 1798 and who had taken refuge in Dublin.[26] They returned with news of greater support in the north than had been expected and assurances that they would turn out if Dublin were captured. Michael Dwyer, who had held out since 1798 in the hills of Wicklow – the county from which the leaders expected most support – said much the same, though laying great stress on success in Dublin prior to any turnout from his men.

By May the secrecy of the preparations still held, but Emmet knew they could not avoid discovery for much longer and Patrick Gallagher (a Dublin shopkeeper) was sent to France to alert Emmet's brother. He was to report that they still intended waiting for the French, but would have to act if attacked. The French should be urged to fix a date for sending help, Thomas should send back some of the exiled leaders, for there was a great shortage of local leadership in Ireland, and extra funds, which were also lacking. Gallagher saw Thomas Emmet in Paris on 31 May. Unofficial negotiations between the Irish and the French government had continued. But they were complicated by the dispute between Emmet and O'Connor, both claiming the status of United Irish chief negotiator, and Emmet was frustrated at getting nowhere near 'the great'. Bonaparte had other things on his mind in these early days of the renewed war, but the delays were exacerbating Thomas Emmet's francophobia. His paranoia about O'Connor and distrust of the French spring from every sentence of his diary of this period. Arthur O'Connor was perhaps not the most reliable person to conduct such negotiations. But he showed a willingness to work with Emmet and even Emmet's supporters were upset by the quarrel, for it was clearly acting as a disincentive on the French authorities. It was unrealistic of all those involved in organising 'Emmet's rebellion' to have expected France to give immediate priority to Ireland on the resumption of hostilities in May and it was not until early August that the first intimation was given of French thinking on the issues raised by Robert Emmet. In that month it was agreed with the French authorities that John Swiney should travel to Ireland to tell the United Irishmen that the First Consul would mount another expedition and that they should avoid partial risings before then. But no dates were given, and Swiney had barely left France when news reached Paris of the rebellion in Dublin.[27]

III

Miles Byrne had attended a funeral in Bishop Street, Dublin, on Saturday 16 July and returned via the Patrick Street depot to ascertain progress. He was horrified to find a crowd assembled outside and to learn that an explosion had taken place. Three of the inmates were sent to hospital, where one died, and the refusal of those left inside to admit the fire-fighters aroused suspicion. A stray spark igniting the combustible material preparing for the rockets had been responsible for the explosion. Much of the ammunition was moved to another safe house acquired on Coal Quay, before the Dublin police arrived the following evening. Even so, they found traces of gunpowder and saltpetre, and clear signs of weapon manufacture; and those moving the ammunition had been involved in a tussle with some watchmen.[28] It was to become one of a long catalogue of incidents on which government failed to act that week and for which it was later pilloried. But Emmet and his co-conspirators were not to know this. Money had already run out before the preparations had been completed and many now must have rued the wastage on the fancy military experiments, to say nothing of those glorious green uniforms being prepared for the leaders. On 17 July Terence Coghlan, a tailor by trade, had fallen asleep in the yard of the Bull Inn after a night of drinking. The following morning he found himself forcibly 'recruited' to make uniforms in the Thomas Street depot. These were the 'regimentals' of the leaders, which Russell told his followers were the uniforms of French generals, and, with their gold epaulets, lace and cocked hats, they certainly impressed the working people being recruited. However much Russell and Emmet disliked the French, the uniforms, and the use of spoken French by Emmet and others, seem to have been designed to create the illusion of French backing.[29]

There were also signs that expectations of socially superior leaders coming forward in numbers comparable with those of 1798 were unrealistic. Some, who had earlier promised support, drew back when this became apparent. The mood was quite different in Ireland now and there were few signs of any desire to turn out again. The Hardwicke administration had continued the conciliatory policy of its predecessor and scaled down both security legislation and the size of the military force in the country. At this stage the leaders began to behave like the impoverished middle class that they were, jeopardising all to preserve what they had already acquired. Only the truly rich and the truly poor know how to cut their losses. Having expended nearly all their resources on preparations and struggling to find more, fear of losing them all at this stage became the prime reason for the decision to rise prematurely.

A meeting of the leaders just after the Patrick Street fiasco was divided on the wisdom of acting without French help. We do not know whether Emmet was one of those in favour of rising before the French arrived. Indeed, the Chief Secretary, William Wickham, was later convinced that he was not, though the slim chance of gaining some control before the French arrived might have been an incentive. It was decided to bring forward the rising to the 23rd – a Saturday, market day in Dublin, when the crowds filling the streets and the taverns would provide a good cover for the increased movement of people. Russell, Hamilton and Hope went north to raise the standard there, though the loss of Hope was soon felt because of his stature among the working people of the Liberties.

Emmet took up residence in the depot behind Thomas Street and spent much of his time composing the various manifestos, proclamations and instructions that have given 'Emmet's rebellion' a gloss of greater sophistication than existed in reality. A rough draft of instructions for military manoeuvres (left unfinished) Wickham thought showed 'talent and judgement'.[30] It reads like the plan of campaign for a regular army and sits strangely beside what we know of a working men's (civilian) conspiracy already beginning to fall apart. Wickham believed it was written with the French army in mind, but that is uncertain and the generalised instructions for manoeuvres in different terrain would hardly have been necessary for a seasoned French force. Was it written for the commanders in the counties, who the leaders thought would respond on the fall of Dublin? Or was this Emmet doing what came most naturally to him, writing about military tactics?

Both the original draft of the manifesto of the provisional government and bundles of printed copies 'quite wet from the press' were also found. The hurry in which it was prepared was evident from the oblique reference in the text to the Patrick Street explosion having removed the advantage of surprise (and surprise at the government's slowness to act upon it). The preamble is excessively long and complicated, lacking the punch and clarity of Tone's public writings. 'You are called upon to shew the world that you are competent to take your place among nations; as an independent country: by the only satisfactory proof you can furnish of your capability of maintaining your independence, your wresting it from England with your own hands.' The system for doing so has been developed 'without the hope of foreign assistance' (a point to which it returns several times) over the past eight months. It is largely on the men of Ulster and Leinster that it calls to take the initiative and those of the other two provinces then to follow their example. They should not sully the 'honour' of the country by 'excesses', 'intoxication, plunder, or revenge' and should give no excuse to their enemies to call it 'a religious contest'. There are disclaimers of any war against property, and there had been heated discussions on this point between followers and leaders in the months before the outbreak. Their only enemy was 'English dominion'. Whilst the provisional government would abolish tithes and take church and government property into the ownership of the nation, there were few carrots held out to the foot soldiers. Rather this was to be as orderly a transfer of power as possible. The generals were to follow strict military codes concerning hostages and prisoners, until the provisional government could hand over power after elections to a parliament like the one just lost, though no longer so 'notoriously bribed' and unrepresentative. The French are nowhere mentioned.[31]

There can have been little time to rest after the decision to bring forward preparations, and Miles Byrne tells of the frantic activities of the secondary leaders to alert people to plans for the 23rd. Some only learnt of the new date on the previous evening – 'the time came on in such a hurry', explained Patrick Farrell, steward to a grocer in Thomas Street, who had been forcibly detained in the depot after he had stumbled upon it on Friday night – and there were still doubts on the day itself about the wisdom of going ahead.[32] The secrecy that had confined knowledge of the preparations to a few and the advance of plans for a turnout before such preparations were complete resulted in utter confusion on 23 July. Because of the losses at the Patrick Street depot and the impossibility of completing arrangements elsewhere in Dublin, plans now concentrated on the capture of the Castle. Men forewarned in Wicklow, Kildare and Wexford were to come in to Dublin and an advance party out of the Thomas Street depot would enter the Castle yard in six hackney coaches, as if they were attending a levee.

But messengers were only sent to the neighbouring counties at the last minute. Some, like the one sent to tell Michael Dwyer in Wicklow, never arrived. Confusion reigned and many who had started to

come in turned back on the false report that the rising had
poned. Ned Conlon acquired the coaches in good time, u
icked and shot a soldier who enquired about their destination
which the drivers took off with their coaches. 'The time of assembly
was from six till nine', Emmet later wrote to his brother; 'and at nine,
instead of two thousands, there were eighty men assembled … Add
to this, the preparations were, from an unfortunate series of disap-
pointments in money, unfinished; scarcely any blunderbusses bought
up. The man who was to turn the fuzes and rammers for the beams
forgot them, and went off to Kildare to bring men, and did not return
till the very day', so that the whole of the 22nd and 23rd 'which
ought to have spent in arrangements, was obliged to be employed in
work. Even this, from the confusion occasioned by men crowding
into the Depot from the country, was almost impossible'. Patrick Farrell tells of people being sent out that morning for flints, powder and
ball cartridge. The various components necessary to complete the arsenal (even if they had been purchased and much had not) were mis-
laid in the mêlée. Gunpowder was everywhere, lying ankle deep,
reported the army officer who investigated the depot later that night.
The people were refusing to act without blunderbusses and money
was only found to purchase some at five o'clock on the 23rd. Late that
evening orders were given to take the arms of the sentries at the Marshalsea debtors' prison (off Thomas Street), but these, like the other
last-minute preparations, could not be completed, because they were
ordered to turn out early.

'To change the day was impossible', Emmet later wrote to his
brother; 'for I expected the counties, and feared to lose the advantage
of surprise. The Kildare men were coming in for three days; and after
that, it was impossible to draw back.' This was confirmed by information later given to government. It was because so many had already
come in from the countryside that Emmet decided to go ahead, even
though he knew the preparations to be incomplete and 'against the
opinion of some of his associates'. Some of these from Kildare met

with him at the White Bull Inn at two o'clock and queried whether he actually had the means to proceed with the insurrection. When he failed to satisfy them as to arms and men and 'not being satisfied with a speech which he made to them', they ordered their men to return to the country.[33] Hearing of the departure of the Kildare men, the Dublin leaders also refused to act. It was now 7 p.m. and differences continued about what action to take. Should they still try to take the Castle? Perhaps it would now be better to take the barracks or other buildings where quantities of arms could be had. But Emmet still wanted to take the Castle and he spoke about it as if it would be relatively easy and bloodless.[34] Did Emmet really believe this, or was it his famous persuasiveness trying to rally the doubters? Whichever way, plans were being constantly altered in the course of the evening.

When the military first arrived at the depot later that evening, they found a single hackney-coach at the door, the horse still breathing heavily as if recently arrived.[35] The last-minute plan had been for Emmet to take a carriage to join with those gathered at Coal Quay and from there to make the attack on the Castle. But preparations were interrupted by a false report that troops were surrounding the depot and they decided to come out and fight in the street. 'It is my opinion they did not intend to break out so soon,' Farrell told his interrogators, 'only something happened then that I could not understand [which] ... made them turn out sooner than they expected.' At around nine o'clock John Fleming, an ostler at the White Bull, in the confidence of those in the depot, saw Emmet, at the door, draw his sword and call out 'come on boys'.[36] Shortly afterwards John Fisher – son of an excise officer – caught sight of Emmet by the lamplight as he looked through his drawing-room window at No. 89 Thomas Street. 'Come on boys, we'll take the Castle', he urged on the crowd, mostly Kildare men, who followed him.[37] Supporters had been gathering at Owen Kirwan's house in Plunkett Street and on the signal of a rocket from Thomas Street, they set off in that direction. Pikes were being let down from the upper storeys of the depot and distributed to

a larger group of rebels. It was these that the watch
as they were leaving Marshalsea Lane. Nearby, two r
been sent to Sylvester Costigin's distillery to open the gate
ing an exchange of fire, looked at their watches and comment
it was 'too soon'.[38]

The hasty decision to turn out and fight was a repeat of a similar
occasion on the 17th, when Emmet had risked all to help rescue a
barrel of ammunition being moved from Patrick Street, which had
been seized by watchmen. These were the actions of a very young
man, idealistic and oblivious to danger. William Colville, a distant relative, thought him 'a very young giddy man (known to be highly eccentric and impractical'). Hope says much the same, though more
charitably, and all the contemporary accounts – hostile and
favourable alike – refer to his extreme youth. Emmet told Quigley in
confidence that unless the numbers turning out were larger than expected 'he would attempt nothing then, but march them off and join
Dwyer in the mountains'. He had counted on some 2,000 men joining him in Thomas Street. Instead some 300 did (only 80 considered
reliable) and even these, according to the baker Nicholas Stafford
(one of the commanders at the depot), would not obey his directions.
They remained in Thomas Street for less than fifteen minutes and by
the time they reached the market house at the top of the street only
18 to 20 followers remained. Shortly afterwards Richard Wornall, a
Patrick Street victualler, caught sight of Robert Emmet in his general's
uniform, waving his sword and urging the men on: 'Turn out my boys,
now is your time for Liberty', he called out, and fired a pistol in the
air. A larger group of around 300 passed by minutes later, breaking
the lamps as they went and demanding to know in what direction
Emmet's party had gone.[39]

Although Myles Byrne waited with a few hundred Wexford men in
Coal Quay for Emmet's men to join them, the authorities had already
been alerted, the Castle gates were closed and troop movements
could be heard in the nearby streets. By now Emmet had abandoned

the attempt and continued up Francis Street out to Butterfield Lane and then into hiding in the Wicklow Mountains, from where countermanding orders were issued to prevent those who had not already turned out from doing so. 'Had I another week – had I one thousand pounds – had I one thousand men, I would have feared nothing', continued Emmet in his explanation to his brother. 'There was redundancy enough in any one part to have made up, if complete, for deficiency in the rest: but there was failure in all – plan, preparation, and men.'[40]

A messenger sent from Coal Quay by Miles Byrne was the first to encounter the signs of confusion in Thomas Street and the pikes strewn about the street. But it was not till eleven o'clock that night that the authorities searched the area and discovered the depot. At dawn – when a difference in width between the external walls and the interior was noted – the full secrets were exposed. Then a false partition wall running through several stories was broken down, huge quantities of pikes discovered, mattresses, blankets, ammunition, grappling irons and a scaling ladder, unfinished items of the officers' uniforms, some green flags trimmed with white, bundles of the proclamation and over 200 freshly baked loaves.[41] Yet even though the authorities were now on full alert, Miles Byrne and his Wexford men were able to scour the streets throughout the night in search for Emmet, without meeting any opposition.

IV

The government had been caught entirely unawares and an almighty clamour broke over their heads in consequence. The Lord Chancellor, Lord Redesdale, told the Prime Minister, Henry Addington, that he had known nothing of the rebellion till knocked up at four o'clock on the morning of the 24th.[42] There are few signs that any extra precautions had been taken as a result of the Patrick Street explosion. The under-secretary, Alexander Marsden, was holding the fort on his

own, for the Chief Secretary, William Wickham, had been on holiday
in Yorkshire and now claimed to be recuperating from illness at his
Norwich home. 'I wish you would say a word in the newspapers', he
wrote to the then Lord Lieutenant, Philip Yorke, 3rd Earl of Hardwicke on the eve of his departure for Ireland, 'announcing my arrival
with my family, to show that we are not afraid, and accounting for my
absence, such as I had been confined for three weeks.'[43] The Lord
Lieutenant was in his official residence in the Phoenix Park, some distance from the Castle across the river. In 1803 there was no one in
Dublin capable of giving the government reliable information, for
Cooke had been treated dismissively by Hardwicke and had resigned
in disgust.[44] Rumours and reports of disaffection were ten a penny
throughout these years and officials had learnt to treat frequent loyalist scares with some scepticism. Moreover, the riotousness of the
Dublin working-class (to say nothing of their frequent intoxication –
a major contributory factor to the scuffles of the night of the 23rd)
was notorious. Just over a week earlier Major Sirr had been stoned by
crowds on the quays as he tried to intervene in Bastille Day celebrations, involving huge bonfires, rockets and firing – which occasioned
his complaint about the usual inactivity of the city magistrates.[45] It
would have been difficult to distinguish this from the real preparations for some kind of uprising. It was only late on the day itself that
reports coming into Marsden convinced him that something was
afoot and it was the series of despatches that he sent out which
brought about the most notorious casualties of 'Emmet's rebellion'.

The new commander-in-chief, General Henry Fox, had only returned from the west of Ireland the night before and was with the
Lord Lieutenant in the viceregal lodge when, at two o'clock, they received an urgent message from Marsden to come to the Castle. But so
indeterminate was the information received about a possible rebellion that at six o'clock the Lord Lieutenant returned to the Park,
passing through the very centre of Emmet's preparations. Later that
evening the military were warned to be on alert, the drums beat to

arms and it was while on his way to the barracks that Lieutenant Colonel Brown was piked to death by the mob, which had now taken over the streets after the departure of the leaders. A carriage bringing to town the Lord Chief Justice, Lord Kilwarden, his daughter and his nephew, the Revd Richard Wolfe, was stopped in Thomas Street and the two men murdered. Kilwarden had been a humane and popular judge and the murders cast particular odium upon the rebellion, so much so that a saving role had to be created for Emmet in the developing legend as rescuing Miss Wolfe, even though he was nowhere near Thomas Street when it happened.[46]

In Ulster the collapse had been even more marked. At first Hamilton parted from Russell and Hope and went into Cavan and Monaghan, but then returned to Antrim and Down, where their efforts were concentrated. However, they found little of the support that they claimed from the earlier visit. Then Hope had only spoken with his social peers and the middle-class leaders of previous years – with whom Russell was friendly and on whom he placed such store – were unimpressed. Things had changed in the north and Russell – out of circulation since 1796 – was completely out of touch. Even had the French landed in force and inspired risings elsewhere in the country, the depth of sectarianism in Ulster would most likely have cancelled out any lingering support there. Russell exhausted himself riding back and forth to former haunts in the two counties. But though he tried to inspire confidence by donning his general's green uniform and issuing proclamations on behalf of the provisional government, he offered no arms, no chance of a French invasion (which witnesses said he seemed positively hostile towards), and no plan of campaign besides an overriding belief that the people would turn out automatically when called upon. It was madness, and some thought in retrospect that years of imprisonment and impoverishment had unhinged Russell's mind. But there was more to it than this and his most recent biographer – James Quinn – makes a compelling case for a dogmatic millennialism. A fatalistic and melancholy man, with an unworldliness and all-embracing religiosity that made him such a foil to his friend Tone, Russell's sense that providence ruled all and would triumph eventually was clearly guiding his now impaired judgement. 'I go this moment', he wrote to Frank McCracken after the collapse, 'for the purpose of … rectifying the mistakes that have taken place. Whether I fail or succeed is in the hands of God, but the cause I will never relinquish. He has for the present stopt our progress … if you here [sic] of my friend [Hamilton] you will tell him or any other person I am gone to join anybody I can find in arms in support of their rights and that of mankind.'[47]

The cult of sacrifice – bequeathed by this era to future Irish republicanism – was fundamental to Russell's psyche. There were many occasions in his life since helping to found the Society of United Irishmen in 1791 when he actively put his well being in jeopardy in pursuit of principle, courting long imprisonment when minor compromises secured the release of others. Now, when defeat was glaringly obvious, he chose not to escape as nearly all the other main leaders of 1803 had done, but, with a price of £1,500 on his head, he travelled to Dublin, to rescue the now imprisoned Emmet. 'There were many United Irishmen who were prepared to sacrifice their lives', writes James Quinn, 'but few embraced their fate as readily as Russell, whose rigid millennialist convictions drove him steadily towards inevitable martyrdom.'[48] Like Emmet, Russell was a noble individual, and they had much in common. Emmet too could have escaped. Instead, he returned to his lodgings at Harold's Cross on 28 July, and was arrested there on 25 August. However, in both men there was an irresponsible belief in their own ability to lead the masses, although they showed little understanding of what these people really wanted, as Jemmy Hope discovered in his conversations with Emmet whom he otherwise admired.

The events in Dublin sparked off a degree of panic among the Protestant gentry in formerly rebellious counties and there were reports from Wexford and Longford of them fleeing to the towns for safety.[49] But apart from a number of attacks by rebels in Kildare, the events in Dublin did not unleash any major disturbances elsewhere in the country, whatever the persistence of low-lying disaffection.[50] However, they did contribute to the religious polarisation in the country, which was such a feature of the early 1800s. Emmet may have argued – and I think genuinely so – that all the leaders were Protestant and he assumed that Catholics would not suffer. But this was part of his self-delusion. The 1803 rebellion only served to throw the anti-popery of both Irish and English ruling classes into ever-sharper focus. Indeed, the very absence of the Irish Parliament (abolished with the Union in 1801) rendered the Irish Protestant ascendancy all the more fearful of the Catholic population.[51]

And just another popish rebellion is how the Protestant ascendancy now saw that of 1803. The Catholic Archbishop of Dublin, John Troy, had written an exhortation denouncing the rising, which was to be read from the altars at mass the next morning, 24 July.[52] But although Troy was the most anti-republican of the Catholic hierarchy, his exhortation was denounced by the Castle as hypocritical. It was believed that the conspirators must have confided their plans to their priests in confession and Troy was brought to the Castle for questioning on the issue. All the old misconceptions about what Catholics believed – generally more muted in the past two decades – were once again aired. An extraordinary exchange of letters took place between the Lord Chancellor, Lord Redesdale, and the Catholic Lord Fingall on the old theme that Catholics could not give allegiance to a Protestant state. In the circumstances Fingall's response was restrained and he wondered why Redesdale – who, as Sir John Mitford, had been responsible for ameliorating the lot of the English Catholics in the early 1790s – should think so differently of *Irish* Catholics. Given that the Fingalls and Troys of Ireland had been invaluable to government in their support of the recent union, and had been denied the restoration of full political rights, which they had been led to believe would be the reward for their loyalty, it was an inauspicious

start to the new century. Lord Cornwallis and Lord Castlereagh –
both now in England and still staunch supporters of Catholic rights –
certainly felt as much. Given the failure of the Irish government to
prevent the attempted insurrection, there was much speculation
about a return of Cornwallis to Ireland in 1803. But, as he later
learnt, the suggestion was suppressed through the influence of 'the violent Protestant feeling in the Cabinet'.[53]

4 Final days

The fathers and mothers of Ireland should often tell their children that story of Robert Emmet and that story of Anne Devlin … To the Irish mothers who hear me I would say that when at night you kiss your children and in your hearts call down a benediction, you could wish for your boys no higher thing than that, should the need come, they may be given the strength to make Emmet's sacrifice, and from your girls no greater gift from God than such fidelity as Anne Devlin's.'

Patrick Pearse, 'Robert Emmet: an address delivered at an Emmet commemoration in New York on March 9 1914'

'I am vexed about my friend Marsden, who will undoubtedly be blamed for not having better channels of intelligence', Cornwallis wrote on 1 August to his old friend Charles Ross. In the event it was General Fox who was moved. Marsden survived, but only just, and Wickham, caught in a vortex of criticism from Irish loyalists and the London government, resigned prematurely some months later. Thirty years later he was still deeply upset by the whole experience. In the evolution of the legend of Robert Emmet there has been a persistent trend to view his rebellion as part of a government conspiracy. The charge is that the government knew about it in advance and let it happen.[1] The claim cannot be sustained against all the evidence to the contrary. Only in the conduct of the subsequent trials and executions can government ministers be accused of hastening events and even then it was as much an effort to cover up its own inadequacies as anything else. Commenting on the attacks made on government for its unpreparedness, Lady Hardwicke wrote to a friend:

> The ignorant or angry letters from Dublin are believed in England ... In their intemperance they loudly declared their belief that no jury would dare to find the rebels guilty, or that, if they did, would Government *dare* to punish them. In spite of all their violence, they have seen that the slow but steady march of justice can overtake the offender, even in this lawless country. No attempt has been made to rescue the prisoners, and the trials and the executions have been undisturbed, though in the midst of multitudes. The sentence being put in force the following day has struck much awe on the minds of those who talked so loud of the fear or weakness of their rulers.[2]

It is hard to escape the conclusion that the treason trials of 1803 were largely staged with government critics in mind.

I

In public, members of the government tried to play down the rebellion and ultimately went along with Emmet's own version that he alone was responsible. In private, however, there was panic and recrimination. Wickham now felt sure that the attempted rising was a prelude to a full French invasion and he criticised London for letting its intelligence channels lapse during the recent peace. A scattergun approach was adopted to arrests and most of the leading people escaped. The messenger sent with news of the outbreak arrived in London on the night of 27–28 July, but so little information accompanied the despatch that ministers were pilloried next day in parliament when they had to announce it. 'Though I have seen several letters from Dublin', complained William Windham (former war minister, now in opposition), 'I learn nothing further than what the papers contain, unless it be that it was a complete surprise.'[3] How could ministers call for emergency security legislation while at the same time dismissing the events of 23 July as the 'contemptible effort of a wild and extravagant young man'?[4] Perhaps 'the ministers would tell them when they should have made up their minds upon the subject', commented Windham, 'whether the late insurrection was really a contemptible riot' or something which had taken deeper root.[5]

Despite all the statements to the contrary, the Irish government was sure that Emmet's attempt was the prelude to something greater and it desperately sought further information. But such was the secrecy of the preparations that few outside the main leaders had any to give. Dowdall, Allen and a number of the other leaders escaped to France. Miles Byrne also made his way there, having been sent by Emmet early in August to tell his brother what had happened and urge renewed efforts to send French help.

Emmet was arrested on 25 August at his lodgings at Harold's Cross, to which he had returned on 28 July. After the failure of the 23rd, Emmet and about a dozen others made their way back to Butterfield Lane, where, Anne Devlin later told Dr Madden, she chastised them for leading the people to destruction and then abandoning them. If so, she told Emmet no more than he was already thinking, for witnesses later spoke of his fatalistic mood and of his refusal even to seek refuge with Dwyer because of the failure. John Patten and Phil Long tried to persuade him to leave at once for France, but he replied 'that it should never be said of him that he had abandoned the brave people implicated through his means'.[6] The owner of one of the houses to which they moved from Butterfield Lane thought him 'rather ill-looking'. Emmet and the other leaders were still in their uniforms when Anne Devlin found them 'sitting on the side of a hill' the following day. Anne brought a change of jacket for Emmet; the many descriptions of what he was wearing would later inform the legend. For, quite apart from the striking green regimentals, Emmet had been fastidious in cutting a figure: white waistcoat and pantaloons (cashmere), new, black and fashionable 'Hessian boots' and black velvet stock or neckcloth being commented upon by a number of witnesses to these events.[7] Emmet decided to return with Anne to Dublin. It is difficult to explain why he should have placed himself in such danger, when he had been offered the chance to remain with Michael Dwyer's men until his escape could be arranged. It has long been assumed that he returned for personal reasons.

A large part of the romance of Robert Emmet involves his relationships with two young women who subsequently acquired the status of tragic heroines in popular tradition. The first was Anne Devlin, a sixteen-year-old farmer's daughter and cousin to Michael Dwyer. She was part of an extended family, most of whom had been out in 1798 and became re-involved in Emmet's rebellion. It was her father who procured the house in Butterfield Lane and Anne was assigned as housekeeper. But she was much more than this; she was fully apprised of the plans and frequently acted as confidential messenger. She lived long enough to tell her tale to Dr Madden and Brother Luke Cullen, and in graphic detail described her half-hanging by the yeomanry to extract information and her long imprisonment in Kilmainham gaol.[8] Today her cell is the centrepiece of the museum, into which Kilmainham was transformed in the1960s.

The other young woman was Sarah Curran, youngest daughter of the celebrated advocate, John Philpot Curran. The Curran family was friendly with the Emmets and Sarah's brother Richard had been at Trinity with Robert Emmet. Sarah, black-haired and dark-eyed, was a rather pensive and melancholic girl, but was said to have had the singing voice of an angel and had been coached by the young Thomas Moore. It was only after Emmet's return to Ireland in1802 that the love affair began and it was Anne Devlin who conveyed the correspondence between them. A friend of Sarah's later explained that Robert Emmet's delay in Ireland had been caused by her refusal to

accompany him to America and she blamed herself for his fate.[9]
Emmet acted like the infatuated young man that he was in his personal relationship with Sarah Curran and had not destroyed her letters. They were found both in the Marshalsea Lane depot and on his
person when captured. They were unsigned and at first they were
thought to be those of his sister, Mary Anne Holmes – the affectionate allusions considered some kind of code. Even so when members
of the Privy Council told Emmet during interrogation that they had
the letters, his composure evaporated. He became extremely agitated,
talked confusingly about having to balance his honour with his duty
and – having until then refused to answer questions – began to hint at
another Kilmainham treaty, making disclosures but concealing names.

Some days later he wrote to Wickham:

> Sir, I have heard of you as an honourable man and as such
> I commit myself to you without reserve. I have weighed
> well the proposal that was made to me … Give me the
> same advantages. Let me have free communication with
> some friends; let the lives of others be spared; let the
> documents affecting another person be suppressed, and I
> will try how far in my conscience, and according to *my*
> notions of duty, I ought to go. But I will stand my trial,
> for I will not purchase my own safety.

Until this break in Emmet's composure, Wickham doubted they had
enough evidence for a case against him. Despite all the documents
found at the depot, no one could assert conclusively that they were in
his handwriting. 'He was very much beloved in private life, so that all
the friends of his family, even those who abhorred his treasons, will be
glad of any pretext to avoid appearing against him.'

On 4 September Wickham replied to Emmet's letter of the 3rd.
Any statement he wished to make would be carefully considered, but
no conditions could be agreed in advance.[10] The same day, Emmet

began seriously to entertain the idea of escape and St John Mason tried to bribe the gaoler George Dunn. Dunn was also entrusted with another letter that Emmet had written to Sarah Curran (this time actually writing her name on the cover).

> My Dearest Love, I don't know how to write to you. I never felt so oppressed in my life as at the cruel injury I have done you. I was seized and searched with a pistol over me before I could destroy your letters. They have been compared with those found before. I was threatened with having them brought forward against me in Court. I offered to plead guilty if they would suppress them. This was refused. Information (without mentioning names) was required. I refused, but offered since, if I would be permitted to consult others … that I would only require for my part of it to have those letters suppressed, and that I would stand my trial. It has been refused. My love, can you forgive me? … I have written to your father to come to me [as his counsel] tomorrow. Had you not better speak to himself to-night? Destroy my letters that there may be nothing against yourself, and deny having any knowledge of me further than seeing me once or twice. For God's sake, write to me by the bearer one line to tell me how you are in spirits. I have no anxiety, no care, about myself; but I am terribly oppressed about you. My dearest love, I would with joy lay down my life, but ought I to do more? … I must send this off at once; I have written it in the dark. My dearest Sarah, forgive me. [11]

Dunn exposed both the escape plan and the letter and on the morning of 9 September Major Sirr raided the Curran house at Rathfarnham. The Castle's correspondence concerning the Curran affair is instructive (as, indeed, is that with Robert Emmet). Anne Devlin and her like could be treated roughly, but the same delicacy towards the genteel, which had impelled even Lord Clare to facilitate a visit by relatives to the imprisoned Lord Edward Fitzgerald, now came into play. Curran had been an active reformer and critic of government all his life. He had defended many of the leading United Irishmen in court and even Emmet had at first named him as counsel. One might have assumed that his fall from grace would have delighted government supporters as much as Grattan's had in 1798. Silencing him was also an end worth achieving, for the arrest of Russell (9 September) threatened to revive the issue of government's 'bad faith' over the Kilmainham treaty.[12]

However, Wickham was embarrassed by it all and sought assurances from London that neither the British nor the Irish government would reveal the name of Sarah Curran. Sirr took a letter to her father from Wickham on the morning of the raid: 'Sir, It is with extreme regret that I find myself under the necessity of informing you that the Lord Lieutenant is obliged to direct that a search should be made in your house for papers connected with the late treasonable conspiracy. The Lord Lieutenant is persuaded that they have been concealed there without your knowledge ...', and he offered to examine Sarah at Curran's town house rather than the Castle as 'less distressing'.[13] Wickham was genuinely dismayed that Curran had not been at home that morning when Sirr arrived and the Town Major had therefore to enter Sarah's room when she was still in bed. The fact that her sister used the embarrassing occasion to start destroying papers seemed less unpleasant than the scene of Sirr invading her bedroom. Sirr sent a despatch to Wickham, who responded instructing him to leave, and the Attorney-General – Standish O'Grady, a personal friend of Curran – was sent in his place. 'I lament exceedingly the circumstance of Mr Curran's absence from his country house on your arrival there', Wickham wrote to Sirr, 'and am much distressed to learn the state of Miss S. Curran's mind as you described in your letter. I think it better on the whole that you should leave the house and return without delay to town.'[14]

Curran had never supported militant republicanism and was appalled by the murder of his friend and mentor Lord Kilwarden. Signs are that illness and a recent visit to France under Bonaparte were altering his former radicalism.[15] However, the whole affair clouded Curran's legal judgment. His refusal to represent Emmet was entirely understandable. But when those of lower social standing also nominated him and were also tried for high treason, he did not give them adequate representation. In an extraordinary statement for the defence in the trial of Owen Kirwan – a 'cast-clothes man' of Plunkett Street in Dublin – he scarcely mentioned the prisoner in a speech occupying almost twelve columns of the trial report. Instead he spoke at length of the total lack of justification for such an insurrection, given the changed situation of the country and the mildness of the present government. He fulminated against Bonaparte and the idiocy of preferring French to British rule, denounced the murder of Kilwarden and the rising as 'a drunken riotous insurrection ... of the most contemptible insignificance'. His conduct surprised the Attorney-General:

> Curran ... made a most extraordinary speech. He set out
> with praising Government, congratulating the court on
> the loyalty of the great majority of the people, professing
> his own loyalty, abusing Buonaparte for his causing the
> present Rebellion, and advising the mob, as an old friend,
> against their present folly. So far his speech did him great
> credit. But then forgetting all he said, he occupied the
> court nearly an hour in proving no Rebellion existed, and
> then sat down, having totally forgotten his client in the
> transaction. I once thought it would have been necessary
> to have spoken to evidence, in reply to Mr. Curran; but
> the latter part of his speech was so extravagant, and the
> witnesses produced for the prisoner were guilty of such
> gross contradictions, that I declined speaking.[16]

Her use of letters is import her melbutty

The scourge of the establishment for decades was silenced.

After Curran's questioning before the Privy Council on 10 September, he wrote to Emmet, withdrawing as his counsel. In response, Emmet wrote at length about how his relationship had developed with Sarah Curran and retelling how he had tried to secure anonymity for her by his various offers to the Privy Council.

> I know that I have done you very severe injury, much greater than I can atone for with my life ... There has been much culpability on my part in all this, but there has also been a great deal of that misfortune which seems uniformly to have accompanied me ... looking upon her as one, whom, if I had lived, I hoped to have had my partner for life ... I know not whether success would have blotted out the recollection of what I have done – but I know that a man, with the coldness of death on him, need not be made to feel any other coldness, and that he may be spared any addition to the misery he feels not for himself, but for those to whom he has left nothing but sorrow.

This letter was published in 1819 in Curran's life by his son William Henry. In this he mistakes the date, assuming it was written at the same time as the letter to his brother Richard after Emmet's conviction. But the correct date appears to have been immediately after his receipt of Curran's as it is mentioned in information sent by Leonard MacNally to Wickham on 12 September: 'Emmet appears deeply affected on account of the young lady whose letters are in the possession of Government ... On this subject his mind seems wholly bent, and cruelly afflicted. For his own personal safety he appears not to entertain an idea. He does not intend to call a single witness, nor to trouble any witness for the Crown with a cross-examination, unless they misrepresent facts.'[17]

In preparing the case against Emmet, the government was having difficulty connecting him with the documents found at the depot and at the house where he was arrested and sought to come to an agreement with Richard Curran to suppress his sister's letters in return for a witness who could identify his handwriting. Richard thought that Emmet himself would admit to writing them in return for such an undertaking.[18] This suggestion was declined and no such witness was produced at the trial. Although by this stage government did not think Sarah's letters of material importance in the prosecution, the pressure on Curran was maintained. It suited government better to depict the letters as coming from a 'brother conspirator' and so they were presented at the trial.

II

We now come to those events that were to form the core of the Emmet legend: his trial and execution, and most of all his speech. Trials of the 'better sort' always attracted great interest, but this trial was attracting an unusual degree of attention.[19] The treason trials of those implicated in the rising opened at the Green Street courthouse on Wednesday 31 August with that of Edward Kearney, a dealer in skins, arrested with a pike in his hand in Thomas Street. Over the following two weeks the trials also took place of Thomas Roche, a slater and plasterer, Owen Kirwan, a tailor and second-hand clothes dealer, James Byrne, a baker, John Begg, an apprentice car and jaunting-car maker, Walter Clare, a labourer in a distillery, Felix Rourke, a small farmer and former shoemaker, John Killen, keeper of a lodging house, John McCann, a publican, Joseph Doran, a labourer in an ordnance yard, Thomas Donnelly and Nicholas Farrell, labourers, Laurence Begley, a hostler, and Michael Kelly, a bricklayer. They had been arrested with pikes in their hands on the night of the 23rd. All except Clare and Doran were found guilty and executed the day after their conviction. Three carpenters, Henry Howley, John MacIntosh and

Thomas Keenan, and coal-factor Denis Redmond were tried and executed after Emmet. Redmond had been due for trial on 5 September, but the gaoler found him 'weltering in blood' on the floor of his cell, where he had attempted to shoot himself. His action prompted the government to take precautionary measures to prevent the other prisoners acting likewise. Emmet was indignant. He wrote to Wickham: 'I find with whatever delicacy it has been done, that the use of a knife and fork or razor has been prohibited to me – I was ignorant from what cause this could have proceeded until I heard of an unfortunate occurrence that has lately taken place and as I presume that this must have been the reason for issuing the order, I request that it may be countermanded, as whatever my situation might be I hope that I should never have so much cowardice nor so little principle as to commit suicide.'[20]

Redmond had only been brought into the conspiracy after the Patrick Street explosion required new premises to which the arms could be moved. He was having a house repaired on Coal Quay, into which he planned to move after his forthcoming marriage. He was flattered to be asked to lend it to Emmet and the arms were duly transferred. He was unusual among those enlisted in being 'a man of some fortune and some education'. It was in this house that Miles Byrne had gathered with the Wexford men on 23 July. After the failure of the rising Redmond panicked and tried to dispose of the pikes into a neighbouring yard. He escaped on board a vessel bound for Chester, only to be taken when it was driven by bad weather into Carlingford.[21] He was the last to be executed on 6 October. All (except perhaps Redmond) were described by Wickham as 'miserably poor. Three and four guineas are given with their briefs. In the year 1798 thirty guineas were usually given to leading Counsel.' [22]

Emmet's trial opened at 10.00 a.m. on Monday 19 September. Contrary to legend it was a fair trial. The case for the prosecution connected him with the Thomas Street depot and the house in Butterfield Lane, the small desk in the depot where he kept his writings and his general's uniform. His escape into the mountains with the other leaders was tracked, the farmer from Ballymeece (Tallaght parish) where they stopped on the 26th identifying 'that young man or boy, or whatever you call him' as the 'French officer' who came that night. The task of his defence team – Tone and Russell's old friend Peter Burrowes and Leonard MacNally – was an impossible one. Emmet instructed them not to call any witnesses, or to make a case. When Burrowes would try to disconcert a witness in cross-examination, Emmet would check him: 'No, no; the man's speaking the truth.' And when he was about to avail himself of the right to reply 'wearied to death with anxiety, and feeling both the painfulness and inutility of what he was about to do', Burrowes later told Thomas Moore, Emmet said, 'Pray do not attempt to defend me; it is all in vain', and Burrowes accordingly desisted.[23] Emmet intervened himself to emphasise that part of the proclamation that stated that no form of torture was to be used and no one executed until the provisional government had pronounced on such.

At the close of the trial, despite a challenge from MacNally, William Coyningham Plunket, counsel for the prosecution, delivered an hour-long speech for which he was later much criticised. It spent as much time complimenting the present mild government and denouncing the French system of 'liberty' as on the case in hand, and he was later pilloried for thus ingratiating himself with a government that he had previously attacked. 'It was delivered on purpose to show his entire and unqualified renunciation of his former principles', wrote Wickham, 'his determination on due and mature reflection, to support the Union after having been its inveterate opposer, and to stand or fall with the present Administration. You may naturally suppose that this is the prelude to closer connection, and that it will be the death-blow to the anti-Union party at the Bar.'[24] His behaviour at the trial was blatantly careerist and he became Solicitor-General shortly afterwards. Plunket had been a reformer in his younger days and a friend to those who went on to become United Irishmen. In the Emmet legend he was portrayed as betraying old friendships and delivering a 'serpent' speech.

The jury did not retire and pronounced a verdict of guilty after a few minutes. Emmet asked for the judgment to be deferred until the next day, but this was denied. There has been some speculation that he did so because of possible escape. It is more likely, however, that he wished to finalise writing his speech, for he already had some notes, and given the late hour (by then the trial had lasted nearly eleven hours), he may have wanted to deliver it in a fresher state. For someone to whom reputation meant everything, this final oration was all important. His request was refused and, on being asked by the Clerk of the Crown, 'What have you therefore now to say, why judgment of death and execution should not be awarded against you according to law?' Emmet delivered his famous speech, his bid for immortality.

The accuracy of contemporary versions has long been disputed. The reason for this is that the earliest published versions were in government prints. Indeed, in 1803 there was no longer any opposition press, all having been either suppressed or cowed by rigorous controls introduced at the time of the last rebellion. The most complete – by William Ridgeway, one of the prosecution team and an experienced law reporter – has been the most quoted and reproduced. Government versions give more prominence to Emmet's criticism of the French, as does an illustration of the trial, commissioned by government. A more sympathetic version appeared in *Walker's Hibernian Magazine*.[25] However, if the United Irishmen had been unsuccessful rebels, they were brilliant publicists and the large number of contemporary editions of Emmet's speech testifies to the real propaganda battle being waged between government and patriotic versions, as well as the high level of public interest. We can be sure that no version was entirely accurate, for law reporting was not highly developed in those days. However, the more exaggerated and defiant phraseology of the patriotic versions accords better with contemporary descriptions of Emmet's demeanour while delivering it. It was said that his words could be heard even outside the courtroom, that he moved backwards and forwards at the bar, swaying as he spoke.

One of the yeomanry guard attending the trial sent an account to his brother. He commenced the letter on the evening of the 18th and told of the great interest Emmet's trial was arousing. He did not believe even the subtlest lawyer could secure an acquittal and thought that Emmet would be brought straight from court to execution. On Monday night he resumed his account. 'It is all over with the unfortunate Emmett ... I was in the Court at 7 this morning and at 7 this evening the Jury brought in its verdict.' He then gives a brief account of the trial and thinks the various addresses and proclamations 'ably put together'. 'What a pity it is that such brilliant talents should yield to an enthusiasm so wild and extravagant ... he behaved throughout with manly firmness and during a very able speech for the Crown', he looked contemptuous when the conspiracy was depicted as insignificant and when the infatuation of his own conduct was alluded to 'he assumed an air of haughty and offended dignity – When the verdict was pronounced, he seemed to consider himself as rising into a Martyr; he addressed the court and the audience declaring with the greatest satisfaction the high station he had held and the active measures he had used in the cause of Liberty, he gloried in having rekindled the flame and was he again at large, he would again strain every nerve to promote its success.'[26]

Emmet did not challenge the decision of the court.

> But I have that to say which interests me more than life,
> and which you have laboured ... to destroy. I have much
> to say why my reputation should be rescued from the
> load of foul accusation and calumny which have been
> heaped upon it ... Was I only to suffer death ... I should
> bow in silence, and meet the fate that awaits me, without
> a murmur. – But the sentence of the law which delivers

my body to the executioner, will … labour, in its own
vindication, to consign my character to obloquy … A
man in my situation, my Lords, has not only to encounter
the difficulties of fortune, and the force of power over
minds which it has corrupted or subjugated, but the
difficulties of established prejudice – the man dies, but
his memory lives: that mine may not perish, that it may
live in the respect of my countrymen, I seize upon this
opportunity to vindicate myself from some of the charges
alleged against me. When my spirit shall be wafted to a
more friendly port; when my shade shall have joined the
bands of those martyred heroes who have shed their
blood on the scaffold and in the field, in defence of their
country and of virtue, this is my hope, I wish that my
memory and name may animate those who survive me,
while I look down with complacency on the destruction
of that perfidious Government, which upholds its
domination by blasphemy of the most high … a
Government which is steeled to barbarity by the cries of
the orphans and the tears of the widows which it has
made.

Here he was interrupted by the presiding judge, Lord Norbury, who
commented on 'the mean and wicked enthusiasts' and 'wild designs'
of the likes of Emmet. There is no record of this in the official account. Emmet was indignant:

I appeal to the immaculate God – I swear by the throne
of Heaven before which I must shortly appear – by the
blood of those murdered patriots who have gone before
me – that my conduct has been through all this peril and
through all my purposes, governed only by the
convictions which I have uttered, and by no other view

than that of their cure, and the emancipation of my
country from the super-inhuman oppression under
which it has so long, and too patiently travailed … Yes,
my Lords, a man who does not wish to have his epitaph
written, until his country is liberated, will not leave a
weapon in the power of envy to impeach the probity
which he means to preserve, even in the grave, to which
tyranny consigns him …

Norbury interrupted again. He did not sit in court to hear treason.
Emmet's tone became angrier.

Where is the boasted freedom of your institutions, and
where is the vaunted impartiality, clemency and mildness
of your Courts of Justice, if an unfortunate prisoner,
whom your policy and not justice is about to deliver into
the hands of the executioner, is not suffered to explain
his motives sincerely and truly, and to vindicate the
principles by which he was actuated. My Lords, it may be
part of the system of angry justice to bow a man's mind
by humiliation to the purposed ignominy of the scaffold;
but worse to me than purposed shame, or the scaffold's
terrors, would be the tame indurance [sic] of charges and
imputations laid against me in this Court: You, my Lord,
are Judge, I am the supposed Culprit; I am a man, you
are a man also; by a revolution of Power, we might change
places, tho' we never could change characters; If I stand
at the Bar of this Court, and dare not vindicate my
character, what a farce is your Justice! If I stand at the Bar
of this Court, and dare not vindicate my character, how
dare you calumniate it? Does the sentence which your
policy inflicts on my Body, also condemn my Tongue to
silence and my reputation to reproach? your executioner

> may abridge the period of my existence, but while I exist,
> I shall not cease to vindicate my character and motives
> from your aspersions; and as a man to whom fame is
> dearer than life, I will make the last use of that life in
> doing justice to that reputation which is to live after me,
> and which is the only legacy I can leave to those I honor
> [sic] and love, and for whom I am proud to perish ...

Emmet resented the accusation that he had acted out of ambition, that he was an emissary of France. His rejection of the charge was the dominant element of the official version of the speech. The patriotic version also has his rejection, though placed less prominently. The French were invited 'as auxiliaries in war, and allies in peace'. Were they to come as invaders, he would meet them 'with all the destructive fury of war'. No, ambition was not the motive, for through his education and 'the rank and consideration of my Family', he could have found a place 'amongst the proudest of my oppressors! My Country was my Idol, to it I sacrifice every selfish, every endearing sentiment; and for it I now offer up my life!' They were wrong in giving him the credit for the conspiracy. He was only a 'subaltern'. There were others infinitely superior 'who would not disgrace themselves by shaking your blood-stained hand ... if it were possible to collect all the innocent blood that you have shed in your unhallowed Ministry in one great reservoir, your Lordship might swim in it! ... Let no man dare, when I am dead, to charge me with dishonour.'

In an interruption detailed in the official account, Norbury spoke of Emmet's family, the respectable situation once held by his father under government, his eldest brother, 'one of the greatest ornaments of the bar', who had defended laws that Robert Emmet now sought to overturn. This prompted an appeal by Emmet to his dead father. 'O! ever dear and venerated shade of my departed father, look down with scrutiny on the conduct of your suffering son; and see if I have even for a moment deviated from those principles ... which it was

1. Emmet's arms depot in Marshalsea Lane (Thomas Street) — hostile image by Cruikshank for Maxwell's History of the Irish Rebellion *(1839).*

2. The murder of Lord Kilwarden during Emmet's rebellion — by Cruikshank for Maxwell's History of the Irish Rebellion *(1839).*

3. *A contemporary (government) print of Robert Emmet's trial by Brocas, highlighting the anti-French comments in Emmet's speech.*

4. *The trial of Robert Emmet, 19 September 1803 as portrayed in the* Shamrock *colour Christmas supplement 1892.*

5. *By James Petrie, c. 1804–5.*

6. *By Henry Brocas, c. 1803.*

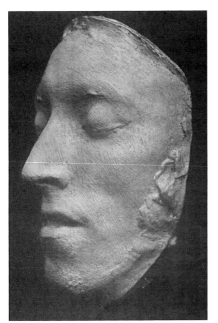

7. *Deathmask of Emmet, from cast said to have been taken by Petrie, 1803.*

8. *By James Petrie, from rough trial sketch, c. 1810.*

9. 'The unfortunate Robert Emmet', from Walker's Hibernian Magazine, September 1803.

10. Portrait of Robert Emmet by William Read (after Petrie), c.1824–37. This is the classic Emmet portrait that informed later representations.

11. 'Robert Emmet heads his men', by J. D. Reigh, from the Shamrock colour supplement, 5 July 1890.

12. From the Shamrock, 16 June 1883. The caption reads: 'Sarah,' interrupted her father, 'here I present you with a husband that is superior to Robert in every way'.

13. From the Shamrock, 5 June 1886. Captioned 'the figure of Robert Emmet seemed to move as if in life, and a clear voice fell on my ear, saying: "Ireland will be Free!"'. It became the dream which attracted the young Irish-American to come to Ireland to join the Fenians.

14. *Sarah Curran, by Edward Corballis.*

15. 'The ordeal of Anne Devlin' by W. C. Miles, from Weekly Freeman,
12 December 1903.

16. 'Anne Devlin is put
to the Test', from
1969 school textbook.

your care to instil into my youthful mind, and for which I am now to offer up my life.' The suggestion in all the versions is that Emmet was not permitted to proceed with his vindication because it was thought inflammatory. He had, therefore, to draw it to a rapid conclusion.

> My Lords – You are impatient for the sacrifice ... be yet
> patient! I have but a few more words to say – I am going
> to my cold and silent grave: my lamp of life is nearly
> extinguished: my race is run: the grave opens to receive
> me, and I sink into its bosom! I have but one request to
> ask at my departure from this world, it is the charity of its
> silence! – let no man write my epitaph, for as no man
> who knows my motives dare now vindicate them. Let
> them and me repose in obscurity and peace, and my
> tomb remain uninscribed, until other times, and other
> men, can do justice to my character; – when my country
> takes her place among the nations of the earth, then and
> not till then – let my epitaph be written – I have done.[27]

At the end of a lengthy trial, it was a remarkable performance. Peter Burrowes later told Thomas Moore 'of the wonderful strength and resolution of Emmett in standing so long (twelve hours, I think), through all the fatigue and anxiety of the trial, and then delivering that noble speech with such energy before the pronouncing of the sentence'.[28] Edward Lees, the Postmaster-General, wrote to Lord Auckland on the evening of the trial. 'Previous to the sentence being passed he addressed the Court in a long and eloquent speech: in which he avowed the justice of the sentence – and declared that his object, and that of the Provisional Government was a separation from England – unconnected with the Politicks of France, and in every respect independent of them.'[29] Even the pro-government press was unusually sympathetic to 'this unfortunate young man', praising his talents though lamenting the use to which he put them.[30] Later tradition has it that Leonard MacNally 'flung his arms around him and kissed him on the forehead', thus creating an-other piece of the legend, 'the kiss of Judas'. I can find no contempo-rary evidence for this, though it is not implausible, even if embellished.

III

In a handbill distributed by the government the following day, it was stated that 'a friend' was admitted to Emmet the morning of his exe-cution. This was almost certainly his counsel, Leonard MacNally, or MacNally's son. The text concentrated on his criticism of France and his comments on the moderation of the present government in Ire-land. However, Emmet made no secret of his feelings on both issues. The distinction drawn between the current government, which he considered conciliatory, and the *form* of government, which he sought to overthrow, he likewise made in conversations with the clergymen who attended him in prison.[31] He also expressed his annoyance at having been searched in the dock as if they suspected an attempted suicide. Emmet was reputedly handed a sprig of lavender to refresh him after the long trial, but it was taken away for fear that it might contain poison. He reprobated the act of self-destruction as one of an unchristian character. He professed 'to hold the tenets of religion as taught by the Established Church ... his hopes of salvation were not on any merits of his, but through the mediation of the Saviour, who died an ignominious death on the cross. With these sentiments he said it would be absurd to suppose him capable of suicide. What had he to apprehend more than death? And as to the obloquy attached to the mode of death, it could but little affect him, when he considered that Sidney and Russell bled on the scaffold in a similar cause.' Alger-non Sidney and William Lord Russell had been found guilty of treason by a packed jury and executed in 1683. They were regarded as heroic martyrs by reformers and radicals, the stories of Russell's heartbroken wife adding a note of tragic romance. The parallels seem not to have been lost on Robert Emmet.[32]

According to Madden, it was MacNally who told Emmet of his mother's death, which had occurred on 9 September. Emmet 'expressed a firm confidence of meeting with her in a state of eternal bliss, where no separation could take place'. But Madden put forward a different version, which he had from a friend of Emmet's and fellow prisoner in Kilmainham and which became the received version. In this, when Emmet expressed a desire to see his mother, MacNally 'pointing upwards, said, "Then, Robert, you will see her this day!" and told him of her death. "It is better so," replied Emmet, expressing "a confident hope that he and his mother would meet in heaven."'[33]

Unlike Tone, who was a deist and critical of established religion, Emmet's sincere Christianity was more amenable to the blood-sacrifice traditions of Irish republicanism, a tradition that he consciously helped create. Two Anglican clergymen attended Emmet in his last hours, the Revd John Grant, prebendary of Kilmactalway, Co. Dublin, and the Revd Thomas Gamble, curate of St Michan's and chaplain of Newgate (and a contemporary of Temple Emmet at Trinity). 'I was very anxious that he should have a fair chance of being brought to a proper temper of mind before his death', wrote Hardwicke to the Home Secretary, 'and it is possibly owing to this circumstance that Mr Gamble ... felt himself justified in administering the Sacrament to a person who professed a general repentance and sense of religion, tho' he did not admit the guilt of the crime for which he suffered.' On his disclaiming any intention of shedding blood, Emmet was urged by the clergymen to admit that if he could have foreseen the murder of Kilwarden and the others who died he would have abandoned his attempt. He replied that 'no one went to battle without being prepared for similar events, always considering his attempt as free from moral reproach, in consequence of what he conceived to be the goodness of the motive that produced it', and 'that though persons professing his principles and acting in the cause in which he had been concerned were generally supposed to be

Deists, that he was a Christian in the true sense of the word, that he had received the Sacrament, though not regularly and habitually, and that he wished to receive it then'.[34] At the time of Emmet's arrest, Sirr had found a handwritten copy of a commentary on the passion of Christ. The reader is invited to reflect on the agony of Jesus in the garden of Gethsemene, 'sweating blood, betrayed', the details of the 'concluding of this astonishing tragedy' outlined, the heavy under-scoring highlighting the sufferings of 'the innocent victim … *oppress'd – afflicted – bleeding – dying*'. The handwriting is careful and formal, rather like a child practising joined-up letters. The wording is not un-like that of Emmet's brooding, messianic verse, an extreme example of which had been found, crumpled up, at the Marshalsea Lane depot. 'The Bastille' resonates with the imagery of Christ's passion and foreshadows the similar strain in the more accomplished poetry of 1916. There is an exaggerated *Boy's Own* quality in this poem – 'the jail mastiffs' howling, the dungeon chains clanking, 'the blood-reek-ing' scene, the 'innocent' 'victim' tortured like Christ, his death in-evitable. Might its fatalism help explain why Robert Emmet took so little care to escape in the weeks after the failed uprising?[35]

After his trial Emmet had been returned to Newgate, which ad-joined the courthouse. Here, according to the *Dublin Evening Post*, a dinner had been prepared for him. However, about 1 a.m., he was moved to Kilmainham, further out of the city – 'for humane motives … to have an apartment to himself with fire and candlelight' (ac-cording to the government press), as a precaution to prevent an es-cape attempt (according to Madden), though Kilmainham, as the county gaol, would have been the normal prison for those commit-ting crimes in Dublin county.[36] He spent much of the time remaining to him in writing letters, which he then gave to Dr Edward Trevor, as-sistant-governor of Kilmainham. He finished a long explanation of the rising that he had been preparing for his brother, detailing the military plan, the arsenal, the points of attack and defence, the streets, the buildings to be taken, etc. It was a 3,000-word strategic document and concluded with a declaration to rival his speech in the projection of the Emmet legend.

> I would have given it the respectability of an insurrection, but I did not wish uselessly to shed blood … I know how men without candour will pronounce on this failure, without knowing one of the circumstances that occasioned it. They will consider only that they predicted it … they will not recollect that they predicted also that no system could be formed – that no secrecy nor confidence could be restored – that no preparations could be made – that no plan could be arranged – that no day could be fixed, without being instantly known at the Castle – that government only waited to let the conspiracy ripen, and crush it at their pleasure – and that on these grounds only did they predict its miscarriage. The very same men that after success would have flattered, will now calumniate.[37]

Emmet was well on his way to snatching victory from defeat and the theme was continued in a personal letter to his brother, Thomas Emmet, and his sister-in-law, Jane Emmet.

> My dearest Tom and Jane,
> I am just going to do my last duty to my country. It can be done as well on the scaffold as on the field. Do not give way to any weak feelings on my account, but rather encourage proud ones that I have possessed fortitude and tranquillity of mind to the last.
> God bless you, and the young hopes that are growing up about you. May they be more fortunate than their uncle, but may they preserve as pure and ardent an attachment to their country as he has done. Give the

watch to little Robert he will not prize it less for having been in the possession of two Roberts before him. I have one dying request to make to you. I was attached to *Sarah Curran*, the youngest daughter of your friend. I did hope to have her my companion for life. I did hope that she would not only have constituted my happiness, but that her heart and understanding would have made her one of Jane's dearest friends. I know that Jane would have loved her on my account, and I feel also that had they been acquainted she must have loved her on her own. No one knew of the attachment till now, nor is it now generally known, therefore do not speak of it to others.

She is now with her Father and Brother, but should those protectors fall off and that no other should replace them, take her as my wife and love her as a sister.

God almighty bless you. Give my love to all my friends.

On the instructions of the Lord Lieutenant, Wickham forwarded an extract of the passage concerning Sarah to her father, asking if it should be sent. 'It is part of a letter addressed to Mr Thomas Emmet the whole of which Government cannot suffer to be forwarded because of the principles avowed in it by the writer, the publication of which might do mischief among his deluded followers.'[38] Government was delighted at making Curran squirm for his past attacks and his response to this communication did him little credit. Curran replied immediately in terms of exaggerated gratitude, asking that the extract be suppressed:

Even on the first falling of the unexpected blow, I had resolved ... that if I found no actual guilt upon her I would act with as much moderation as possible towards a poor creature that had once held the warmest place in my heart. I did even then recollect that there was a point to which nothing but actual turpitude or the actual death of a parent ought to make the child an orphan. But even had I then thought otherwise I feel that this extract would have produced the effect it was intended to have, and that I should think so now. I feel now I should shrink from the idea of letting her sink so low as to become the subject of a testamentary order of a miscreant who could labour by so foul means and under such odious circumstances to connect her with his infamy and to acquire any posthumous interest in her person or her fate. Blotted therefore as she may irretrievably be from my society or the place she once held in my affection, she must not go adrift. So far at least 'these protectors will not fall off'.[39]

Emmet's letter, in other words, had served to rupture irretrievably Sarah's relationship with her father and she was effectively expelled from the family home. She seems to have suffered a nervous break-down, and, after several months recovering with Dublin friends, she went to live with the Penrose family in Cork. Long after her death in 1808, her friend – thought by Madden to have been the daughter of the Revd Thomas Crawford, with whom she had stayed after her mother left when she was fourteen – published an account of their long friendship. She told of the death of Sarah's twin sister, Gertrude, at the age of eight, the coldness of her father, the desertion of an adored mother. After the failure of the rebellion Emmet had asked her to go to America with him. Her refusal was, it seems, the reason for his decision to remain in Ireland, and she afterwards held herself responsible for his fate.[40] It was only her father who spurned her, for the general sympathy for Emmet made her an object of interest and attracted the attentions of Captain Henry Sturgeon, nephew to the Marquess of Rockingham, then stationed in Cork. They were married there in November 1805, and although this friend testified to her continuing attachment to Emmet ('she was – in truth – a mourning bride'), Sarah's correspondence shows that the marriage became a loving one.[41] She accompanied Sturgeon first to England, then to postings in Malta and Sicily. It was on board ship back to England from Sicily that she gave birth prematurely to a son. The baby died after their arrival at Hythe in Kent. She did not long survive him and died on 5 May 1808. The news was conveyed to the friend three days later in a distraught letter from her brother Richard. 'I am now on my way with her afflicted widower, accompanying her remains, which she wished to lie in her native land.'[42] She was buried beside her grand-mother at Newmarket, Co. Cork, her desire to be buried with Gertrude in the Priory garden having been rejected by her father. Sturgeon was to figure as the gallant rescuer in the legend.

Wickham was amused by the extravagance of Curran's compli-ments and by 2 October considered him 'completely in Govern-ment's power'.[43] It was quite a coup, for a week earlier he still thought the likes of Curran and Ponsonby could have embarrassed government by raking up all the old accusations over the Kilmainham treaty.[44] The letter was never sent and Thomas Emmet only learnt of it when it was published in 1819 by Curran's son William Henry. Emmet had also written to his friend, Sarah's brother Richard.

> My Dearest Richard,
> I find I have but a few hours to live, but if it was the last
> moment, and that the power of utterance was leaving me,
> I would thank you from the bottom of my heart for your
> generous expressions of affection and forgiveness to me.
> If there was anyone in the world in whose breast my
> death might be supposed not to stifle every spark of
> resentment, it might be you – I have deeply injured you –
> I have injured the happiness of a sister that you love, and
> who was formed to give happiness to every one about
> her, instead of having her own mind a prey to affliction.

Oh! Richard, I have no excuse to offer, but that I meant the reverse; I intended as much happiness for Sarah as the most ardent love could have given her: − it was not with a wild or unfounded passion, but it was an attachment increasing every hour, from an admiration of the purity of her mind, and respect for her talents. I did dwell in secret upon the prospect of our union. I did hope that success, while it afforded the opportunity of our union, might be the means of confirming an attachment, which misfortune had called forth. I did not look to honours for myself − praise I would have asked from the lips of no man: but I would have wished to read in the glow of Sarah's countenance that her husband was respected. My love, Sarah! it was not thus that I thought to have requited your affection. I did hope to be a prop round which your affections might have clung, and which would never have been shaken: but a rude blast has snapped it, and they have fallen over a grave. This is no time for affliction. I have had public motives to sustain my mind, and I have not suffered it to sink: but there have been moments in my imprisonment when my mind was so sunk by grief on her account, that death would have been a refuge.

God bless you, my dearest Richard. I am obliged to leave off immediately, Robert Emmet[45]

Although the two letters to Emmet's brother are among the official papers of the period, this one to Richard is not. Nor is there a copy in Wickham's private papers, although he diligently kept copies of everything else. Is it possible that this letter was given instead to Mac-Nally, a close friend of John Philpot Curran, or to the Revd Gamble, whereas the others had been given to Dr Trevor, who delivered them to the Castle?

Much of the Emmet legend centres on the contrast of the noble young man writing such words within minutes of execution, and a tyrannical government sending in spies in the guise of friends and legitimate clergymen to extract information that might then be used in the propaganda battle. A battle it most certainly was, but one that Emmet won decisively. There is no reason to doubt Gamble's claim that Emmet himself had asked for the two clergymen to remain with him in his final hours – despite the treacherous gloss put on their role by later tradition. 'Persons engaged as I have been', he told Gamble, 'in attempting to subvert political establishments are too generally stigmatized with the reproach of Deism. This title I disclaim, and am proud to call myself a Christian.' On being asked how he reconciled this with his conduct, he replied, condemning the murder of Lord Kilwarden: 'I expected other resources but found myself entangled with a rabble.' Gamble, according to the descendant of a friend to the Emmets, had more than a passing acquaintance with the family and the account sent to government after the execution was very largely a sympathetic one.

What MacNally told the government about Emmet's attitudes towards the French would not have borne publicity. Emmet told him that he expected the French to come in force and that he had wanted his trial deferred for ten days, for they would certainly then have arrived. 'Mr Emmet assured *my friend* on the very day of his execution', Wickham later reported, 'that his brother and others in Paris had negotiated for a French Force. That if they came with a Treaty they ought to be joined and, and [sic] that if Ireland was once separated from England, by the means of France, then Ireland, connecting with England by Treaty ought to establish her independence against both France and England, by beating the French out of the Island – if they remained as Conquerors. Emmet had no objections to French aid by Treaty – he only objected to France conquering Ireland for herself.'[46] Emmet also repeated his claims that he only had the command of the Dublin area and that all the money used in the preparations was his own.

IV

At around 1.30 p.m. when the sheriff arrived at Kilmainham to take Emmet to execution, he was reported to have met him with 'composure and ... easy politeness'.[47] At the last moment he asked to return to his cell to pen a note to Wickham.

> Sir, Had I been permitted to proceed with my vindication, it was my intention, not only to have acknowledged the delicacy with which I feel with gratitude, that I have been personally treated; but also to have done the most public justice to the mildness of the present administration of this country, and at the same time to have acquitted them ... of any charge of remissness in not having previously detected a conspiracy, which from its closeness, I know it was impossible to have done.

He would have liked to have been given the opportunity to explain why he still wanted to overthrow such a government. He does not do so adequately here – though he did elsewhere. 'However, as I have been deprived of that opportunity, I think it right now to make an acknowledgement which justice requires from me as a man, and which I do not feel to be in the least derogatory from my decided principles as an Irishman.'[48] Russell was to speak in similar terms after his own trial some weeks later. This letter was to cause some confusion in nationalist historiography. Alone of Emmet's final writings, it was not produced in its entirety by MacDonagh and it does not figure at all in Madden.

All those condemned in 1803 were executed at the spot where their action on the 23 July had occurred. Accordingly, on 20 September a temporary scaffold was erected before St Catherine's church in Thomas Street. Emmet's carriage left Kilmainham accompanied by a strong guard, progressed 'at a slow, solemn pace' over Sarah's Bridge, along Barrack Street and over Queen's Bridge to Thomas Street. The best account of the events of that day comes again from the pen of Edward Lees, the Postmaster-General, one of the many on the government side deeply affected by the entire situation.

> From the time he left the cell to the last moment of his existence, he conducted himself with a degree of hardihood bordering on insanity, and of which I could not have supposed any Human Being, in the awful situation he was, could have manifested − From the jail to the place of execution, he appeared engaged in a serious argument with 2 clerical gentlemen, who accompanied him in a carriage, whose exhortations never appeared to produce the smallest effect on his countenance − It never once suffered dejection. − Arrived at the fatal spot where thousands of the populace were assembled to behold the Execution, he ascended the platform with the most undaunted resolution, and determined resignation to his fate − He looked round him with the utmost composure and beheld his numerous *Friends*, everyone of whom … were at this moment without their Hats. − It was expected by most people that he would address them − I believe he was prevented − he uttered not a word.[49]

The government newspapers were not quite so complimentary, though they hardly measure up to Madden's accusation of 'memory-murdering' and in general they confirm Lees's report about Emmet's firmness and composure.[50] A former college friend (Revd Dr Haydn) who was near the scaffold later told Madden that he heard him utter the words, 'My friends I die in peace − and with sentiments of universal love and kindness towards all men'. This is confirmed in other contemporary reports.[51] He had been dissuaded from making an address by the clergymen, anxious lest his desire to state that he had been loyal to his oath as a United Irishman might 'produce tumult and bloodshed'.[52] He seems to have made no objection to his hands being tied and the use of the black cap, although all accounts agree that matters were delayed while he queried the positioning of the rope with the executioner. He was hanged shortly after 3 p.m. and thirty minutes later the rest of the sentence for high treason was carried out. Emmet was beheaded by the executioner and his head then held aloft. Assisted by Madden, eyewitnesses later recalled small details from the day: Mrs McCready told of the dogs lapping up the blood from the paving stones; John Fisher remembered the table on which he was beheaded ('a deal table like a common kitchen table') being taken to the market house where anyone could see it.[53]

What happened to his remains thereafter is a mystery, and a fundamental part of the Emmet legend. Immediately after the execution they were removed to Newgate. The gaoler of Kilmainham later informed Madden that the remains were taken there, where they would normally have been claimed by a family member. However, the only family members remaining were his sister Mary Anne Holmes and his niece, Kitty, then sixteen years of age and, according to Dr Drennan, 'subject to nervous attacks, increased much at night since her Uncle Robert's lamentable end'.[54] Mary Anne's husband, Robert Holmes, had been imprisoned as part of the government sweep after the rebellion and his wife had sought permission to join him in prison. We do not know whether her request was granted. However, neither she nor her niece were in good health and Mary Anne was several months' pregnant. At some stage on the evening of Emmet's execution a death mask was taken. Then the body – which remained unclaimed – was buried behind the prison in a plot reserved for paupers and executed criminals, but, according to the gaoler, was later reburied elsewhere. Head and body were not interred together and so the search for head, body and burial place was interwoven with the developing legend, in an age fascinated by the gothic and the macabre.

The messenger who conveyed Emmet's last letter to Wickham also brought news that the execution had taken place. Wickham was told the story of Emmet's request to return to his cell to write to him and was struck that, even in such circumstances, it was 'in a strong, firm hand, without blot, correction or erasure'. Shortly afterwards he drafted his letter of resignation as Chief Secretary. He criticised the established church in Ireland as prejudiced and exclusive and spoke of the exclusion of Catholics from parliament as 'one of the grossest injustices'. But his main reason for resigning was the letter that he had just received from 'the unfortunate Robert Emmett':

> No consideration upon earth would induce me to remain after having maturely reflected on the contents of this letter … in what honours or other earthly advantages could I find compensation for what I must suffer were I again compelled by my official duty to prosecute to death men capable of thinking and acting as Emmett has done in his last moments for making an effort to liberate their country from grievances the existence of many of which none can deny of which I have myself acknowledged to be unjust, oppressive and unchristian. I well know that the manner in which I have suffered myself to be affected by this letter will be attributed to a sort of morbid sensibility, rather than to its real cause, but no one can be capable of forming a right judgement on my motives who has not like myself been condemned by his official duty to dip his hands in the blood of his fellow countrymen, in execution of a portion of the laws and institutions of his country of which, in his conscience he cannot approve.

He did not, in the event, tender his resignation until four months later and exhaustion and recent illness may have been colouring his outlook. But three decades later he still spoke in similar terms of the impact Emmet's execution had had on him. From his then residence,

Geneva, he wrote to a friend in Ireland, enclosing a copy of the letter he had received from Emmet and which 'for the long space of thirty years has been my constant companion'. He spoke of the difficulty in overcoming prejudice in Ireland, 'but let such persons consider how light the strongest of such feelings must appear when compared with those which Emmet so nobly overcame even at his last hour, on his very march to the scaffold'.[55]

IV

Thomas Russell was the only other major leader of the 1803 rising to be tried for high treason and executed. He had arrived in Dublin on 7 September and taken lodgings near the Castle at 28 Parliament Street, in the house of a sympathiser who was frequently under surveillance from the authorities. He intended organising the escape of Emmet, though there is no indication that his own bid was co-ordinated with that of St John Mason, and with a £1,500 reward on his head his presence there could not for long have gone undetected. He was arrested at his lodgings on 9 September and there ensued a protracted row in print over which of the three involved in the arrest merited the reward.

Even more so than Emmet, Russell was courting fate in these final days, to the extent that his friends thought they detected signs of insanity. Like Emmet, he believed a French attack would soon take place (whatever his personal reservations); like Emmet he proclaimed his desire to minimise bloodshed and his trust in the patriotism of the 'lower orders'; like Emmet he acknowledged Wickham's 'gentlemanly conduct' towards him. Although imprisoned in Kilmainham after 12 September, no evidence has been found that he was able to communicate with Emmet, though he did with Anne Devlin. On 12 October he was transferred north for trial in Downpatrick, Co. Down – the main scene of his activities – and there tried and convicted on 19 October. He too offered no defence, though defended ably by

Henry Joy, relative of his close friends the McCrackens, who paid for his defence. In his own speech he spoke of his religious feelings, called on the rich to look after the poor and declared that several members of the jury had once shared the beliefs for which he was about to die. He spoke of past empires rising and falling and yet many governments of his day acted as if they were 'immutable'. The laws of God he had always followed. The 'laws of state' frequently clashed with these and he cited, pointedly, the Roman laws that had crucified Christ. 'By my conduct I do not consider that I have incurred any moral guilt. I have committed no moral evil. I do not want many and bright examples of those who have gone before me, but did I want this encouragement the recent example of a youthful hero, a martyr in the cause of liberty, who has just died for his country, would inspire me.' Russell spoke then of their difference in age. Whilst Russell had had time to experience the realities and delusions of the world (he was thirty-seven), Emmet 'was surrounded by everything that could endear this world to him, in the bloom of youth, with fond attachments, and with all the fascinating charms of health and innocence; to his death I look back, even in this, with rapture'.[56]

Russell was convicted of high treason and was hanged and beheaded the following day at Downpatrick gaol. His remains were then buried in the nearby Protestant parish church. Four others were also executed for their part in the attempted northern rising. Despite Russell's reputation among the disaffected, his end was low profile in comparison with that of Emmet. His speech lasted but twenty minutes and though considered 'eloquent and energetic', the press thought it 'unconnected' and it never became the stuff of legend like Emmet's. No propaganda machine (republican or government) was employed for Russell. He was not 'society' like Emmet was and his execution took place within the gaol's precinct, the doors opened only briefly to the public.

There were no more executions after this, even though many more suspects were later arrested. The example had been made; the government's credibility restored. Altogether 23 had been executed and 500 sent out of Ireland to serve in the crown forces. Around 50 people had been killed in Dublin on the night of the attempted rising. But the government was still very unclear as to what had actually happened, how extensive disaffection was in the country and just how far France was involved. Consequently it was prepared to forgo the chance of bringing others to the scaffold in return for information or exile, and many complied (for which they were dammed as informers as the Emmet legend developed). Most now accepted that there was little appetite in Ireland for another rebellion, and even Michael Dwyer accepted government terms and exiled himself to Australia in 1804. Hamilton went into hiding and was later arrested in Monaghan. He was not brought to trial and was liberated with the other state prisoners in 1806.

News of the rising caused a sensation in Paris and it was used to great effect to argue English tyranny.[57] John Swiney was commissioned by the French government to travel to Ireland to say that French help was coming and to urge against partial risings. Swiney was able to travel to Cork unimpeded, and, though the Dublin government had wind of an agent in the country, it could not identify him. In Ireland Swiney learnt the news of the collapse of the rebellion and his freedom of movement was impeded by the resultant security measures. He returned to Paris on 20 October, bringing Thomas Addis Emmet news of his younger brother's trial and execution. Thomas Emmet was worried about the impact of the speech on the continuing negotiations with the French authorities. It was certainly contributing to the French belief that Emmet himself was anti-French and that O'Connor's party should be given greater credence. Only on 12 December did he receive the different version of the speech put out by Emmet's 'friends', which he sent to the Minister of War, asking if he could publish it in the *Argus*, which he did on 11 January 1804. In a lengthy article the *Argus* argued that the English had misrepresented the speech to create distrust between the Irish and the French. 'As one mode of accomplishing this infernal policy it falsified and misrepresented the speech pronounced by the young and unfortunate Robert Emmet, before he received sentence of death. It did so, by inserting abuse of the French Government and Nation, which was never uttered, by suppressing the greater part of what was said, and by misrepresenting the remainder' and it now offered 'some authentic fragments of what Mr Robert Emmet really said on that occasion'. There are some similarities with the government version and the passage about meeting the French on the beach and immolating them in their boats if they came as enemies, is here. 'But Frenchmen will not come as foreign enemies; they will come as friends and allies, to assist you in expelling a foreign enemy.' The guarantee given to America had already been procured and the French were preparing in every port. 'I acted as an Irishman desirous of delivering his Country, from the yoke of a domestic unprincipled faction, and the accursed influence of a foreign and unrelenting tyranny ... Irishmen! your most implacable and deadly foes are in the heart of your country.'[58]

However, O'Connor had no reservations whatsoever about French aid, and Thomas Emmet's diary reveals mounting disillusionment at the way that his old foe's advice was accepted over his own. Despite the propaganda to the contrary, Robert Emmet's rebellion and speech confirmed the French government in its belief that his brother's friends could not be trusted. In February 1804 Arthur O'Connor was made commander of the new Irish Legion being formed in France. Emmet had no more meetings with the French government after that and he finally sailed for America in October, there to give the most powerful stimulus to the Emmet legend.

'Emmet's rebellion' was a leftover from that of 1798, following plans developed in reaction to the defeat that year. But without a French invasion, it was stillborn, whatever Emmet's propaganda to the contrary. Even though discontent continued to respond to events in France until Napoleon's defeat in 1815, the rebellion of 1803 marked the end of the United Irishmen. The French never did arrive and they became irrelevant to the development of the legend. The future of Irish republicanism lay with Emmet's romantic legend of the noble victim and the imperialist tyrant. It was not the message of the original United Irish Society, but it was far more powerful and Emmet had largely fashioned it himself. Had it emerged in the immediate aftermath of the 1798 rebellion it might have sunk without trace. But as the threat of serious political disturbance receded, the memory of the terror of those years did likewise and it became possible to subscribe to the legend without necessarily being considered a dangerous republican.

Emmet's boyish looks, good stock, eloquence and desperate sincerity aroused the sympathy of those who had witnessed the events outlined above. Less recognised is the anger and dismay of many Catholics and Protestants alike at the re-imposition of strict security measures, when there had been a welcome period of mild government. There were other ways of achieving reform, and Daniel O'Connell, whose family was threatened by the 1803 outbreak, thought Emmet should hang.[59] Yet even the achievements of O'Connell – undoubtedly the most important politician in the making of modern Ireland – would be swept away in the romantic revolutionism that had Emmet at its centre.

5 The legend: romantic beginnings

There is a certain poetical halo about Emmet that makes
many persons of opposite politics compassionate towards
his memory. His romantic passion for Miss Curran and
his enthusiasm for Ireland has made him a sort of hero
with many sentimentalists.

D. O. Madden, Ireland and Its Rulers since 1829, 3 vols.
(London, 1844), iii, 133

The legend of Robert Emmet took off almost immediately after his
death, gaining pride of place in a new martyrology developing around
the memory of the fallen United Irishmen of 1798 and 1803. He fitted easily into a long-standing tradition linking the deaths of successive generations of fallen leaders with that of the ancient mythic hero
Cú Chulainn. Cú Chulainn, the model of youthful courage, dies
young in the face of great odds, laughing at death as it comes.[1] Perhaps somewhat surprisingly, it was establishment figures that contributed more than others to the legend's early development. I cannot
find an attack on Emmet himself, even in hostile accounts. Trinity's
literati were particularly to the fore, former students inspiring both
conservative and nationalist literary revivals in the 1830s and 1840s.
Both recalled the shock of his trial and execution. 'It was in truth a
piteous and heartrending spectacle,' wrote a reviewer in the Tory
Dublin University Magazine. 'Such a youth, in such a plight, would have
moved a heart of stone.'[2] A string of publications and libel actions in
the decades after 1803 kept Emmet in the news and firmly rooted the

image of the romantic young hero surrounded by villains. It was these publications that informed almost everything written about Emmet over the following two centuries.

I

Government propaganda had made versions of the speech immediately available to the public. But while the intention of disabusing the disaffected about the French succeeded well enough,[3] even the government versions carried the 'Let no man write my epitaph' section, and we know from the many editions of the contemporary pamphlets covering his trial and speech that there was a ready market.[4] Much like the radical pamphlets of the 1790s, such Emmetania may have been used by sympathetic teachers in the hedge schools.[5] And then there was the verse and song, by far the most effective educator prior to widespread literacy. In December 1803 the Dublin government was sent an epitaph to Emmet, reported to be circulating among the disaffected.

> By *regal murder* 'neath the humble sod,
> (Oh, gentle Copyist of the living *God!*)
> A headless form in mould'ring ashes his,
> Whose blood for vengeance to its maker cries.
> Illustrious Emmet! – here's thy last retreat,
> Oh, unmatched victim of untoward fate!
> 'In other times' some loftier bard will sing –
> 'And better men' – around thy arm will cling.
> Enough for me to mark the – fatal place,
> Which on a *tarnished crown* reflects disgrace.[6]

Although Plunket remained a liberal in outlook, and championed the Catholic cause, his reputation was badly damaged by his speech at Emmet's trial. Some versions of Emmet's speech circulating after the trial contained Emmet's accusation that Plunket was betraying past friendship, and even if he had not made the statement, others did. William Drennan and his sister Martha McTier – though on friendly terms with Plunket – were critical. Drennan sent his sister 'a severe epigram on that business'.

> Prostrate, unarmed, no more alive,
> Had ceased Kilwarden's breath,
> The savage strife was then to give
> A death-wound after death.
>
> When Emmet self-convicted, stood,
> In fate, already hung,
> Plunket still longed to taste the blood
> And piked him, with his tongue.
>
> Now which of these barbarians say
> Waged the most cruel war,
> The savage of the bloody fray
> Or savage of the *bar*?[7]

Plunket won a number of libel cases against printers and publishers who continued to make the charge, including legendary English political writer William Cobbett. In 1812 he succeeded in having it removed from John Gamble's *Sketches of Dublin and the North of Ireland* (1811). Gamble, commenting on his observations of the Dublin bar in 1810, had written:

> Mr Plunket, the late Attorney-General, is an admirable
> public speaker. This gentleman, however, was severely
> reprobated for his conduct at the trial of Mr Emmet, for
> high treason, about seven years ago. Mr Plunket, who was
> then only King's Counsel, conducted the prosecution

against this unfortunate young man, with a rancour and virulence that shocked and surprised every person acquainted with his obligations to his father and family. Mr Plunket's reasons for his conduct have never been made known, though it injured him very much in public estimation. Crown Lawyers have at all times been of the bloodhound tribe; they seldom lose scent of their prey, either from considerations of gratitude or humanity.[8]

Madden, after consulting John Patten and William St John Mason, eventually accepted Plunket's claim that he had not been intimate with the Emmets, as did Watty Cox, his most dogged accuser. But Cox still thought the speech unnecessary and was simply to curry favour with the government. Indeed, doubts about his conduct never did vanish and even supporters continued to criticise him for it. In 1812, while canvassing support for one of Trinity College's parliamentary seats, he was obliged to explain 'the part you took on the trial of the unfortunate Robert Emmett' by Dr Stephen Sandes, a fellow of the college, and later bishop of Cashel, before he would lend his support. When fellow lawyer (and admirer) Charles Phillips, in the 1818 edition of his *Curran and his Contemporaries*, queried whether Emmet had made such an attack, Plunket thanked him, only to be subjected to a lengthy chastisement for having made the speech in the first place. If such a speech was necessary, argued Phillips (and he doubted that, for Emmet admitted his guilt), it was the role of the Attorney-General to deliver it, not the prosecuting counsel. In addition, he thought his somewhat slavish profession of loyalty to the British constitution sat uneasily with his much-admired speech against the Union a few years previously.[9]

At the time of Emmet's execution Phillips was a second-year student at Trinity and his fate made a particular impression on this generation of young intellectuals.

Every one loved – every one respected him – his fate made an impression on the University that has not yet been obliterated. His mind was naturally melancholy and romantic – he had fed it from the pure fountain of classic literature, and might be said to have lived, not so much in the scene around him as in the society of the illustrious and sainted dead.[10]

Such sentiments were echoed the following year by William Henry Curran in the biography of his father, John Philpot. Despite the traumatic effects on the Curran family of Emmet's attachment to Sarah Curran, this too is remarkably sympathetic.

He met his fate with unostentatious fortitude; and although few could ever think of justifying his projects or regretting their failure, yet his youth, his talents, the great respectability of his connexions, and the evident delusion of which he was a victim, have excited more general sympathy for his unfortunate end, and more forbearance towards his memory, than is usually extended to the errors or sufferings of political offenders.[11]

W. H. Curran also published in full Emmet's final letters to Richard Curran and their father, with a facsimile of the original of the former, written just before he was taken out to execution.

At the time of Cobbett's attack on Plunket, the Irish government had sought clarification about what Emmet had actually said at his trial.[12] Indeed, it was to remain sensitive about issues surrounding the events of 1803 for many years to come, for there was rarely a year in the early decades of the century when associated issues were not aired by opponents. The long detention without trial of those arrested in 1803 was a running sore and they conducted their complaints against government in a very public manner. Wickham had been brought to parliament from his sick bed in July 1805 to answer charges brought against the government on this issue by Charles James Fox.[13]

Emmet's first cousin and fellow Trinity student, William St John Mason, made it something of a lifelong campaign. He was one of a group of Irish law students in London who had become involved in subversive activities after 1798, although there was no evidence to link him directly with Emmet's activities. He had been called to the bar in 1803 and was arrested on his first circuit. He soon put his undoubted legal and literary talents to use and, with the other state prisoners, successfully sued for a judicial investigation into the petty tyrannies of the gaolers in Kilmainham (June 1804), notably Dr Edward Trevor. It was this campaign that first brought to public attention the mistreatment of Anne Devlin. Trevor was lampooned as *Pedro Zendono, Inquisitor of Kilmainham*, and Mason sustained the attack for much of the rest of his life, living long enough to tell it all to Dr Madden. Having returned to London after his release, Mason became involved with the opposition press and his case was taken up by government opponents in the House of Commons, most notably the radical Irish-born dramatist and MP Richard Brinsley Sheridan.[14] Because of her fearlessness and sharp tongue, Anne Devlin attracted the particular ire of Trevor and Sirr and she was kept in solitary confinement for much of Mason's three-year imprisonment. It was only after the personal intervention of Chief Secretary Charles Long, on an appeal from the wife of one of the gaolers, that she was finally liberated. Sheridan wanted to lay her case 'before the world' and sent 'a gentleman' to secure her agreement. Unfamiliar with Sheridan's reputation, she declined, though later regretted having done so, when 'a gentleman who had been a state prisoner (possibly Mason)' came and explained it to her. However, the opportunity passed and it was not until 1842, when Dr Madden found her living in poverty in John's-lane, Dublin, that the opportunity returned. Madden had communicated with Brother Luke Cullen, then gathering information from survivors of the rebellion in Wexford and Wicklow, who told him of her existence, and between them they brought her story to the world. Although Cullen's interviews were not published till the next century, they informed a number of the works that underpinned the Emmet legend, most notably that of Madden.[15]

At a more popular level, it was Cox's *Irish Magazine* (1808–15) that helped create the image of Robert Emmet as the romantic idealist, betrayed by his friends. Son of a Catholic bricklayer and himself a Dublin gunsmith, Watty Cox was typical of those disaffected artisans who worshipped the likes of Lord Edward Fitzgerald. However, Cox's opinions were more extreme than his mentors', and when he produced the newspaper the *Union Star* (1797), identifying informers and others for assassination, the United Irishmen thought that he was a Castle spy. But Cox was an eccentric, utterly oblivious, it seems, to his own personal safety, infuriating successive governments, yet largely outwitting them. When in 1797 the Castle was trying to discover the identity of the proprietor of the *Star*, Cox agreed to reveal the name in return for his own safety, only to dumbfound the normally astute spymaster, Edward Cooke, by revealing it as himself. At the time of Emmet's rebellion, he was suspected of involvement and courted by the Castle in its desperate search for information. Brian Inglis has suggested that he was simply playing them along and mocking their stupidity – and such would have been in character. Ultimately the authorities did not quite know what to do with the irrepressible Cox. Years of imprisonment for libel seemed to make no difference and he simply continued to produce his *Irish Magazine* from inside Newgate.

Witty, scurrilous, anti-English, anti-establishment and utterly irreverent, his *Magazine* was as popular with the working people as the United Irishmen's earlier publications had been. It was largely written by himself, those he chose to pursue (like Major Sirr and an informer called Jemmy O'Brien) becoming popular villains, its illustrations (by Brocas) informing historical accounts, even today.

One of his villains was Plunket and it was Cox who in.
phrase the 'serpent' speech. In an early number of the M.
told Emmet's story, declaring to his readers that 'Enemies'   .-
luded to prevent publication of his portrait. The image presented was
to become the traditional one – a rebellion hopeless of success, a
young man credulous but honourable, misled and abandoned by
those around him, then accepting his fate and meeting his death with
fortitude, only to be tortured by a degenerate bar at his trial.

> To the disgrace of the bar, to the duties of hospitality, a
> man appeared who formerly lived, by the bounty of the
> prisoner's father, out of his place, and beyond the duties
> of his office, to stand up, and in a studied speech of
> considerable length attacked the unprotected youth, in
> the severest tone of legal and political asperity; so
> unnecessary was the effusion of artificial loyalty and such
> was the atrocity of this violation of former friendships,
> and early intimacy, that the conduct of the man, has been
> spoken of in terms of the liveliest abhorrence, by persons
> of every party … this pleader who so strenuously
> demanded the life of the prisoner, was the tutor of that
> prisoner and actually taught him, those very political
> lessons … which formed so prominent a part of the
> accusation … at the table of Dr Emmett the prisoner's
> hospitable father.

Cox opened the next issue of the *Magazine* with a portrait of Emmet
and returned to this charge in a lengthy poem 'Elegy on the death of
Robert E—t'.

> Behold, Hibernia, Freedom's victim son,
> Whom power debauch'd not, nor foul faction won,
> Thou P—, second Judas! oh forbear,

> To draw from mem'ry's eye the gushing tear!
> Unbidden base accuser, couldst thou lend
> Thy purchas'd voice to sacrifice a friend
> How of the youth thine indigence he fed?
> But serpent venom fill'd thy foster'd head:

Then follows an account of the execution and Emmet's apparent fearlessness.

> Pure spotless spirit that now sit'st on high,
> Bend on our isle thy bliss illumin'd eye;
> If parted shades depart this earth below,
> Watch o'er the length'ning measure of our woe
> Forgive my zeal which breaks thy last command,
> The unrecording silence of the land;
> Be this thy Epitaph till other times,
> Convey thy deathless name to other climes.

Several other poems on Robert Emmet (largely on the uninscribed tomb and epitaph theme) appeared in Cox's *Irish Magazine*. Predictably the treatment of Emmet was one of the issues around which battle was engaged by the pro-government *Milesian Magazine* (an equally irreverent and witty periodical). Run by another eccentric, Dr John Brenan, with government support, it was anti-Catholic and anti-Cox. A number of its issues focused on Cox's inconsistent career, using material from an earlier pamphlet to show how (in a print as graphic as anything in Cox's *Magazine*) he had vilified the reputation of the dead Emmet. However, Brenan's magazine was too ephemeral (and too anti-Catholic) to make much of a dent in the developing Emmet legend, even though the *Irish Magazine* itself was effectively shut down in 1815 (when Cox was let out of prison in return for an agreement to leave for America).[16]

II

The qualities that Emmet came pre-eminently to symbo
new to Irish popular culture. Heroic death and heroic
themes as old as the legend of Cú Chulainn, suffering for his people
(a theme to become peculiarly associated with Emmet), and they
were already present in Gaelic poetry.[17] Yet by the end of the nineteenth century Emmet's story came to supplant the old favourites of
several centuries. The main reason was his repackaging by the
Romantic movement and the symbiotic relationship between it and
the rise of modern nationalism. Fundamental to this process was
Thomas Moore. There is little agreement on *when* nationalism and
romanticism 'start', but full agreement on their association. According to Tom Nairn, nationalism is 'not necessarily democratic in outlook, but it is invariably populist ... it had to function through highly
rhetorical forms, through a sentimental culture sufficiently accessible
to the lower strata now being called into battle. This is why a romantic culture quite remote from Enlightenment rationalism always went
hand in hand with the spread of nationalism.[18]

Romanticism extolled the power of imagination, permitting the
creation of 'Forms more real than living man, Nurslings of immortality' (Shelley). The strong puritanical streak in Irish nationalism and
republicanism is often attributed to its Catholic ethos. However, it is
equally attributable to its romantic underpinnings. It could not have
flourished in the irreverent atmosphere of the Enlightenment. At the
risk of caricaturing a complex movement, Romanticism glorified the
emotional and irrational, the sublime and atmospheric, individual-
ism, passion and revolt. Byron, Moore's friend, was its embodiment,
his own early death the living out of the ideal. It became interwoven
with the malaise of the post-revolutionary generation, a malaise born
of the disillusionment at how the hopes of the French Revolution had
been disappointed. Yet their admiration of the ideal remained and it
was Thomas Moore, above all others, whose projection of Emmet as
tragic romantic hero set the tone for the legend. Emmet himself,

brooding and rather humourless, was Ireland's perfect romantic hero.

Moore was once dismissed as too insipid, too middle class, and later Irish nationalists disliked the manner in which he became the darling of the English glitterati.[19] And who can deny that the words of his *Irish Melodies* are kitsch to modern ears? However, their subversive undertones were recognised and denounced by anti-nationalists during his lifetime and a number of nationalist writers rallied to his defence, including T. D. Sullivan, one of the most influential of them all.

> His thoughts were, perhaps not as deep as a well,
>   Nor rose they as high as a steeple;
> But his songs will abide – where he wished them to dwell–
>   In the homes and the hearts of his people.[20]

At first Moore's melodies were confined to the drawing room, but in time were popularised and well into the twentieth century most would have encountered the legend of Robert Emmet first in Moore's songs. As for the accusation that he was too fond of English lords, wrote the *Shamrock* in 1868, it was Moore who immortalised Emmet, 'when Emmett's blood was yet red on the scaffold'.[21] Moore was already establishing a reputation as a writer and poet before his first *Irish Melodies* appeared in 1808, a reputation that, ironically, brought an offer from Lord Lieutenant Hardwicke to create an Irish poet laureateship for him in spring 1803.[22] No evidence has been found of Moore's immediate reaction to Emmet's rebellion, at the time of which he was in London preparing to take up a post in Bermuda, arranged by his patron Lord Moira. In Philadelphia he visited his old friend Edward Hudson in the summer of 1806 and felt uneasy at no longer sharing his republicanism. But he does not eschew his 'rebel' past and, as his fame increased, was to take positive delight in rehabilitating Emmet's reputation in official circles. He recalled with pleasure being given the chance 'to pronounce an eulogium upon Robert

Emmett at the Irish Chief Secretary's table', at a d.
Irish administration. If this was, as it seems, in 18
courageous than his account suggests, for with the revo.
Continent, even his Whig friends were trying to stop him.
his *Life and Death of Lord Edward Fitzgerald*, which also contain.   u-
logium on Emmet cited earlier. It would be reproduced repeatedly
thereafter as a faithful description of Emmet's character and abilities.

Taken together, Moore's works on Ireland are much more politically radical than sometimes recognised;[23] appearing in 1808, his *Melodies*, dedicated to Emmet, are the most radical of all.

> Oh! breathe not his name, let it sleep in the shade,
> Where cold and unhonour'd his relics are laid;
> Sad, silent and dark, be the tears that we shed,
> As the night dew that falls on the grass o'er his head.
>
> But the night-dew that falls, though in silence it weeps,
> Shall brighten with verdure the grave where he sleeps;
> And the tear that we shed, though in secret it rolls,
> Shall long keep his memory green in our souls.

This has taken the famous passage from Emmet's speech as its theme, linking it to the significance of the unmarked tomb. It echoes Emmet's own call to suspend action, but not memory, until such times as Ireland became an independent nation. In 'When he who adores thee' (also appearing in the first number, 1808) and 'She is far from the land', the tragic love affair with Sarah Curran and happiness deferred till the next life again echoes the theme of destiny deferred. These are melancholy laments, in tune with the times, and, given Moore's own horror of violent means, hardly a call to action. But dying for a cause was something deemed admirable by the Romantics (even Moore) and the idea of heroic sacrifice, of dying for one's country is as much extolled here as it would be in any Irish 'rebel song'.

She is far from the land, where her young hero sleeps,
And lovers are round her sighing,
But coldly she turns from their gaze and weeps,
For her heart in his grave is lying!

...

He had lived for his love, for his country he died,
They were all that to life had entwined him;
Nor soon shall the tears of his country be dried,
Nor long will his love stay behind him.

Oh! make her a grave where the sunbeams rest
When they promise a glorious morrow;
They'll shine oe'er her sleep, like a smile from the West,
From her own lov'd island of sorrow.

Moore's *Irish Melodies* (written in eight parts between 1808 and 1834) were best-sellers in his own lifetime and brought him the public recognition accorded a modern rock star. Robert Southey recognised their inflammatory potential, but at the time their political contribution was largely that of creating a climate where Ireland could be represented as oppressed, rather than rebellious, and Moore's biographer thinks that they helped pave the way for Catholic emancipation (for which Moore had been a lifelong campaigner). However, more successfully than any prose text they perpetuated the basic elements of the Emmet legend, were sung at every major gathering during the centenary commemorations of 1898 and 1903 and became such standard fare that they were lampooned by Seán O'Casey, James Joyce and Samuel Beckett in the reaction against romantic nationalism in the twentieth century.

Moore's melodies about Emmet struck a particular chord with fellow Romantics. Byron wrote to his friend that if he died during the struggle in Naples, he hoped that Moore 'would at least celebrate him by another "Oh breathe not his name"'.[24] Washington Irving –

recovering from the loss of his betrothed – was also inspired by Moore to include an essay on Sarah Curran and the ill-fated love affair in his *Sketch Book* of 1819–20. 'Every one must recollect the tragical story of young E——, the Irish patriot; it was too touching to be soon forgotten ... His fate made a deep impression on public sympathy. He was so young – so intelligent – so generous – so brave – so everything that we are apt to like in a young man. His conduct under trial, too, was so lofty and intrepid.' He spoke with 'noble indignation', appealing to posterity in 'the eloquent vindication of his name'. He then comes to the real subject of his essay, the 'broken heart' of Sarah Curran, describing graphically the finality of the grave suddenly and irretrievably separating the two lovers. She remained wretched and joyless, despite every effort by friends. She married Sturgeon on the understanding 'that her heart was unalterably another's' and she died through 'devouring melancholy ... the victim of a broken heart'.[25] Irving's reflections were reproduced in every work on Emmet thereafter and with Moore's melodies came to inform the accepted version of the Sarah Curran story.

'The early Romantics' admiration for Thomas Moore is one of those crazes that a later age finds baffling.' Thus writes David Cairns in his magisterial biography of composer Hector Berlioz (2000). He suggests a 'crypto-erotic vein' in Moore at a time when such matters could not be expressed openly. Certainly Byron made a direct connection between the impact of Moore's melodies and his own heightened sexuality. A movement that sought to take the emotions into uncharted territory found resonance in Moore's treatment of the Emmet story of heroic death and unrequited love. His melodies were translated into a number of languages, including the French edition of 1823 by the grandmother of Hilaire Belloc, Louise Swanton Belloc – herself daughter to the exiled United Irishman John Swanton.[26] Berlioz first encountered the *Irish Melodies* through this translation in 1826 and he immediately made the connection with his passion for the unattainable Irish Shakespearian actress, Harriet

Smithson. Quotations from Moore began immediately to appear in his scores and in 1829 he began to compose his *Neuf Mélodies irlandaises*, to accompany translations of Moore's *Irish Melodies*. The ninth, his *Elégie en prose*, was a last-minute addition. In January 1830 his hopeless passion for Harriet Smithson had resulted in one of his long expeditions into the countryside. On his return he lifted his volume of Moore, lying open at one of the songs dedicated to Emmet, 'When he who adores thee', and there and then wrote the setting to his *Elégie*, dedicating it to Harriet Smithson, and the *Mélodies* as a whole to Moore. The peculiar intensity of *Elégie* sets it apart from the other melodies. Berlioz himself fretted about his ability 'to recreate ... the mood of pride and tenderness and deep despair which Moore must have experienced when he wrote the words, which I felt when my music flooded out and took possession of them ... works of this kind are not meant for the ordinary concert-going public; to expose them to its indifference would be a kind of sacrilege'.[27]

Berlioz later sought further information on Emmet and rededicated *Elégie* to him. Significantly the information came from Leigh Hunt, friend and inspiration to Moore and to most of the English romantics. Hunt also sent the patriotic version of the closing part of Emmet's speech, which Berlioz reproduced in a new preface to his work, along with an explanation of the inspiration behind it. He told of the deep impression Moore's song had made, spurring him to investigate its inspiration. He discovered that it was about a real person, Robert Emmet. 'He belonged to an honorable (sic) family. His character was noble and dignified, his mind spirited, his heart ardent and dedicated, he was seduced by brilliant hopes and betrayed by false friends.... and suffered the most severe consequences of defeat. He was condemned to death and executed at the age of 24. He was thought to have been in love with Miss Curran', and Berlioz thought that Moore portrayed Emmet as addressing both her and Ireland in the words of his song. Berlioz's admiration for Moore would dim somewhat in later life, but towards its close he refers again to the extrasensory emotional plane to which Moore's *Melodies* seemed to bring the young Romantics. Berlioz's fascination with Robert Emmet owed something to his empathy with other gifted young men cut short brutally during the revolutionary era. But John Crabbe – in a psychological study of Berlioz – is so impressed by it that he suggests a form of telepathic communication between the two across time and has even suggested the possibility of Berlioz having been the reincarnation of Emmet.[28]

Contrary to myth, the Irish are not natural rebels, even if they like to think they are. What they are are romantic rebels, lamenting the unattainable, eulogising the heroic failure and speaking of oppression. This trait, already long established in Gaelic poetry and oral traditions, was repackaged for a new age by Thomas Moore. It was a repackaging of potentially dangerous ideas, 'softening and sugaring'[29] them in such a way that militant and constitutional nationalism could take what they liked from them. The confusion that the blood-letting of the 1798 period had brought to English and Irish reformers alike was gradually dispelled and Moore was making it possible once more to admire the ideals of the United Irishmen. The withholding of the expected Catholic emancipation at the time of the Union and the sympathy for the Irish Catholics (not least among Moore's friends, the Whigs and his fellow Romantics) perpetuated the idea of unjust oppression. Moore never forgot his early experiences as one of the first Catholic students permitted to enter Trinity. There is a resentment that suggests a lingering Catholic inferiority complex and, almost certainly, taunts about not quite fitting in at this former bastion of Protestant privilege. As late as 1821 he records, with some bitterness, Trinity's reluctance to acknowledge his fame.[30] He was, as W. J. McCormack comments on his profound influence on Victorian Ireland's style of writing, 'that most discontented of types, the recently liberated man who has just grasped how thoroughly his past has been enslaved'.[31] Nearly all Moore's works – not just the *Melodies* – call for remembrance of past oppression and of those who resisted.

> Forget not the field where they perished
>
> (Poetical Works, 166)

> Forget not our wounded companions, who stood
>   In the day of distress by our side;
> While the moss of the valley grew red with their blood,
>   They stirr'd not, but conquer'd and died.
>
> (Poetical Works, 144)

Norman Vance, who has studied this aspect most closely, finds the ghost of Emmet pervasive in Moore's works, even in his exotic eastern tale *Lallah Rookh* (1819).

> Farewell – farewell –until Pity's sweet fountain
>   Is lost in the hearts of the fair and the brave,
> They'll weep for the Chieftain who died on that mountain,
>   They'll weep for the Maiden who sleeps in this wave.
>
> (Poetical Works, 316)

Byron, Moore and their Whig friends liked to lampoon those earlier Romantics whose radicalism dimmed as the 'early dawn' of revolution brought bloodshed, tyranny and repression. They particularly disliked Robert Southey (Poet Laureate from 1813), for his Toryism and anti-Catholicism. Yet he was the first in the field with a poetic tribute to Emmet. It is a somewhat confused poem, penned as soon as he read Emmet's speech in the press and conveying something of the mixed emotions felt by even those on the political right at his death. At this stage Southey still retained some of the radicalism (particularly on social issues) that had fired his youth and there is admiration still for the ideal. Opening with the final lines of Emmet's speech, he points to the irony of someone like he being so moved, a son of England, 'To

which in thy young virtue's erring zeal/Thou wert so perilous an
enemy', and asks if he should 'Build thy imperishable monument'. He
praises Emmet's idealism and criticises his execution, for was this not
just the error of youth, certain to be cured by maturity?

> So young, so glowing for the general good,
> Oh what a lovely manhood had been thine,
> When all the violent workings of thy youth
> Had pass'd away, had thou been wisely spared,
> Left to the slow and certain influences
> Of silent feeling and maturing thought.
>   But the blow
> Hath fallen, the indiscriminating blow,
> That for its portion to the Grave consign'd
> Youth, Genius, generous Virtue. Oh, grief, grief!
> Oh, sorrow and reproach! Have ye to learn,
> Deaf to the past, and to the future blind,
> Ye who thus irremissibly exact
> The forfeit life, how lightly life is staked,
> When in distempered times the feverish mind
> To strong delusion yields? Have ye to learn
> With what a deep and spirit-stirring voice
> Pity doth call Revenge? Have ye no hearts
> To feel and understand how Mercy tames
> The rebel nature, madden'd by old wrongs;
> And binds it in the gentle bands of love,
> When steel and adamant were weak to hold
> That Samson-strength subdued!
>   Let no man write
> Thy epitaph! Emmet, nay: thou shalt not go
> Without thy funeral strain! O young and good
> And wise, though erring here, thou shalt not go
> Unhonour'd nor unsung.

Yet what if Emmet had succeeded? Surely his heroic death, leaving his memory unsullied, was preferable to the demons success would have unleashed?

> Better to fall, than to have lived to mourn,
> As sure thou wouldst, in misery and remorse,
> Thine own disastrous triumph; to have seen,
> If the Almighty at that aweful hour
> Had turn'd away his face, wild Ignorance
> Let loose, and frantic Vengeance, and dark Zeal,
> And all bad passions tyrannous, and the fires
> Of persecution once again ablaze
> How had it sunk into thy soul to see,
> Last curse of all, the ruffian slaves of France
> In thy dear native country lording it!
> How happier thus, in that heroic mood
> That takes away the sting of death, to die,
> By all the good and all the wise forgiven,
> Yea, in all ages by the wise and good
> To be remember'd, mourn'd, and honour'd still.[32]

Southey was far more disturbed by Ireland than his friend Coleridge, fearing its people certainly – joking on the eve of going there in 1801 that he was leaving for the 'Land of Pistols & Potatoes' – but blaming government more than the rebels for what happened in 1798 and for the repression that followed. His visit in October 1801 was to investigate a post that Isaac Corry, the Irish Chancellor, offered to create for him. He thought Dublin a beautiful city, set in a magical landscape, yet one devoid of trees, suggesting 'an instinctive dread of the gallows in the people'.[33] It was a theme to which he returned in his reaction to Emmet's execution: 'If they mean to extirpate disaffection in Ireland by the gallows, they must sow the whole island with hemp.'[34] Southey had learnt much about Emmet 'from a young man who was his most intimate friend and loved him dearly. He told me that there did not and could not live a purer nor more enlightened man.' Southey tried to persuade him of the 'ruinous objects' of Emmet's party, 'but it was in vain. There is a strange warp in every Irishman's nature, they are all either wrong headed or wrong hearted, and the genius which they all possess serves only to render them more mischievous.'[35]

The newspaper reports on Emmet's trial and execution also produced disturbed reactions in Coleridge: 'Emmet = mad Raphael painting Ideals of Beauty on the walls of a cell with human Excrement.'[36] He too likened Emmet's youthful enthusiasm to his own in the 1790s and reflected how he might have suffered a similar fate had he fallen foul of the law. 'I have been extremely affected by the death of young Emmett,' he wrote to his friends Sir George and Lady Beaumont on 1 October, 'just 24! – at that age, dear Sir George! I was retiring from Politics, disgusted beyond measure by the manners & morals of the Democrats ... Alas! alas! unlike me, he did not awake!' Yet he felt Emmet had more cause for his actions than the radicals in England because of 'the state of Society & to the Orange Faction holding together that State of Society, which he believed to be the cause of these Vices! Ah woe is me! & in this mood the poor young Enthusiast sent forth that unjustifiable Proclamation, one sentence of which clearly permitted unlimited assassination.' This he thought led directly to Lord Kilwarden's murder, but he was sure that Emmet had not intended that. Even so he shuddered at the chaos and 'Fiends of Anarchy' that this 'most mistaken and bewildered young Man' almost unleashed. Again he associates his own early radicalism with Emmet's and thinks his attack on the French and his declared Christian attributes would likewise have redeemed him had he lived. Like Southey, he too thought the sentence excessive. 'O if our Ministers had saved him, and taken his oath & word of honor, to have remained in America or some of our Colonies for the next 10 years of his Life, we might have had in him a sublimely great man, we assuredly sh[ould] have had in him a good man, & [in a phrase that shows how little Coleridge actually knew of Emmet's true thinking] heart & soul an *Englishman*!'[37]

Shelley had missed the events of the 1790s, which had caused such a change of heart in the early Romantics, and was still a schoolboy when Emmet was executed. His 1812 poem 'On Robert Emmet's Tomb' lacks the sense of shock and lament for the loss of young talent of Southey's and Coleridge's immediate responses. Possibly inspired by Moore (and certainly by Southey, whose library at Grasmere he raided for information on Ireland prior to his visit), it picks up the 'let no man write my epitaph theme' and predicts the power of the uninscribed tomb against 'the tyrant, the coward, the slave'.

> No trump tells thy virtues – the grave where they rest
> With thy dust shall remain unpolluted by fame,
> Till thy foes, by the world and by fortune caressed,
> Shall pass like a mist from the light of thy name.
> When the storm-cloud that lowers o'er the daybeam is gone,
> Unchanged, unextinguished its life-spring will shine;
> When Erin has ceased with their memory to groan
> She will smile through the tears of revival on thine.[38]

Moore was baffled by Shelley, possibly overwhelmed by his mad, often opium-driven aristocratic brilliance; whilst Moore never quite lost that Catholic lack of confidence from his youth. Perhaps too he worried about Shelley's fascination with the more militant side of the United Irishmen as inspiration for his own anarchism. Not yet twenty years of age, it was to Ireland (ironically in the person of Emmet's printer John Stockdale) that Shelley looked to publish an early collection of poems on liberty. He was also writing a pamphlet in favour of Catholic emancipation, which became his *An Address to the Irish People*. Shelley thought Ireland was ripe for revolution and he set about alerting its populace by distributing free copies of his pamphlet in

Dublin's public houses, throwing them into carriages, pushing them into the hands of beggars. The pamphlet oscillated between the gradualism of Catholic emancipation and a call for popular resistance against oppression. Attracted first by his support for Catholic emancipation (which he had advertised in the Dublin press), the Catholic Committee invited him to address one of their 'aggregate meetings'. However, the Dublin audience was as baffled by the rhetoric of this pale young Englishman as many a future Irish audience would be by other non-Irish intellectuals seeing revolution where there was none and Shelley was alternately cheered and booed. He returned to England somewhat chastened, though with an undimmed reverence for the United Irishmen and the power of revolution.[39]

The Shelleys (he had been accompanied by his first wife, Harriet) had been deeply disturbed by the poverty and persecution that they found in Ireland. It (and indeed Emmet) was to haunt the poet's life, a metaphor for what was wrong in England. Shortly after their return from Dublin, they sought out Shelley's old college friend, James Hogg. Harriet showed him a broadside of Emmet's trial, expecting him to share their sympathy. Hogg's retort that the sooner all such 'rascals' were hanged the better produced a rift in the friendship.[40] Shelley also tried to start a subscription in England to republish William MacNeven and Thomas Emmet's *Pieces of Irish History*, which he thought a model of radical propaganda.[41] Predictably he gravitated to the most radical politicians and writers in the circles in which most of the Romantics (Moore included) moved. From his exile in Italy he continued to read and write about political issues; his outrage at the Peterloo Massacre of 1819 produced one of his most savage attacks on the establishment, in the person of Lord Castlereagh. This was 'The Mask of Anarchy', a poem of ninety-one stanzas described by Shelley's biographer, Richard Holmes, as 'the greatest poem of political protest ever written in English'. His friend Leigh Hunt, editor of the *Examiner* to which Shelley sent it – who had already served a sentence for publishing seditious literature – thought otherwise, and did not publish it until 1832, ten years after Shelley's death. It would have been sweet revenge for the United Irishmen:

> I met with murder on the way
> He had a mask like Castlereagh –
> Very smooth he looked, yet grim:
> seven blood-hounds followed him:
>
> All were fat; and well they might
> Be in admirable plight,
> For one by one, and two by two,
> He tossed them human hearts to chew
> Which from his wide cloak he drew.

And so any memory of Castlereagh's 'liberalism' in Ireland was erased by the clever epigram based on his reputed impassiveness.

Shortly before writing it, Shelley renewed an acquaintance initiated during the Irish visit of 1812 with Amelia Curran – the clever and fiercely independent eldest daughter of John Philpot Curran, who had attempted to destroy Emmet's letters during Sirr's raid. Shelley's second wife Mary (daughter of Mary Wollstonecraft and William Godwin) was already a friend through the long-standing relationship between their fathers. The Shelleys moved next door to Amelia in Rome, where she was a regular companion, painting their portraits (hers of Shelley now hanging in the National Portrait Gallery, London) and participating in their discussions. Just as Temple Emmet's daughter, Catherine, lately returned from visiting her uncle Thomas's American Emmet family, was then residing in Bath with the parents of the English radical essayist, William Hazlitt,[42] so the relationship between Amelia Curran and the Shelleys was emblematic of how echoes of the Irish past were continuing to have an impact on a new generation of thinkers.

III

Between January and December 1825 a new periodical, *and London Magazine*, ran a series of articles, later describe ᴏy Madden as 'remarkable' and used by himself and others to bridge the void in information about Emmet's character. The narrator (an Englishman with an Irish family) claimed as a young man to have taken part in Emmet's rebellion. Lengthy passages of dialogue and discourse, sounding very much like speeches to the Trinity historical society, appeared to provide a unique insight into Emmet's beliefs and plans. In these Emmet speaks of liberty and oppression, discusses at great length the state of agriculture, population and absenteeism and proclaims the ascendancy of physical over moral force. The narrator's tone is similar to that of Lady Morgan's novels, and there is much about a fallen yet heroic Gaelic race seeking justice from England. In fact, the writer was the Wexford-born editor of the new periodical and subsequent editor of the *Liverpool Journal*, Michael James Whitty (1795–1873), and the selling potential of such a popular topic was, as he later admitted, a motivating factor. That much of the dialogue was derived from the likes of Curran's speeches or accounts of military atrocities from Hay's *History of the Insurrection of Wexford* (1803) seems not to have been noticed at the time or later.

This fictional (if plausible) work became the most important source of information about Emmet's character just in the period when the essential aspects of the legend were taking shape. The account of the rebellion is a paraphrase of Emmet's plan, which had appeared six years previously in Curran's life by his son, in which Emmet had distanced himself from its bloodshed and confusion. The picture of Emmet the man, painted from the likes of Cox, Phillips and Curran, is that of the legend and it particularly influenced Dr Madden. There is not a fault attributed to him, gentleness, kindness, manliness and above all total sincerity being the attributes constantly referred to. And just as constitutional nationalists for the next two centuries nevertheless glorified in the rebellions of this era, so Whitty presents Emmet as glorifying in the idea of martyrdom before he chose to do so after his conviction.

Whitty later republished this as a toned-down work of fiction, admitting his authorship of the earlier series, and expressing his surprise that they had been taken as authentic by so many people. Because 'Robert Emmet was a charmed name', the new periodical was assured commercial success. The articles 'were published by the small printers in every possible form, and circulated most extensively; and when the last paper appeared the whole were very promptly published in a small volume'. This was then republished in America in a number of different forms and in Manchester, and, as Whitty admits with evident surprise, 'Curiosity did not yield to the usual effect of time' by discovery. Perhaps people wanted to believe it. Most surprising in this respect was the credulity of Dr Madden — whose work Whitty greatly admired — who 'seems to have regarded some parts of the Emmet papers as veritable and authentic, for he not only refers to them constantly, but largely quotes from them'.

Almost half a century on, with the Fenians reviving militant republicanism and citing Emmet as their inspiration, Whitty had mellowed and preferred to emphasise the romantic element in the legend to suggest that Emmet would not have approved of the use to which later militants had put his reputation.

> Of all the good men, bad men, and great men engaged in national conspiracies in Ireland, not one has acquired by their patriotism or their deaths, the fame which, from the hour of the rebellion, surrounded and seemed to halo the name of Robert Emmet. His rebellion was an abortion — his preparations for it boyish; but his youth and obvious love for Ireland, and his ardent and daring love for Sarah Curran, had about them all the elements which in all ages have sufficed to constitute personal heroism. The story of his fate and the story of his love challenged, at first — pity,

then sympathy, and, lastly – national regard. His young friend, Thomas Moore, in wedding immortal verse to national song, helped, after a pagan fashion, to deify the memory of Emmet. Moore did this when it was treason to love him; but the poet of all circles never dreamt that his admiration and his melodies would help, not only to perpetuate his memory, but to convert adoration into a means of inciting to rebellion.[43]

Whitty's *Dublin and London Magazine* inspired the most enduring popular work on Emmet, *The Life, Trial and Conversations of Robert Emmet, Esq.* (1836), a chapbook that went into numerous reprints. These little booklets seem to have had a lengthy commercial market. The popular booksellers in Dublin and Belfast stocked them throughout the following decade.[44] 'Poor Emmett is the Irish darling still', wrote Thackeray of Dublin in his *Irish Sketchbook* (of his tour in Ireland in 1842), 'his history is on every book-stall in the city.' His comments on Emmet were sympathetic and he picked out the sites associated with his imprisonment and execution for specific comment.[45]

This 1836 chapbook is largely a compilation (and plagiarism) of much that has gone before and was the most popular of an outpouring of works on Emmet in the 1830s and 1840s. It reproduces Moore's 'Oh, Breathe not his Name', 'She is far from the Land' and a number of other verses and songs. Most notable is Thomas Kennedy's 'The Uninscribed Tomb of Emmet' – a wistful lament in the style of Gray's 'Elegy in a Country Churchyard' and destined to become a favourite in the many later collections of Emmet songs and poems. It was another product of Trinity students' continued fascination with Emmet, appearing in their Comet Club's reformist-literary magazine the *Comet*, in 1830. It is significant in showing that the basic elements of the romantic legend of Robert Emmet are already in place this early: the kindly, gentle, yet manly Emmet from Whitty, the love story from Moore, Curran and Irving, the details of the rebellion largely ignored (save through Emmet's own description of the military plans as explained in the undelivered letter to his brother), and the speech in full – the patriotic version. The romance of Emmet and Sarah Curran is more touchingly related here than previously, with the emphasis on the finality of separation by death, following Irving. Here is reproduced the ballad 'My Emmet's no more' – which Zimmermann has identified as the earliest broadsheet ballad on Emmet (prior to the popularising of Moore's), in which Sarah Curran's lament is equated with that of Erin:

> 'Despair in her wild eye, a daughter of Erin
>   Appeared on the cliff of a bleak rocky shore ...
> Loud rang her harp in wild tones of despairing ...
>   She sang Erin's woes and her Emmet's no more.
>   ...
> Brave was his spirit, yet mild as the Brahmin,
>   His heart bled in anguish at the wrongs of the poor ...
> But, alas! he is gone, he has fallen a young flower,
>   They have murdered my Emmet – my Emmet's no more! [46]

This little book also contains some anecdotes of Emmet's time in prison, which had appeared in a privately printed poem by M. E. Dudley of Mount Dudley, Roscrea, King's County.[47] These told of Sarah Curran visiting him the evening before his death, 'the heavy clanking of his chains' contrasting with the tearful farewell of the lovers. Emmet was said to have been discovered by the prison governor at his 'little deal table' plaiting a tress of hair that he planned 'to wear next my bosom on the day of my execution'. After his execution a drawing was found on the same table of his own likeness, a severed head, the scaffold, axe and other instruments of executions for high treason. Other details of his last hours told of his steadfastness and calmness and of the emotional impact of his character even on the hardened gaolers.

And so the image of Emmet as a noble and gentle hero, and of Sarah Curran as tragic heroine, was almost complete, the popularity of this booklet testimony to a story already vying with those long-standing favourites of romance and banditry. It was reprinted many times over by the most prolific popular publisher of the day, James Duffy. Works on Emmet would figure prominently in his output, not least those by R. R. Madden, and Duffy's company remained 'the flagship of Irish literary nationalism' into the twentieth century.[48] The new introduction to Duffy's version of the 1836 pamphlet, *The Life, Trial and Conversations of Robert Emmet, Esq.*, has Emmet already approaching the status of the irreproachable and unblemished icon of tradition. But the finishing touches to the legend awaited the endeavours of Madden a few years later.

IV

Madden was born on 20 August 1798, during a raid by Major Sirr on the house of his father, a Catholic silk merchant in Dublin. However, the nearest his family came to involvement with the United Irishmen was a minor role played by a first cousin in Emmet's rebellion.[49] Madden is very much part of that post-revolutionary generation of Irish intellectuals who decried violent means, but idolised the United Irishmen and portrayed them as victims of a vicious system, often tricked into revolt by *agents provocateurs* and spies. Madden was a passionate admirer of Thomas Moore. They first met at a dinner given in Moore's honour in Dublin, August 1835. Madden told him of his youthful admiration of the poet when apprenticed to Moore's apothecary in Paris. He would walk out to where Moore lived in the Allée des Veuves just to look at their house and wrote of his admiration around the perimeter of a box of pills being prepared for him.[50] The admiration never dimmed. Madden appears to have been inspired to write his multiple biography of the United Irishmen by the popular reception of Moore's *Lord Edward Fitzgerald* (1831), and wrote to him in 1841 expressing the hope that it would in no way compete with his own *History of Ireland* (the first three volumes having appeared). Moore responded graciously. In no way would their works compete; indeed, Moore hoped that Madden's work would supply him with much of the factual material for future volumes. He never did reach the volume that would have dealt with Emmet. Indeed his reputation was already on the wane because of the pedestrian nature of the *History*. But Madden remained loyal, dedicating his *Literary Remains of the United Irishmen* (1846) to Moore, 'Among the last surviving friends of William Corbet, Edward Hudson, and Robert Emmet'.[51]

Madden was a medical doctor by profession and spent much of his earlier life practising outside Ireland, including a fashionable part of London in the late 1820s. However, he abandoned the medical profession shortly afterwards to oversee the abolition of slavery, in the West Indies, the United States and West Africa and in 1847 and 1850 was colonial secretary in Western Australia. During this time, he nevertheless managed a steady flow of publications. He began collecting material for his *Lives and Times of the United Irishmen* in 1835 while in the United States, where he met a number of the United Irish exiles. Thus he amassed a library of over 7,000 volumes and part of his pamphlet collection currently occupies seventy volumes in the Royal Irish Academy.[52] Most importantly he tracked down surviving United Irishmen and their relatives – at least those who wanted to be found. Emmet's brother-in-law Robert Holmes did not and wrote telling Madden quite firmly that he greatly disapproved of the 'Memoir' he proposed. Those who did were eager to vindicate their forebears and a significant portion of the original documents used by Madden for his 'Memoir' on Robert Emmet came from the Emmets in America, who would continue to play a prominent part in developing and promoting the Emmet legend for well over a century.

Madden's work was Carlyle's heroic history *par excellence*. In his influential *On Heroes, Hero-Worship and the Heroic in History*, Carlyle identified the cult of the hero with the philosophy of nation building. The most significant trait of the hero was sincerity and through his ideas he influenced future generations beyond the grave. A nation's history should be that of great men. The eleven volumes of Madden's *United Irishmen* consisted largely of multiple biographies. Twelve were singled out for particular attention, the volume on Robert Emmet being reissued as a separate biography in 1846. The general approach of Madden was to set the tone for all the popular biographies of Emmet thereafter, and that tone was rather like that found in traditional saints' lives. C. Litton Falkiner identified it as 'Madden's persistent attribution to his heroes of impossible perfection in character and to their opponents of equally unobtainable depravity'.[53]

Even within such hagiography, Madden's treatment of Emmet is excessively uncritical, if not unreal. It reads like a work of bad fiction, because much of it is just that. It also epitomises the reason why Robert Emmet became such a legend in a way that Wolfe Tone or Lord Edward Fitzgerald could not. So little was known about him – he did after all leave behind only a few documents, and those written in dramatic circumstances – that the heroic icon could be constructed to reflect the needs of the nation. Emmet became a legend almost immediately after his death. Fiction and fact were intermixed and became indistinguishable as time went by and the more it was retold. Unlike his biographies of other United Irishmen, there is little that is new about Emmet himself in Madden's volume, though there is new material on the rebellion. Even the information sent by the Emmets of New York was largely concerned with his brother Thomas. Robert Emmet himself occupies only about a third of the book, and that third largely taken up with accounts of the rebellion, trial, speech, imprisonment and execution. It is a life delineated by the few high points of patriotic sacrifice and his entire life up to 1800 has been told by page nine. As for a sense of Emmet's character, this comes over as strangely plaster-cast and (apart from Anne Devlin's personal account) other assessments come largely from recycled,

often dubious sources, tending to accommodate Madden's presenta-
tion of Emmet as the pure, romantic hero, duped by treachery.
Thomas Moore's tribute from his *Life and Death of Lord Edward Fitzgerald* is reproduced in full along with his relevant melodies (several
times), the sympathetic accounts from the sons of Curran and Grattan, Irving's 'Broken Heart' and Whitty's 'Robert Emmet and his
Contemporaries'.

The use Madden makes of this piece of fiction is surprising. Madden was impressed by these 'very remarkable' articles, and uses
Whitty's phraseology liberally in describing Emmet. Whitty was already recycling the language used by the likes of Cox, Curran jr,
Phillips and Moore, with Emmet as kind, gentle, affectionate, sincere,
noble, dignified, calm, yet manly, enthusiastic, animated when speaking (adjectives used repeatedly). But Madden takes such hyperbole to
extremes. He also takes some of his storylines from Whitty, which he
then presents as fact, and because of his influence these enter the
legend. The most important such is what Madden makes of the
'Malachy' character in Whitty's fiction. In the story Malachy is the
Catholic cousin of the narrator and is at the centre of Emmet's
Dublin plans. It is he who tries to bring more people out on the night
of the rising by sending up more signal rockets and is stopped by
Emmet. He then betrays the rebels' refuge in the Wicklow hills and
ultimately Emmet's hiding place. Madden identifies this fictional
character with the real Malachy Delaney. It accords well with Madden's obsession with spies and informers and, although a number of
others are mentioned as the possible betrayer of Emmet, the behaviour of Whitty's Malachy on the night of the rebellion becomes part
of Madden's claim that it was really a government plot and Emmet
himself innocent of any bloodshed. He inquires of two old gardeners
who had worked for the Emmets and who remembered mention of a
Delaney, and so the fictitious character of Whitty becomes fact, even
though Anne Devlin, when questioned by Madden, denied such
charges. In reality Delaney seems to have returned to Ireland after the

premature rebellion, was arrested after the execution
others made a compact with government to desist in re
ities when it became clear that the authorities were anxio
line under the entire business. But Madden was the most
tive work to appear in the decades when the legend was takii _o shape
and this fiction–fact of Malachy Delaney as the ultimate betrayer took
root, to be repeated in every major work thereafter.[54]

Madden opens his biography cautiously, by arguing that the time
was safe to speak of Emmet because the success of 'moral means of
resistance' (i.e. O'Connell's campaigns) had removed the danger of
any similar event occurring. There is a sketchy account of Emmet's
life up to 1802, before Madden moves rapidly to the rebellion. He
then backdates post-rebellion compacts made between some of the
leaders and the government to insinuate that Emmet was the victim
of treachery all along. 'Emmet had no knowledge of the world. He
placed trust in every man; but he was the most honest and single-
minded of human beings' (p. 90). Madden was less fortunate in finding surviving witnesses to Emmet's rebellion than he was for the 1798
period. Apart from the trial reports and Emmet's own statement to
his brother (here reproduced in full) none of his informants were
present in the depots that night and, unusually, he did not contact
Myles Byrne, then living in Paris. Everything that goes wrong Madden
attributes to 'treachery, tracking Robert Emmet's footsteps, dogging
him from place to place, unseen, unsuspected, but perfidy nevertheless embodied in the form of patriotism, basely employed in deluding
its victims, making the most of its foul means, of betraying its unwary
victims' (p. 119).

In 1842 Madden tracked down Anne Devlin, with the help of
Brother Luke Cullen, who had been gathering material on the Wick-
low rebels and who lent Madden his papers, including his work on
Anne Devlin. It was Madden who brought her story to public atten-
tion. In 1842 he found her living in very poor circumstances in the
Liberties. She described at length her sufferings in prison, her refusal

to identify Emmet, her transport to the Castle for interrogation the day after the execution and being shown the blood still visible on the temporary scaffold. Madden has a number of versions of this aspect of Emmet's story, people dipping their handkerchiefs in the blood to keep as mementoes, dogs and pigs lapping it up. The following summer Anne Devlin accompanied Madden to the house in Butterfield Lane and they were permitted by the occupier to tour it. Anne Devlin recalled various details about those who had lived there in the months before the rebellion. But it was the story of her lengthy imprisonment and sufferings that – as with Cullen – occupied most of his account and he used his third volume to recall nationalists to their duty.

> The extraordinary sufferings endured, and the courage and fidelity displayed by this young woman, have few parallels … the heroism of this woman is a matter for Irishmen of any rank, aye, of the highest rank in the land, to be proud of. The true nobility of nature displayed by this poor creature, of plebeian origin, under all her sufferings; the courage exhibited in the face of death, in the midst of torture, of this low-born woman; the fidelity and attachment of this menial servant [a description that Anne Devlin herself would not have tolerated] to a beloved master … will not be forgotten. The day will come, when the name of Anne Devlin, the poor neglected creature who now drags out a miserable existence, struggling with infirmity and poverty, will be spoken of with feelings of kindness, not unmixed with admiration (pp. 184–5).

Luke Cullen later credited Madden with bringing Anne Devlin's story to public light and such was the interest aroused that the *Nation* newspaper opened a subscription for her. But the response was hardly overwhelming and Anne Devlin found the experience demeaning, for they paid the total raised (£5) in paltry instalments and only then when she asked for it. Madden had helped her financially but she died in considerable poverty in 1851 and was at first buried in the paupers' section of Glasnevin cemetery. When Luke Cullen went in search of her grave some months later, he found that her remains had been removed to the more distinguished part of the cemetery and a tombstone erected:

> To the Memory of
> ANNE DEVLIN
> The Faithful Servant of
> Robert Emmet, who possessed
> some rare and many noble
> qualities.
> Who lived in obscurity and
> poverty and so died on the
> 18th of September, 1851,
> aged 70 years.
> May she rest in peace.

Thus was the process of commemoration gathering ground through Madden's efforts. Indeed, Luke Cullen assumed that the claiming of Anne Devlin's resting place for the legend was done by Madden himself. Certainly, her obituary in the *Nation* reproduced Madden's account at some length, thereby adding Anne Devlin's story – absent from previous accounts – to the legend.[55]

Madden's surprise at finding noble virtues in someone of 'menial' standing would in itself surprise were it not for his tendency to excessively romanticise those of the 'gentle' class of patriot. If the virtues attributed to Robert Emmet seem unreal, those attributed to Sarah Curran by Madden are more so. Again there is almost a sense of a fictional tragic heroine. We know that she was not a conventional beauty and her letters show her to have been no shrinking violet. Yet for Madden 'she was one of the gentlest, the most amiable, the simplest-minded, the freest from affectation, the most patient, the least wilful of womankind, and yet there was no sacrifice she was not capable of making for the man she loved'. This account of Sarah Curran ushers in Madden's most extravagant claims for Emmet's character and a reproduction of Irving's 'Broken Heart' and the songs devoted to the doomed love affair, including Moore's. 'Who thinks of the young heroic man of 1803; who talks of the child of the heart of Ireland; who loves and cherishes the memory of the youth "who perished in his pride on the scaffold" ... who reads the story of Robert Emmet, and does not recall the name of Sarah Curran, and all that is sad, as well as beautiful, that is associated with it?'(p. 257) And added to the tragedy were a host of poignant, though largely inaccurate details. These too would enter the legend, catching the imagination in particular of the popular illustrated weeklies, which began to appear towards the end of the century. Madden heard of a tradition that a young woman, believed to be Sarah Curran, had been seen in a coach near to Kilmainham as Emmet's carriage passed en route to his execution, and the two had waved to each other. Even more influential was to be the story of Sarah visiting Emmet's grave at dusk, some days after the execution – a story related to Madden by the elderly former gardener to the Emmets, Michael Leonard. Madden himself wrote a song about this incident, 'Miss Curran's Lament Over the Grave of Robert Emmet'.[56] Neither could have been true because of Sarah's illness. However, there is some evidence that such a visit to Emmet's grave may have happened after her recovery, some months later.[57]

Madden concludes by telling the reader that his book was designed to justify Emmet's character and he uses 'evidence' from Whitty to do so. Apart from a brief denial of any attempt to justify the rising, he tries to distance Emmet from 'moral' culpability. 'No motive of Robert Emmet could be impure, selfish, venal, or ambitious'. Rather 'he was the victim of deception ... he was deluded, misled, and sacrificed by designing men, whose machinations, his youth, his inexpe-

rience, his confiding nature, were unfit to cope
claims, already shown how the authorities knew abo
tion preparing (which he had not) and then quotes at len
mund Spenser's *View of the State of Ireland* to argue
Government has always fomented conspiracies the better to pu
down. To add further credibility to this line of argument he compared
pictures of the death mask of Emmet with that of Jemmy O'Brien, the
notorious informer subsequently executed for murder.

Thus were the various aspects of the legend of Robert Emmet
brought together in accessible and compelling form by Dr Madden.
This *ingénu*, this pure, gentle, cultivated and youthful hero was not really responsible at all for the bloodshed, but was entrapped and betrayed, the gentle victim of a foul oppressor. The picture of the
faultless hero was even more exaggerated in Madden's 1860 edition
of the volume on Emmet, and this would remain the standard treatment until a reassessment of the plaster-cast image began to appear in
the twentieth century.[58] Madden's was not a popular work. It was too
expensive for that. But it was crucial in bringing together earlier
works, anecdotes and traditions into a coherent story and as time
went by it was regarded as something of a bible on Emmet. It was extracted repeatedly in the press (initially by the *Nation*, immediately
after publication), and informed many of the pictorial representations in the explosion of popular print that occurred in the later
decades of the nineteenth century.[59]

V

It was the Trinity College romantics who revived the ideal of the
United Irishmen in the Young Ireland movement and its newspaper
the *Nation*.[60] Thomas Davis, the movement's founder, mapped out its
agenda in a famous address in 1839 to Trinity's Historical Society. He
chastised his listeners for their neglect of Irish history. 'I never heard
of any famous nation which did not honor the names of its departed

great,' he told them, and he set himself the task of moulding the 'historic memory' which he argued was the essence of nation-building.[61] Through illustrations, song and populist histories he sought 'to set up in our souls the memory of great men' and 'make Irish History familiar to the minds and powerful over the taste and conduct of the Irish people in days to come'.[62] It was Davis and his colleagues on the *Nation* who conceived the idea of raising, indeed creating, popular national consciousness through poetry, song, illustration and simplified historical narrative.

Madden met Davis during his visit to Dublin in 1842–3 and gave the younger man access to the papers that he was using for his volume on Emmet. Davis's intention of himself writing a history of the United Irishmen was cut short by his early death in September 1845.[63] Although Madden's first and second series were published in London, his third (that on Emmet) and subsequent series were published in Dublin by James Duffy. They had been introduced by Davis, and it was Duffy who implemented the *Nation*'s mission of producing potted historical stories for the mass market. He came to that mission with an established pedigree producing chapbooks and Catholic devotional material. In the *Pictorial History of Ireland* (1843), *Spirit of the Nation* (1843) and the Library of Ireland series – monthly volumes retailing at 1s. – Duffy and the Young Irelanders set the pattern for the mixture of pictures, songs and simple stories that created and informed popular Irish nationalism, or as the Tory *Dublin University Magazine* put it, 'treason made easy'.[64]

Madden's volume on Emmet was applauded by and serialised in the *Nation* (the first of many such serialisations). Echoing Carlyle, its reviewer proclaimed: 'The history of every land is the history of its great men', not only those who have brought about successful revolutions, but those involved in 'an unsuccessful struggle, especially for the freedom of a land not yet free' – for which Emmet's 'let no man write my epitaph' words are cited as the symbol. If the successful conflict brings monuments, yearly holidays, insignia, the unsuccessful must be commemorated in a 'compound of individual memories', narratives of 'dead heroes' such as Madden had produced. Did they think that when the dogs of Thomas Street lapped Emmet's blood 'a nation would never write his epitaph? Fools. Presumptuous fools!' No, 'men of noble soul ... [would] uphold his memory as a duty, and derive from his failure ... lessons in future conquest. Would you have a cause eternal, let its youth be trained in defeat.'[65] This was written in 1846, but it could easily be transposed to the early twentieth century and not sound out of place. The 1916 generation of republicans were as much products of romantic Young Irelandism as of militant Fenianism. The Young Irelanders were not in favour of militant force initially and co-operated with Daniel O'Connell in the constitutional movement to repeal the Act of Union. But they did see themselves as inheritors of the United Irishmen and were incensed by O'Connell's 1841 attack on the men of 1798 as 'weak and wicked men' who used 'sanguinary violence' to improve Ireland's situation. Among those who resigned from the repeal movement were the Emmets of New York.[66]

In Dublin another young Protestant Trinity man, John Kells Ingram, disgusted by the failure of the O'Connellites to respect the memory of the United Irishmen, dashed off his historic poem 'The Memory of the Dead' and sent it to the *Nation*.

> Who fears to speak of Ninety-Eight?
>   Who blushes at the name?
> When cowards mock the patriots' fate,
>   Who hangs his head in shame?
> He's all a knave, or half a slave,
>   Who slights his country thus;
> But a true man, like you, man,
>   Will fill your glass with us.
>
> . . .
>
> They rose in dark and evil days

o right their native land;
y kindled there a living blaze
That nothing shall withstand.
Alas! that Might can vanquish Right –
They fell, and pass'd away;
But true men, like you, men,
Are plenty here to-day.[67]

Ingram was a nineteen-year-old student when he composed his famous verses and in later life was more unionist than nationalist. Indeed, he did not publicly acknowledge authorship of the poem until
1900.[68] But Ingram's early Young Irelandism was representative of
that continuation of romantic nationalism in Emmet's old college.

The power of the Emmet legend came from its reduction to a very
basic narrative. It is a story of heroes and villains, romance and betrayal and a process of saturation, simplification and hyperbole. The
acceptance of new facts ceases with Madden, the intermittent press
references assuming familiarity. Ignored is St John Mason's exonera-
tion of Norbury or the succession of official papers published from
mid-century onwards clearly showing that there was no government
plot against the young rebel. Much has been written about elite creation of tradition/memory and the making of the Emmet legend
partly falls into this category. To folklorists the assimilation of print
culture into oral traditions is a well-recognised process. However, the
huge popularity of collections of United Irish songs in the early nineteenth century, or the cheap booklets noted by Thackeray, can
scarcely be attributed to elite culture. In urban Ireland at least the cult
was already there before its widespread popularisation from mid-century. Emmet too was easily incorporated into traditional folk narrative, and Ireland was not unique in privileging the story of the
underdog, the victim, the oppressed above others. Gaelic oral culture

had long damned the English and Scots, spoke of oppression and extolled the messianic hero, even if the gentleness, purity and sobriety attributed to Emmet in the growing legend were most definitely Victorian values. By 1858 when Madame de Staël's daughter published her work on Emmet, it was as a 'martyr to liberty' and 'a sort of heroic and romantic legend' that she depicted him.[69]

6 The 'Uninscribed Tomb': the search for Emmet's grave

No rising column marks this spot
   Where many a victim lies,
But oh! the blood which here has streamed,
   To heaven for justice cries.
  …

It claims it on the callous Judge,
   Whose hands in blood are dyed,
Who arms injustice with the sword,
   The balance throws aside.
  …

Nor shall a tyrant's ashes mix,
   With those our martyred dead;
This is the place where Erin's sons,
   In Erin's cause have bled
  …

Unconsecrated is this ground,
   Unblessed by holy hands;
No bell here tolls its solemn sound,
   No monument here stands.

But here the patriot's tears are shed,
   The poor man's blessing given;
These consecrate the virtuous dead,
   These waft their fame to Heaven.[1]

This is part of a poem written by Robert Emmet in 1798. It refers to the many executions and burials in the 'Croppies' hole' of Arbour Hill in the summer of 1798. For some it seemed prophetic of his own fate, a suggestion even that he intended his burial place not to be found. All Emmet's poetry was inspired by dark gothic themes, themes that – second only to the romance – would dominate the legend. The absence of a grave (which to this day has never been located) added extra meaning to his speech, and, just as the absence of detail about his life and thought permitted all manner of embellishment, so the non-existent grave enhanced the legend. A violent, ignominious death, heroically confronted, and a common criminal's burial placed Emmet to the fore of developing Irish nationalism, which valued suffering and death above all other attributes for iconic status. Although all his fellow defendants were beheaded, as were many in 1798, *his* death made an awful impact on the generation of 1803. An 'appalling sensation ... pervaded his country on the occasion of his lamented death', wrote the anonymous author of the bestselling *Life and Actions of Robert Emmet* (1840), 'his removal in one unexpected moment from this busy life's vocations to the oblivious silence of the tomb' produced 'a general burst of sorrow, and a common sense of bereavement'.[2]

Emmet's execution and the manner in which he confronted it became the defining element in the legend. If the government had simply banished him to Australia as it did with Michael Dwyer and many others, a later critic was to argue, he would never have become such a martyr and inspiration to others.[3] It was a criticism that would also be made of the execution of Patrick Pearse, the man who, above anyone else, had modelled himself on Robert Emmet. 'I cannot too strongly condemn Emmet's execution. From his grave sprang a bitter plant that yet bears blossom and fruit', lamented the author of *The Island of Sorrow*, Mary Lucy Arthur – no friend to militant nationalism. 'The death of this boy, deserving as maybe it was, has brought a most bitter punishment, for, instead of being known as a silly, pretending, grandiloquent youth, the name of Robert Emmet, for all times, is revered as a martyr ... His death gives a dignity nothing else could have given to the extreme silliness of his behaviour.'[4]

I

'I am going to my cold and silent grave ... let no man write my epitaph, for as no man who knows my motives dare now vindicate them. Let them and me repose in obscurity and peace, and my tomb remain uninscribed, until ... my country takes her place among the nations of the earth.' Emmet's injunction inspired everything written about him, with little sense of the irony involved in the absence of any tomb on which an epitapth could or could not be written. Even Southey's poem, the most powerful of the Romantics' treatment of Emmet, felt the need to erect a monument. Moore's 'O Breathe not his Name' and Thomas Kennedy's 'The Uninscribed Tomb' locate the grave in the idealised country graveyard setting of much nineteenth-century literature.[5] At a time when nationalism still flourished among the Protestant intellectuals, Kennedy's elegy is an early version of Irish nationalists' interpretation of Emmet's command that his epitaph could only be written in a free Ireland.

The fiction of a decent burial of sorts sustained the image of Sarah Curran paying a night-time visit to the grave, which became a recurrent image in the popular weeklies.[6] In the general run of nationalist comment, the absence of a grave was not mentioned. The writing of an epitaph on his tomb remained emblematic of a future independence, a 'silent reproach' reminding future generations of Emmet's last injunction.[7] 'What are you doing in Dublin to find Emmet's grave?' asked the chairman of the centenary committee in Melbourne, in a letter to the *Irish People* in August 1903. The Irish in Melbourne had taken the Exhibition Building for the 'grand Centenary night' on 21 September and a series of tableaux would depict Ireland's past and future:

I –   Ireland in the days of her glory (VIII Century).

II –   Invasion by the Normans.

III – Ireland in bondage. Penal Times.

IV –   Ireland in mourning at the foot of an uninscribed
       tomb visited successively by the Angels of
       Sympathy, of Hope, of Succour, and of Liberty.

V –   Erin a Nation (with the tomb inscribed).[8]

What matter that there is no grave, thought others, the loss of the body adding force to the 'let no man write my epitaph' request, ensuring that 'under all the present circumstances it is better that mystery should continue to guarantee respect for the martyr's last desire'.[9]

Despite the richness of new research that proves an underlying Jacobitism in much of Irish Catholic thinking and corresponding lack of perceived legitimacy in the ruling system, this research has not yet extended to an examination of popular reactions to capital punishments in cases of high treason. Admittedly it has only recently been addressed by English historians and even they struggle to explain the gulf between the growing public disapproval of the butchery of those executed for treason and the insistence of the ruling class in retaining the grisly clauses on the statute book. Even V. A. C. Gatrell – who is unusual among historians in addressing this point – struggles to explain it, suggesting that it was an unconscious 'ancestral inheritance' and respect for such symbols of state power among the elite. Not all countries had such a straightforward view of treason as Britain. 'None of us is certain that tomorrow the situation won't be different, or that it won't change again the day after next,' argued Friedrich Scheller in 1848 in a debate on capital punishment in the Frankfurt Parliament. 'Yesterday the death penalty for treason was meted out to deeds that are rewarded with civic honours today.'[10] It was an argument that Emmet himself had touched upon in his speech and one that emerged increasingly in nationalist commentary on Emmet.[11]

Robert Emmet and the others hanged for their involvement in the 1803 rebellion were the last in Ireland (though not in England) to be publicly executed and beheaded for treason. As such its treatment in print and song set a pattern for the construction of a martyrology, largely lacking in figures as genteel or prominent as Robert Emmet. Hanging is a most brutal form of death, robbing the victim of dignity as well as life. Death was rarely quick and those in the know had learnt to position the knot of the noose in such a way as to obviate frequent bungling by the executioner. Emmet was one of these. Muscular convulsions were common, as was involuntary defecation, urination and erection of the penis in men.[12] Perhaps this is why Charles Maturin's rebel hero (*The Milesian Chief* [1812]) is executed by firing squad (highly unlikely) rather than hanging. On this aspect of public executions there is silence, both in public print and by witnesses of executions – a taboo unbroken in Ireland until Joyce's irreverent take on Emmet's execution in *Ulysses*.

Every other detail of Emmet's execution, however, was lingeringly detailed. Madden obtained a first-hand account from a fellow student. The makeshift scaffold of planks placed across empty barrels was erected overnight in the middle of Thomas Street in front of St Catherine's church. Through the planks two posts rose some 12 to 15 feet, across which a beam was placed horizontally. Another single plank was balanced about three feet above the platform, where the prisoner was to stand. Emmet mounted the steps to the first platform, delivered the short statement mentioned earlier, removed his cravat and adjusted the rope himself, before being placed on the second plank and having the usual thin cap pulled over his head. He was said to have lifted this and exchanged a few words with the executioner. Then on being asked if he was ready, he replied 'not yet' twice, but on the third 'not ...' the executioner tilted the plank, and Emmet 'was dangling like a dog, writhing in the agonies of the most revolting and degrading to humanity of all deaths ... After hanging for a moment motionless, life terminated with a convulsive movement of the body. At the expiration of the usual time the remains were taken down and extended on the scaffold, the head was struck from the body, grasped by the hair, and paraded along the front of the gallows by the hangman.' Madden's informant added that 'there was no distortion of the features, but an extraordinary palor [sic], (the result of the flow of blood from the head after decapitation), he never saw a more perfect expression of placidity and composure'. Mrs McCready, passing through the street shortly after the execution, told Madden that she saw dogs lapping up the blood from below the scaffold and some spectators dipping their handkerchiefs in it to take away as mementoes.[13] Later, nationalists interpreted this as sympathisers securing relics of the martyr. However, this too was normal practice at executions, belief in the healing blood of the executed being part of the 'magico-religious' culture of pre-modern societies everywhere in Europe.[14]

These descriptions, given forty years after the event, came to inform every popular account of Emmet's execution thereafter. For Madden was collecting memories just when the Emmet legend was taking off and very largely informed it, one of the more notable examples of booklorish Irish folklore. John Fisher of Inn's Quay thought the beheading took place on a table, 'a deal table, like a common kitchen table', and afterwards it was simply returned to the market house opposite John Street and there left exposed.[15] The more enduring and brutally suggestive tradition is that Emmet was beheaded on a butcher's block. Only in 2002 was I told of the sensation caused when visitors to the Hermitage in Rathfarnham were told that a large block on display was that on which Robert Emmet had been beheaded. My informant then confided that he regularly walked past St Catherine's on his way home, the dark edifice reminding him of what had happened Robert Emmet.[16]

There is very little contemporary evidence about the behaviour of the crowd. They were said to have removed their hats at the end, and 'moaned' when the head was cut off.[17] This would have been typical of execution crowds generally and not specific to Emmet. The legend assumes that those present were sympathisers and Watson's 1870 illustration has the military attacking the spectators. But this is highly unlikely and probably owes more to the pictorial representations of the 1819 Peterloo massacre in Manchester. In 1914 Dr Thomas Addis Emmet, grand-nephew to Robert Emmet, was sent the recollections of an eyewitness to the execution. They came from a reputable optician and told of how his aged grandmother had watched from a friend's house on the opposite side of the street. It is a horrific account of the severing of the head – as indeed, it would have been – and the soldiers pushing aside those who dipped their handkerchiefs in the blood.[18] This image may have been the origin of the account of the soldiers attacking the crowd, for execution crowds rarely rioted, except when the executioner bungled the process. The psychology of execution crowds was extraordinarily complex. Support for the victim was the norm and recognition that the theatre of execution had failed in its deterrence factor was key to the decision in 1868 to end public executions.

With the removal of executions from the public space to the interior of the prisons after 1868, public spectacle gave way to a more heightened fascination with the detail. Indeed, the growth in literacy and a popular press transferred a rich oral to a print culture.[19] Madden's account is reproduced repeatedly and added to. The *Shamrock* devoted its St Patrick's Day 1887 double issue to Robert Emmet and Michael Dwyer. It was lavishly illustrated by John D. Reigh, the frontispiece depicting Emmet in his cell on the day of execution. His attire meticulously reproduces that of the traditional portrayal and he holds the black velvet stock into which the lock of Sarah Curran's hair was said to have been sewn. A story-book angel prepares a victory crown of laurel, pointing to the figure of liberty breaking his chains. The accompanying story opens with traditions of the execution in the anonymous author's family: 'The noblest Roman of them all, the martyr-hero, the boy with pale, firm, predestined face, who was strangled and decapitated in Thomas-street for the crime of having loved his country with a passion pure and enthusiastic.' His grandfather had witnessed the execution as a child, 'got quite close to the grisly cross-beam', and he had heard the story with a childhood fascination, the execution of Robert Emmet becoming part of that cupboard of ghostly tales so beloved by generations of children. He told of Emmet ascending the scaffold 'without faltering', 'a gleam of serene brightness in his look'. 'The verdict of posterity has reversed the pronouncement of the ruthless judge and no character is more prized among those who have written their names in the luminous pages of history than that of the gallant stripling, whose head was chopped off by the felon hangman and exhibited as a dripping trophy to a horrified mob.'[20]

'We wish to turn our faces from the scene', wrote the author of another lengthy article in the *Weekly Freeman* for 17 October 1891, 'but we cannot; it has a horrible fascination for us.' And so it had. This author takes up the story in Thomas Street on 23 July and imagines Emmet having a premonition of his fate as he saw St Catherine's church, the 'Protestant place of worship ... black, gloomy and forbidding'. By now the scaffold was being treated as an 'altar' on which Emmet 'the martyr' had been sacrificed. The handkerchiefs dipped in his blood are 'holy souvenirs', the visit to St Catherine's a 'pilgrimage' in honour of 'the greatest saint in the calendar of Irish political martyrology', the place where his life was 'sacrificed ... the holiest spot in all Ireland'.[21] As such it becomes a surrogate grave, a site where wreaths were laid and pilgrimage-like processions and mock funerals routed past, even, by the time of the centenary in 1903, a tourist attraction.[22]

Such Christ-like references were not unusual in the making of heroic legends. Even so, the lingering discussion of bodily suffering in the Emmet legend has a very Catholic ring to it, a mirror image (at a time of steady catholicising of Irish nationalism) of the Catholic Church's growing emphasis on Christ's wounds and passion.[23] Typical was a flyer in 1903 for 'The Chance of a Lifetime: A Romance of the Days of Robert Emmet', by popular Catholic fiction writer Mrs M. T. Pender; it spoke of 'the hero and martyr climbing ... Calvary in the steps of Christ'.[24] There is also an unmistakeable necrophilia, or, at the very least, an interpretation of the Emmet legend through Ireland's 'gothic mode', with its 'emotional intensity ... feelings of terror or horror', often linking the 'sexual and violent aspects of human experience'.[25] The obsession with the beheading part of the execution drama is one example, though there are others.

The initial interest may have been prompted by the works of Eugene O'Curry and Standish O'Grady into ancient Irish society and the cult of the severed head. Emmet was said to have drawn an image of a severed head on the eve of his execution, which is almost certainly a confusion with the heads sketched by Petrie at the trial. The features of the head were described in detail, the method of decapitation, the instruments used, the nature of the blood flow perhaps suggesting that Emmet was not dead when the decapitation took place. 'Almost before life was extinct', wrote M. McD. Bodkin, nationalist MP and journalist, 'the rope was cut and the head was hacked from the still quivering body while the gush of warm blood flooded the platform and dripped down upon the pavement. Clutching the ghastly head, from which the blood still dripped the hangman paraded it in front of the scaffold.'[26] It was a theme continued in Bodkin's popular historical novel, *True Man and Traitor: or The Rising of Emmet* (1921), the crowd taking away mementoes of his 'sacred blood, to pass on as a rich legacy from generation to generation, in memory of him who died for Erin's sake'.[27] The image of this 'still warm blood' reddening the streets of Dublin carried suggestions of the hero's 'manhood' and 'virility' draining away, an association of manliness and the blood sacrifice particularly noticeable in republican literature:

Robert Emmet! Robert Emmet!
  When the tyrant struck you down
In the springtime of your manhood,

> In the heart of Dublin town;
>   When she gave the dogs your life-blood,
>   When she mocked your dying moan,
>   Did she think the power of Emmet
>   Was for all time overthrown.[28]

The most famous example of this association is in the writings of Patrick Pearse. His fascination with Emmet was more than just an admiration for the hero who had sacrificed all for the national ideal. Much has been written about Pearse's suppressed homosexuality.[29] Here I want to show that, in addition to this, the key points of the Emmet legend, and particularly those surrounding the execution, were crucial to his (and republicanism's) mesmerisation with death, violence and the blood sacrifice. Pearse provides the best-known example of necrophilia in the making of the Emmet legend, Emmet (until his later identification with Cú Chulainn) taking pride of place in the 'homoeroticism' of his writings.[30] Images of the doomed but noble hero came easily to Pearse. He grew up surrounded by the funereal monuments and tombstones of his father's workshop, and was something of a recluse who was deeply influenced by the sentimental nationalism of his mother and great-aunt. His morbidly devout Catholicism lent itself easily to reflections on suffering and redemptive death, and his admiration for Emmet became an obsession after he moved his private school, St Enda's, to the former Curran family home at Rathfarnham. Here Pearse became haunted by the love story. He believed their spirits survived in the places where they lived. He imagined the presence of Sarah Curran and Emmet in its grounds and rooms, and pictured the 'young, slight figure' of Emmet walking there from Harold's Cross, his 'noble ... head', *à la* Petrie, 'bent a little upon the breast'. He 'communed with the spirit of him who had been there more than a hundred years before and lived every hour of that heroic life over again ... He reverenced Tone and Mitchel and Lalor and Davis, but he loved Emmet as a brother living beneath the same roof as him.'[31]

Pearse recounted this obsession in a famous speech delivered at the Emmet Commemoration in the Academy of Music, Brooklyn, New York, on 2 March 1914. He painted an Emmet trail, taking his listeners through the landscape and buildings and the high points of the Emmet legend. From such animism the equation of his hero with Christ was not such a leap. 'Patriotism is in a large part a memory of heroic dead men', whose 'ultimate sacrifice' placed them 'midway between God and men'. They would not have sacrificed nationhood for peace, like those who parleyed today with the enemy for an element of home rule. 'But the soil of Ireland, yea, the very stones of our cities' – much like those over which Emmet's blood had dripped – 'cried out against' such 'infidelity'. 'No failure, judged as the world judges such things, was ever more complete, more pathetic than Emmet's. And yet he has left us a prouder memory than the memory of Brian victorious at Clontarf or of Owen Roe victorious at Benburb. It is the memory of a sacrifice Christ-like in its perfection.' Emmet, in the dock at Green Street, stood alone 'face to face with England', his speech, 'the most memorable words ever uttered by an Irishman' echoed down the generations, a reminder of 'a task left unfinished'. But it was the manner of his death that redeemed his country and Pearse relives the scene, much as the stations of the cross invited the congregation to retrace Christ's steps to Calvary. 'And his [Emmet's] death was august. In the great space of Thomas Street an immense silent crowd; in front of Saint Catherine's church a gallows upon a platform; a young man climbs to it, quiet, serene, almost smiling, they say – ah, he was very brave! There is no cheer from the crowd, no groan; this man is to die for them, but no man dares to say aloud: "God bless you, Robert Emmet!" Dublin must one day wash out in blood the shameful memory of that quiescence.' Why was no rescue attempt made? Emmet seemed to expect one. 'He was saying "Not yet", when the hangman kicked aside the plank and his body was launched into the air. They say it swung for half-an-hour, with terrible contortions, before he died. When he was dead the comely head was severed from the body. A friend of mine knew an old woman who told him how the blood flowed down upon the pavement, and how she sickened with horror as she saw the dogs of the street lap up that noble blood. The hangman showed the pale head to the people and announced: "This is the head of a traitor, Robert Emmet." A traitor? No, but a true man. O my brothers, this was one of the truest men that ever lived. This was one of the bravest spirits that Ireland has ever nurtured. This man was faithful even unto the ignominy of the gallows, dying that his people might live, even as Christ died. Be assured that such a death always means a redemption.'[32]

A week later, in another speech in New York, Pearse returned to lessons of the Emmet story 'urging the generations to perilous bloody attempts, nerving men to give up life for the death-in-life of dungeons, teaching little boys to die with laughing lips, giving courage to young girls to bare their backs to the lashes of a soldiery, ... the memory of that splendid death of his ... that young figure, serene and smiling, climbing to the gallows above that sea of silent men in Thomas Street' urging the young men of today towards a similar 'heroic purpose'.[33] And, it seems, it was Emmet's plan that he was following in Easter 1916, when he 'washed out in blood the stain of shame that had defiled the fame of Baile Atha Cliath [Dublin] since 1803. At the last moment men failed in 1916 as in Emmet's day, but the brave and heroic fight was made, the story of which will echo down the ages along with the story of him who swung into undying fame from that sombre gallows in Thomas Street.'[34]

Since the involvement of two young women contributed to the romantic element of the Emmet legend, it should not surprise that they also figured in the necrophilic/erotic element of the legend. There were periodic exchanges in the press about the location of Sarah Curran's grave and something of a cult had developed around the grave of her sister Gertude, mistaken as her own.[35] However, she remained a shadowy figure in the legend and it was the Anne Devlin story that fired popular imagination. After Madden, interest focused on the report of Anne's sufferings before her arrest at Butterfield Lane, accounts telling of brutalised redcoats torturing the defenceless female, often in unmistakeably erotic terms. Thus she was dragged into the outer yard with 'indecent savagery, men disgracing man's form' and as they prepared the mock gallows, 'the fiends kept their sharp bayonets pointed to her naked bosom, pressing them as it were with gentle touches against her tender skin until the blood flowed freely down her person ... And ever as they pressed her to tell, they pierced her woman-skin with soldier-weapons to torture the secret from her.'[36] It is this image of Anne Devlin that is highlighted in the legend. Pearse described it in graphic, and exaggerated, terms in his New York speech. 'They swung her up to a cart and half hanged her several times ... They pricked her breast with bayonets until the blood spurted out in their faces. They dragged her to prison and tortured her for days.'[37] It lent itself well to dramatic visual representation and so popular visual memory becomes informed almost exclusively by images of suffering and death.[38]

> *I* had died for you gladly, my courage never quailed,
> When their swords pierced my bosom, their wild threats
>   assailed
> Nor did their prison torture win from me a single tear –
> *That* memory of grief and pain would fade if you were
>   here.
> ...
> Oh! had the cruel spoiler spared your young dark head,
> The tramp of your United hosts had waked the very
>   dead,
> The shouts of your triumph had thundered to the sky –
> But alas! and alas! in the cold grave you lie.[39]

Much as the authority figures in the Anne Devlin story are depicted as brutish, so the villains pollute Emmet's purity.[40] The 'Elegy on the Death of Robert E....', from Cox's *Irish Magazine,* is reproduced in the centenary songbooks; Emmet the 'hero immolated ... rudely torn/By felon hands', like 'parasitic hungry plants' strangling 'the tendril stems'. Plunket's 'serpent venom' and 'Hell's sulphureous steam' corrupts that 'pure spotless spirit' and Emmet 'His soul unconscious of a guilty thought/Smiles at his doom which self-sold Erin wrought'.[41] The idea that Trevor or Fitzgibbon might be buried beside Emmet added a new horror to the putrefaction of death and decay. The attempt by Sirr's grandson to prove that his grandfather had shown some delicacy towards Sarah Curran was greeted by outrage in the Irish press.[42]

In depictions of the execution the horror is emphasised by images of the youthful features of the dead head, contrasted to 'the brutal fingers' of the hangman clutching its hair, portrayal of the range of instruments available for beheadings, the butcher's block conveying the image of bestial carnage. 'In half an hour the still quivering body is cut down, and extended on a butcher's block, and from it the head is rudely hacked with a butcher's knife. The brutal fingers of the executioner grip its hair, and holding it up, bloody and dripping, exposing the waxen features and glazed eyes of the dishonoured thing to the moaning crowd, he exclaims, as he parades in front of the scaffold: "This is the head of a traitor!"'[43]

When writing this, Michael McDonagh appears to have had before him the 1870 print of Emmet's execution by Watson and there are signs that accounts of Emmet from this period are increasingly influenced by such visual images. In this illustration the butcher's block is prominently positioned. Emmet's head and neck gush blood, the brutality of the scene heightened by the executioner's axe. Pictorial representations concentrate on the beheading rather than the hanging, the life-blood sacrificial image more appropriate to heroic martyrdom.[44] It is a gruesome sight, but not half as gruesome as it probably was in reality. 'Probably', because I have found no detailed contemporary account of the execution (nor that of any of the others executed for their part in Emmet's rebellion). This is baffling, as executions for high treason in England attracted an enormous amount of publicity – that of Despard, and those convicted with him, meriting several columns in the Dublin press some months earlier, giving all the grim detail of the beheadings.[45] There was no opposition press at the time that might have given voice to growing popular disgust at such barbaric vestiges of the ancient laws of treason, as happened in England. Had the beheadings in the 1798 period blunted sensitivities, or the twelve executions that had preceded Emmet's in September 1803, six of these also in Thomas Street? [46]

Predictably, the identity of Emmet's executioner was a frequent topic in the press and elsewhere, and just as predictably a curse was said to follow his descendants. He was thought to have been Tom Galvin, and Madden was told that he had been a postilion with the Duke of Leinster, convicted of highway robbery and offered the post of hangman instead of deportation. For fifty years he was said to have conducted the task until his death in 1830.[47] In 1878 the dying 'confession' of Barney Moran, a pauper in Ballina workhouse, sparked off a new debate. Barney claimed to have been a soldier in Dublin in 1803 and subsequently fought in the Peninsular War. However, he was largely known in Ballina as a harmless tramp and ballad-monger. The story is implausible, one of the many such dubious stories taken into the Emmet legend. But it resulted in another press exchange on the execution with many reproductions of Emmet's death mask and more chill-inspiring reflections on the horrors of the execution. 'It seems hard to believe', mused the *Connaught Telegraph*, 'that ... poor old harmless Barney, whom the children used to crowd round in the street to listen to and laugh at his quaint old comic ballads and jokes – could ever have been the hardened and blood-stained wretch who swung the devoted young patriot into eternity, cut down the body while yet warm, severed from it the head, and held up the poor pale blood-streaked face to the gaze of the callous-hearted soldiery, of the

awe-stricken, pitying people, and, saddest of all, to that of the ago-
nised and broken-hearted Sarah Curran.'[48]

II

In the context of such morbid fascination, it is perhaps not surprising
that there should have been periodic searches for Emmet's grave.

> What erring mortal sleeps beneath
>   This rude, unlettered stone?
> Some felon sure, whose life and death
>   The world would wish unknown:
> For see the grave-stone careless thrown
>   Along the lonely bed,
> Rudely uncared for, and alone,
> Nameless amongst the dead.
>   . . .
> No, child of Ireland, o'er this grave
>   Give free the flowing tear:
> For truthful, trusting, pure and brave,
>   Was he who slumbers here.
> Ah, Heaven! 'tis bitter joy they quaff
>   Whose swelling bosoms know
> Meet pride that scorns the epitaph,
> Was his who sleeps below.[49]

Every heroic reputation depends on successive generations of friends
and family to promote it. It is unlikely that Tone would have found
such fame without the drive and longevity of his widow. Similarly it
was the American Emmets who made Robert Emmet such an icon in
the United States and informed the legend's development at key
stages in Ireland. The United Irishmen who ended up in America determined the bitter anti-Englishness of developing American–Irish

nationalism and few were as embittered as Thomas Addis Emmet. Having himself opposed premature rebellion in 1798, he with William James MacNeven developed the idea that its explosion in 1798 was a government plot, much as his descendants were to argue in the case of Emmet's rebellion. The first public performance of Robert Emmet's speech was in New York in 1806, while the New York Irish newspaper, the *Shamrock*, was filled with United Irish poetry and reflections, much of it on Robert Emmet.[50]

While things improved in Ireland, and Holmes, Patten and Hope, grown old, thought such rebellions no longer necessary, the attitudes of the Irish exiles had frozen in the bad times of 1798. Thomas Moore was told of an incident in which Thomas Emmet's daughter had broken down when singing one of Moore's songs, 'and starting up from the pianoforte gave at once full vent to all her feelings about Ireland, execrating England in the most passionate manner, and wishing that America and the other nations of the earth would join to avenge Ireland's cause on her'.[51] Her brother became president of the Repeal Association of New York and in 1841 resigned in protest at O'Connell's denunciation of the United Irishmen.[52]

Madden befriended the former United Irishmen in New York in the 1830s. Although Thomas Addis Emmet had died in 1827, he was survived by nine children and Madden was particularly assisted in his searches by his sons Robert and Thomas. Madden made enquiries about Emmet's burial place in 1836, 1846 and again in 1859. It seems that Emmet's body was probably buried in Bully's Acre (Hospital Fields) near Kilmainham, when it remained unclaimed. In 1836 Madden sent Leonard, Dr Emmet's old gardener, to question the former gaoler of Kilmainham, George Dunn. Dunn had been accused of petty tyranny by the former prisoners (not least St John Mason and Anne Devlin). However, the posthumous popularity of Robert Emmet sees Dunn actively reinventing himself and his account needs to be treated with scepticism. Dunn sent word to Madden that the body was kept in the 'outer entry of the prison', and he was ordered that if it was not claimed immediately to have it interred in Bully's Acre. Dunn claimed to have 'kept the body for several hours' notwithstanding such orders and, when no one came forward, he had it buried in Bully's Acre, beside the grave of Felix Rourke. Thereafter Emmet's remains were removed in private and in the presence of Revd Thomas Gamble and re-interred some-where in Dublin – other evidence suggesting St Michan's, to which Gamble was attached as curate – possibly until the family vault in St Peter's could be opened.

The descendant of an Emmet family friend, Mrs Elizabeth Ham-mond, née Fisher, published a series of articles in the 1940s, largely based on family traditions, though partially supported by sources from the Rebellion Papers. In these Dunn's story about Bully's Acre is endorsed, though he seems to have had no part in the burial. Rather the governor of Newgate, Tresham Gregg, submitted an in-voice to government for a military party detailed to conduct the bur-ial. Emmet's friends believed his sister, Mary Anne Holmes, would claim the body – normal procedure and the bodies of those executed were usually released to relatives – and consequently did nothing. The Revd Gamble wrote a report to Marsden, and then rode out of town to Donnybrook to see Mary Anne Holmes, probably to secure the necessary permit for her brother's burial.[53] If Hammond is to be be-lieved, Gamble's actions after this would have been consistent with the story of the body having been buried unknown to the family. On the following day he paid visits to a number of family friends, includ-ing John Patten's mother and Joseph Hammond's great-grand-mother, Elizabeth Hammond, then returned to Mary Anne Holmes and on to Rathfarnham to convey Emmet's farewell missive to Sarah Curran (also possibly his letter to Richard Curran). Mrs Patten called on her son – then under arrest – and told him that a porter in the family business had taken Emmet's remains from 'Kilmainham' and buried them in Bully's Acre . This seems implausible. Patten had not given Madden such information when first contacted in 1846, but rather in 1859, when 'he gave me [Madden] the ... account of all the circumstances he could remember, *which had been brought to his knowledge*' [my italics]. Whatever the origin of the Bully's Acre story, it added another melodramatic element to the gothic tale. Then all the traditions converge to claim that Gamble had the remains re-interred temporarily in St Michan's until the Emmet family vault at St Peter's could be opened.[54]

Madden sought information from Robert Holmes. But Holmes refused to talk to him; indeed, in a terse reply he told Madden that he 'greatly' disapproved of his publishing project.[55] Holmes had suffered considerably from his association with the Emmet family. Dr Emmet's legal affairs were not in order when he died and Holmes had been in London to sort out matters relating to Kitty Emmet, a ward of court, when Robert Emmet was in the last stages of organising the rebellion. He was arrested off the boat on his return for no other reason than his relationship and both his and his wife's health deteriorated during his imprisonment. On his release in 1804, his career as a barrister was in disarray. Over the next year the Holmeses lost two infants and there appears to have been some fears of association with Mary Anne, even by the 'patriotic'. 'It is a long winter to the E[mmet] family', commented William Drennan – the Holmeses' friend and physician – and the source of this information. Mary Anne died on 9 March 1805, after a protracted illness, and was buried at 7 a.m. on 13 March.[56] The precise time and place of her burial would become part of the Emmet mystery. Although Madden believed the intention was to have eventually placed Robert Emmet's remains in the St Peter's family vault, he visited St Michan's churchyard on his return to Ireland in 1840. There he located the large flat (and uninscribed) stone slab said to be Emmet's grave and so it was accepted for a generation or more and Gladstone was taken there during his visit to Ireland in 1877.[57]

Tradition also had it that the head was not interred with the body, a tradition chronicled as early as 1811. 'Some of the keepers [of

Newgate] have been accused of detaining in their possession, the heads and bodies of such as were executed for high treason, till they were putrid, in order to enhance the sums first demanded from their relatives for them. It was rumoured through the prison, that Emmet's head sold for £45 10s.'[58] Another, more enduring, tradition had Petrie taking the head away to make the cast, finding the body already gone when he returned and eventually passing on the head to a physician in Galway.[59] Gruesome stuff, though not entirely implausible. Whatever the truth of it all, such traditions added an extra frisson to the legend and few popular accounts were to be complete without drawings of the death mask and reputed grave.

In 1880 the American Emmet most active in the promotion of the legend arrived in Ireland, determined to discover the location of the grave. This was Dr Thomas Addis Emmet of New York, grandson of Robert Emmet's elder brother. As a young doctor at New York's Immigrants' Hospital, he had encountered many of the famine sick and was to discover Anne Devlin's daughter among the paupers, though he hardly needed this to add to the family's existing dislike of England.[60] Dr Emmet was a passionate Irish–American nationalist. He was President of the Irish National Federation of America and active supporter of the Irish Parliamentary [National] Party.[61] Later in life he converted to Catholicism and learnt the Irish language because he believed the two synonymous with Irishness. 'I think there will be a great deal of it spoken in heaven,' he told his friend and fellow convert to Catholicism, Nationalist parliamentary candidate Shane Leslie.[62] He left $25,000 in his will for his body to be buried in Glasnevin, and at the request of his former librarian, two American flags were placed on the grave every year on his anniversary.[63] He was made a Knight Commander of the Order of St Gregory by Pope Pius X. Between 1898 and 1915 Dr Emmet published privately a stream of books arguing English tyranny in Ireland and locating the history of the Emmet family firmly within that theme. In 1903, as he booked his transatlantic passage to return to Ireland in another search for the grave, he wrote of his plans of publishing the results in his *Ireland Under English Rule*.

> I hope the account of it would make a stir among the
> Irish people all over the world. My book is to show what
> the Irish people have suffered and efforts will be made to
> reach the native Americans [by which he did not mean
> the indigenous population, but the descendants of the
> early colonists] more than the Irish people for educational
> purposes to shew from the standpoint any one of my
> name would occupy what has been the course of England
> for 500 years in Ireland. Notwithstanding that you seem
> to be having a 'love feast' [largely due to the government's
> progressive economic policy] in your part of the world I
> do not believe the time is yet near for the millennium nor
> that the past history of Ireland should be forgotten.[64]

Central to this was the idea that Robert Emmet was the innocent victim of a British plot. Dr Emmet had secured permission from the British government to examine official documents for the period of Emmet's rebellion, but found that they had disappeared from Dublin Castle. There Sir Bernard Burke, Ulster King-at-Arms, claimed to have seen a letter from Pitt to Marsden that substantiated the accusation. The implausibility of Pitt (even had he still been in office – he resigned in 1801) communicating such to an under-secretary makes this improbable. However, Dr Emmet was on a mission, and he placed his publications in those institutions where he thought they would wield maximum influence, including the House of Commons Library and the British Library.[65]

His influence over American contributions to the legend was particularly strong, Helen Landreth's controversial, though influential, 1948 book acknowledging her debt. Dr Emmet had turned his home in Madison Avenue, New York, into a shrine to his forebear. It was in reverential tones that the president of the Ladies Auxiliary of the Ancient Order of Hibernians reported her 1913 visit to the house of 'the most celebrated Catholic gentleman living in America today'. 'Every spot of a veritable shrine filled with sacred relics of the martyred dead' including 'the sacred spot on the wall near his desk where hangs the original death mask of Robert Emmet ... standing out in startling distinctness from the dark velvet background, fixing itself on the vision with ghastly reality'. Her account is full of images of the mangled body and Dr Emmet assured her that the head would come forward when Ireland became a nation.[66]

Between 1878 (the centenary of Emmet's birth) and 1903 (the centenary of his death) something of an Emmet memorial industry developed in association with preparations for the centenaries of the two rebellions. Dr Emmet's books were well written, and in their own way compelling. They were full of new pictures, family relics and revelations and fed into this, the most heated period for the fine tuning of the legend, not least the more sustained search for the grave. When Dr Emmet visited Dublin in 1880, the old family friend and fellow physician, R. R. Madden, was nearing the end of his life. By now reports about Emmet's last resting place were coming thick and fast. Old peoples' memories were treated like missing pieces of the jigsaw, and Madden was giving credence to a new theory that Robert Emmet was buried in the graveyard of the old Protestant church at Glasnevin. The Old Glasnevin suggestion had appeared in W. J. Fitzpatrick's *Sham Squire* (1865). It had come third hand from someone who had heard someone else at a dinner party tell how his father, the minister there in 1803, was roused from his bed 'at the dead of night' to perform Emmet's burial service. Two men and two women were present; one of these was Sarah Curran. Fitzpatrick went to investigate. The gardener confirmed the tradition and pointed to 'a grass-grown grave and uninscribed head-stone' as that of Emmet. Fitzpatrick thought this fitted Moore's description in 'Oh, breathe not his name', and on such flimsy evidence he aired his new theory.[67]

This was the source for the dramatic representation of the midnight burial in the *Irish Fireside,* August 1885. It was Fitzpatrick's claim that drew Drs Emmet and Madden to Glasnevin in 1880, as if the care-taking of the legend was being handed on, Moore to Madden, Madden to Dr Emmet. Certainly Dr Emmet showed the same sleuth-like tenaciousness as Madden. Refused permission to photograph inside Green Street Courthouse, he did so secretly, by bribing an official on a Sunday afternoon.[68]

As public interest grew in the approach to the 1903 centennial, more people asked why so little effort had been made to locate the grave and further sites were added to the list of possibilities.[69] Dr Emmet was contacted by a group of professional people: J. F. Fuller, a distant cousin, who had taken the initiative in laying a white marble slab on the St Michan's site and surrounding it with iron railings; Francis Joseph Bigger, a prominent Ulster nationalist and man of letters; and David A. Quaid, a solicitor and author of a 1902 book, opting for St Peter's and denouncing every other theory. Dr Emmet developed a special friendship with Bigger and through him made arrangements for a return to Ireland in 1903 to investigate the main three sites, St Michan's, St Peter's and Old Glasnevin. In 1880 – at the height of the Land War – he had not received a sympathetic hearing when suggesting such to the incumbent of Old Glasnevin.[70] However, in 1903 the climate of opinion was more favourable and the Church of Ireland authorities readily cleared the permissions. Fuller was an asset here, as the architect to the Representative Church Body. Even Lord Justice Fitzgibbon 'gave friendly assistance'. Dr Emmet, now an elderly man, arrived with his son Robert early in July 1903 and took up residence at the Shelburne Hotel on St Stephen's Green. He was anxious to avoid publicity, as he wanted to reveal the findings in his *Ireland Under English Rule*, due out that September. 'I hope the account of it would make a stir among the Irish people all over the world', he wrote to Quaid on 23 April. 'My book is to show what the Irish people have suffered', and he is critical of the positive Irish response to British reforms of these years.[71] At 'an early hour' on Monday 6 July, the two Emmets, Bigger, Quaid, Fuller and the Revd Stanford assembled at St Peter's (the favourite site) and digging began, following the questionable clues provided by Madden and Fitzpatrick. The problem was that an extension to the church in 1867 had spread concrete over the targeted area and removed all the physical signs of pre-existing graves. None of the coffins found had Emmet associations. Investigations under the church's transept found a headstone to Christopher Temple Emmet. So Fuller arranged with the church vestry to have a brass plate placed within the church to mark the spot. Again it was Fuller who eased the way, for Dr Emmet was convinced conspiracy had been involved and the family vault 'destroyed, filled in, and covered over with cement so that its locality could never be identified', and he wanted the word 'destroyed' to be engraved on the plate.[72] But the church vestry insisted on the less-loaded term 'removal'.

Emmet and his son then had to leave Ireland, but agreed to fund further investigations. On 1 August the St Michan's grave was opened in the presence of Quaid, Fuller, and two senior medical men: Lambert Ormsby, President of the Royal College of Surgeons of Ireland, and Alexander Frazer, Professor of Anatomy there. Thus had Robert Emmet become a national treasure, even before the ideal nation had emerged. Two bodies were found, a girl of about thirteen, and below her a male skeleton. The bones of both were exhumed and examined *in situ* by the medical men, particular attention being paid to the cervical vertebrae. However, these were found to be in perfect condition and other signs showed the skeleton to be that of a man in his seventies. Moreover, the symbolic presence of an uninscribed tombstone seemed less significant when it was discovered that the graves of women who had borne children out of wedlock were so marked. Accordingly, the bones were re-interred and St Michan's confidently dismissed. The rector of St Michan's, the Revd Long, was very unhappy at this conclusion. He had been curate there as long ago as 1855 and the traditions handed down by sextons over a century had told of the Revd Gamble burying Emmet's remains in the churchyard at night-time.[73] A dig at Old Glasnevin went down eight feet below the supposed tombstone, but to no avail. Such investigations could not have been kept secret for long and the curious began to gather at the sites.[74] Not everyone was pleased. T. D. Sullivan – a major player in promoting the Emmet legend – published his attack in verse:

'EMMET'
Respectively inscribed to the Investigators of his alleged burial places.

I
Search ye no more, for vain the quest
To find where Emmet's relics rest;
And after all, perhaps, so best:
    He lived and died for Ireland –
What matter now for parish bounds,
Neglected plots, or tended grounds,
Unlettered slabs or grassy mounds –
    His burial place is IRELAND.

II
The island is his monument;
Of him the hills are eloquent;
His spirit with the air is blent
    That fans the fields of Ireland.
We deem his presence ever near,
His deathless words we still can hear,
We see his face, pale, calm and clear,
    Where'er we be in Ireland.

III
For Emmet lives! His patriot soul
Is with us; and while ages roll,

Be Erin's fortune joy or dole,
 'Twill cheer the heart of Ireland –
Upturn no more sods, wood, or stones
In pious hope to find his bones;
He is not dead! In trumpet tones
 So speaks the voice of Ireland.[75]

In 1905 the search was resumed, this time pursuing a new theory, and with the addition of another member to the team. This was J. J. Reynolds, author of a very readable book on Emmet published for the 1903 centenary. Press reports of the search being made in 1903 triggered the memory of Thomas Barnett, a former sexton of St Paul's church in North King Street, who claimed that Emmet's body had been secreted by Dr Trevor in his family vault at St Paul's.[76] This time a plausible skeleton was found. Early on the morning of 10 August 1905, Fuller, Reynolds and the former and current sextons entered the vault. On top of some of the older coffins they found 'a rough coffin of the common kind such as would be provided in Workhouses or by the Crown for its victims'. Inside were the remains of a headless skeleton, which was then examined by the two surgeons who had been sent for. The bones were confirmed as those of a young male of medium height, but since the cervical vertebrae were deemed intact, the mode of decapitation became an issue. Here Dr Emmet, as a surgeon himself, pronounced that no injury would have been sustained had the executioner used a knife. Dr Emmet still preferred to believe that the family would have ensured interment in the family vault at St Peter's, but was prepared to accept that Trevor had been persuaded by 'Pitt's ministry' to secrete the body, and that the Revd Gamble had taken away a different body.[77]

Dr Emmet became even more impassioned in his last years, working constantly, though in poor health, to publish new editions of his works, issuing instructions to his old friend Francis Joseph Bigger for the books and articles required to complete these. He had secured a property deal whereby his Madison Avenue home was demolished and a sixteen-storey block erected in its place (of which he would retain the top floor).[78] It was here that he passed on his passions to his assistants, Anna Frances Levins and Thomas Tuite. Both continued to influence the Emmet legend long after Dr Emmet's death in 1919 at the age of eighty-nine. Shane Leslie attended his funeral and requiem mass in the presence of the Catholic archbishop-elect. 'I saw him last December', he wrote to Bigger. 'He was as bright as ever and only living in order to see the freedom of Ireland. Shrunk and wizened he was sitting at the top of the skyscraper erected on the site of the Emmet mansion with a Sinn Féin flag in his button hole … surely the Emmets are the uncrowned royal family of Ireland.'[79] Bigger also heard from Anna Levins. 'I could not have sat beside Dr Emmet without becoming a Fenian. The day Patrick Pearse was shot the noble old doctor sat back in his chair and murmured – "Would to God I could have stood beside Pearse."'[80]

Although the location of the grave remained a recurrent theme in the press and elsewhere, the next serious search was made in the 1960s by Dr Emmet's great-grandson, James Emmet. Then farming family land in Wicklow, he had been invited to become president of a new Robert Emmet Society. In 1967 the society reopened the Trevor vault, and once again surgeons were used to examine the box of bones. This time they pronounced them to be those of an elderly man suffering from arthritis. The following year a new report that the body had been taken by a relative to Kerry was also followed up. James Emmet employed a diviner, but the result was negative and no further searches were made. The times were thought inauspicious given the onset of the Troubles in Northern Ireland. James Emmet had not inherited the obsessions of his great-grandfather, though he was proud of his ancestry much as the descendants of Tone are. In the 1970s he had no interest in erecting shrines or monuments, simply a family desire for a decent burial. Moreover, the Troubles had cast a shadow over the Emmet legend. The time was not yet ripe for Robert

Emmet's epitaph to be written, he commented, for Ireland's people had not yet learnt to 'live together in peace'.[81]

The search for Emmet's grave is a perfect example of 'booklore' forming popular memory. Every theory was based on the extraordinary credulity of Dr Madden (and later W. J. Fitzpatrick). So little was known about him that every mildly plausible piece of information was seized upon and publicised, soon entering popular consciousness as 'fact', much as Madden had collected for his influential books. Parts of the legend began to be challenged in the twentieth century, but in the nineteenth there was no serious criticism until the controversy over the location of the grave. Over two decades before the beginning of the reaction against the legend, an article in the *Weekly Independent* – 'Robert Emmet's Grave. A Nation Searching for her Martyr's Clay' – challenged the story underpinning the search for the grave. Citing Cowper, 'For it is truth well known to most/That whatsoever thing is lost/We seek it ere it come to light/In every cranny but the right', the author pointed out that every theory rested on little more than an 'assertion of opinions'. It all started with Dunn, hardly a credible witness, and thereafter each new piece of information entered popular folklore, so that any number of grave-diggers and sextons imagined that their churchyard was the location of Emmet's grave. Why do you think Emmet is buried here? the writer had asked of one of these. 'Well ... everybody believed it, and besides, Mr Fitzpatrick had said it.' [82] The truth of the matter is that there really is no firm evidence to sustain any of the theories. The government had no reason to deny Emmet's family possession of his remains. Those of Wolfe Tone had been released straight away to his family five years earlier. The Emmet family's sense that the body did probably end up in St Peter's is as good a theory as any. However, St Michan's remained the preferred site in popular imagination and was still being venerated in the 1950s and 1960s.[83]

But what of Emmet's head? 'When the time comes for writing Robert Emmet's epitaph', wrote Dr Emmet after the disappointing search for the grave, 'this relic will certainly be forthcoming, and it may prove the only portion of his body obtainable.'[84] Despite the strength of the tradition that this had been removed by Petrie, who then was unable to reunite it with Emmet's remains, the source of this anecdote is dubious. Again it is Madden who made such a deduction from the premise that a death mask cast, presumed to be that of Emmet, was sold among Petrie's effects after his death. Madden then acquired it after John Patten saw it displayed by a dealer in curiosities in Liffey Street.[85] Because it was reproduced in the 1846 edition of Madden's *United Irishmen*, the death mask of Robert Emmet becomes part of the fascination with his death. It was carried in the main procession in Dublin during the 1903 centenary and representations of it appeared regularly in the press thereafter.[86] Today there are a number of reputed death masks of Emmet in existence. However, since his very appearance is a matter for conjecture, we may never know whether any of these really is the death mask of Robert Emmet.

Moore and the Romantics' fascination with death had set the tone for subsequent treatment of Emmet. It was the form of death that ensured the speech's fame and the loss of the body that added extra meaning. 'It would seem that some friendly fate lends aid to the securing of the patriot's wish as expressed in his last injunction to his countrymen', commented the *Irish Weekly and Ulster Examiner* on the 1903 report on the search for the grave, 'there are many Irishmen who ... will feel that, under all the present circumstances it is better that mystery should continue to guarantee respect for the martyr's last desire.'[87] For republicans, however, the very mystery was a 'silent reproach', speaking to every generation and reminding them of the task left unfinished.[88]

7 Commemoration, 1878–1922

> The tradition of all the dead generations weighs like a
> nightmare on the brain of the living. And just when they
> seem engaged in revolutionising themselves … they
> anxiously conjure up the spirits of the past … in order to
> present the new scene of world history in this time-
> honoured disguise and this borrowed language.
>
> *Marx, 'Eighteenth Brumaire'*

In Ireland the ascendancy of parliamentary nationalism had collapsed with the fall of Parnell in 1890 and his death a year later. As disillusionment with politics set in, a new messianic and romantic separatism emerged over the next two decades. The legend of Robert Emmet was well suited to the new nationalism, informing the young men of Pearse's generation and through them the imagination of independent Ireland. The essential story had not changed, but the climate of opinion and the medium had and the 1903 centennial of the rebellion produced saturation coverage in the press and popular journals. Visual images – often by the best illustrators of the period – retold the story, and these in turn informed (and narrowed) its recollection. It would have been difficult to miss the outpouring of posters, pictures, songbooks, plays and pageants, press reports, and the many other Emmet centenary-related publications. Preparations had been ongoing since the anniversary of his birth in 1878 and Emmet anniversary meetings continued for at least two decades after the 1903 centenary. The centenary spawned a new crop of literature on Emmet and the fascination showed no sign of abating in succeeding years. More books about Emmet were published in the decade after 1903 than in the entire century preceding it, and most continued in the same vein, largely romantic and sentimental, reproducing the same early nineteenth-century sources. Even the priests were supportive, deeming the story of pure love and sacrifice a good antidote to the 'penny dreadfuls' from England. Admiration for Robert Emmet and the anglophobic statements that often accompanied the retelling of the legend (and increasingly so from the last decades of the nineteenth century) did not necessarily denote militant separatism. But the widespread reverence for cult figures like Robert Emmet and an underlying and longstanding sense of having been wronged, established an undercurrent of resentment, which militant republicans could always draw on, even today.

I

With the phenomenal growth of cheap print from the middle of the nineteenth century, the Emmet story as romance took off. Every work published on Emmet was serialised in the press, often accompanied by simple pen-drawings. Most are wistful, though there were also political and macabre themes, which would intensify during and after the 1903 centenary commemorations. In hindsight the romantic idealisation seems quite unreal and it is difficult to find the real Robert Emmet beneath it all. Madden was not alone in attributing quite unrealistic virtues to him. References to the young 'godlike' hero are legion, and repetitive. 'The history of Robert Emmet is well known to Irishmen. His name is a household name. The memory of the noble young martyr-patriot is treasured in the hearts of his countrymen.' The 'godlike young patriot' is pitted against 'the drunken, sanguinary Norbury ... that ruffianly minion of the English tyranny'.[1] Thus wrote the *Shamrock* in 1868, but the commentary could have been translated to any number of printed works over the next half century and not seemed out of place. He had 'lived without stain and died without reproach', according to the *Nation's* 1878 reviewer of Whitty's *Robert Emmet*, which he takes as accurate.[2] According to another of the many Whitty-inspired commentaries, Emmet was 'the patron saint of Ireland. He was so young, so gifted, so pure in nature' that even his critics could not prevent 'sympathy ... from stealing into their hearts'.[3] While the *Evening Telegraph* in 1902 said much the same: 'In the long headroll of Irish political heroes and martyrs it may be fairly questioned if any other name is so dear to the true Irish heart as that of Robert Emmet ... His high-souled daring and devoted patriotism, his romantic and passionate love-story, his tragic and early death, all form, so to say, an imperishable halo around his name and fame that gives him a position in the love and reverence of the Irish people wonderfully touching and unique. The songs that tell of his love and death are known and sung in every house and cabin in the land.'[4]

In the process of simplification that accompanied the assimilation of the Emmet legend into folk memory, it is Norbury, MacNally and Sirr who are the arch villains, with Castlereagh as the ultimate evil genius – his move to England and non-involvement with the Emmet episode overlooked – and Curran and Plunket are berated as false friends. By the time of the 1903 centenary their villainy was such a part of the legend that catchphrases such as 'the Judas kiss', or 'the serpent speech' required no further explanation. Lord Norbury was deemed 'one of the most loathed of all names in modern Irish history ... a descendant of the Cromwellian planters', a 'Pontius Pilate' to the sacrificial Emmet.[5] Popular legend had him dying without issue and drowning in the bath, mentioned in Emmet's speech.[6] MacNally was a 'black-hearted scoundrel ... Surely, in the black record of human baseness and treachery, there is no viler name than that of "Leonard MacNally the incorruptible"'[7] – villainous reputations that the picture supplements further fixed in popular tradition. The *Weekly Freeman*'s 1892 Christmas supplement carried a vividly coloured representation of the trial. 'Robert Emmet and Norbury. The Night scene in the courthouse ... depicts powerfully the weird and tragic scene enacted in Green Street Courthouse ... In the thronged and breathless court the brave young Irishman, Robert Emmet, poured his vehement invective on the British government, or rather mis-government, of Ireland, typified by the infamous Judge Norbury ... while Leonard MacNally, the informer, crouched in the shade.' A storm of indignation greeted an effort by the grandson of Sirr to ex-onerate his ancestor by claiming that it was he in an act of compassion who had destroyed the letters between Emmet and Sarah Curran. A lengthy critique in the *Evening Telegraph* for 3 September 1910 won-dered at the wisdom of the author in thus raking up the ashes of the most 'infamous' member of his family. 'Few names amongst ... Castlereagh's gang are more detestable than that of Sirr ... a black-guard whose villainies seem to us incredible.'[8]

The three Sullivan brothers, two of them editors of the *Nation*, have been credited with a particularly important role in the develop-ment of Irish nationalism in this period. This is largely because of their influential books *The Story of Ireland* and *Speeches from the Dock*, both of which went through so many editions that they informed Irish nationalism into the second half of the twentieth century. But they were popularisers rather than creators and in the evolution of the Emmet legend their main contribution was the synthesising of Madden and rendering it available in cheap print – very cheap. The individual speeches sold as penny (then twopenny) pamphlets and when brought together as *Speeches from the Dock* retailed at 2s. 6d. The version of the speech was the patriotic one. A. M. Sullivan's *The Story of Ireland* became one of the most popular Irish works of all time, a favourite in the Catholic Young Men's Societies and Land League reading rooms.[9] It sees Irish history as a prolonged struggle against the morally corrupt and tyrannical English, Ireland's purity of soul, noble endurance and sacrifice ensuring ultimate victory. 'Under cir-cumstances where any other nation would have resigned itself to sub-

jugation and accepted death, the Irish nation scorns to yield, and re-
fuses to die.' The 'story' is exemplified in the life and death of Robert
Emmet, and 'the all-absorbing, all-indulging love of a people for
those who purely give up life on the altar of a Country'. Sullivan does
not glorify the rebellion itself. Rather he sees Emmet as rescued from
possible censure for 'the criminal hopelessness of his scheme' by 'his
extreme youth, his pure and gentle nature, his lofty and noble aims,
his beautiful and touching speech from the dock, and his tragic death
upon the scaffold'. This is followed by the standard account, with the
emphasis on the love story and Emmet's noble sacrifice at the end.
The killing of Kilwarden is a blot, but relieved by Emmet's abandon-
ment of the attempt because of 'his aversion to useless sacrifice'.

The penny pamphlets and subsequent collection *Speeches from the
Dock* appeared against the background of the 'Manchester Martyrs'
episode. In September 1867 an unarmed policeman was killed during
the rescue of Fenian prisoners in Manchester, and three Fenians were
subsequently executed for it. The executions caused a furore in Ireland, tens of thousands turning out to take part in mock funerals and
other protests, even though most did not support Fenianism. The parallel with Emmet was not lost.[10] The *Shamrock* had compared the killing
of the policeman to that of Lord Kilwarden, arguing that both, while
regrettable, were accidents. Sullivan's pamphlet avoided any discussion of the events of 23 July 1803, except to repeat the apocryphal
story of Emmet's rescue of Miss Wolfe. Otherwise the long historical
introduction to the speech itself is the Emmet legend fully formed. The
frontispiece is a romanticised version of the Read portrait, discussed
below, with Emmet in the same pose, but softened and made to look
handsome. This was no ragged-trousered rebel, but a young man of
refinement and standing, someone with much to sacrifice.[11] 'In all
Irish history there is no name which touches the Irish heart, like that
of Robert Emmet.' Some died on battlefields, some in exile. 'But in the
character of Robert Emmet there was such a rare combination of
admirable qualities, and in his history there are so many elements of

romance, that the man stands before our mental vision as a peculiarly noble and loveable being, with claims upon our sympathies that are absolutely without a parallel.' He had everything to live for: 'youth, talent, social position, a fair share of fortune'. Yet he sacrificed all this 'in the service of a cause'. He was a man of 'courage, enthusiasm ... strong affections ... sweetened by a nature utterly free from guile'; 'an orator and a poet ... a true patriot, true soldier, and true lover ... Truly, "there's not a line, but hath been wept upon". So it is, that of all the heroic men who risked and lost everything for Ireland, none is so frequently remembered, none is thought of so tenderly as Robert Emmet. Poetry has cast a halo of light upon the name of the youthful martyr, and some of the sweetest strains of Irish music are consecrated to his memory.' A brief rendering of the Emmet story followed, with Moore's ('our national poet') eulogy reproduced from his *Life and Death of Lord Edward Fitzgerald*.[12] This is the romantic account. A year later, when the penny pamphlets were brought together in *Speeches from the Dock*, the language switches to that of Victorian melodrama. Emmet is hunted by 'British spies and bloodhounds', his fate the product of 'English vengeance', his 'lifeless remains ... strangled by the enemies of his country'. 'No traitor was he, but a true and noble gentleman ... a martyr for Ireland.' The background was the national outcry at the executions of three Fenians in Manchester.

Fenianism, or the IRB (Irish Republican Brotherhood) had grown out of the Emmet Monument Association in New York, and was subsequently exported to Ireland.[13] It was to have a long life, despite its spectacularly unsuccessful insurrectionary activities. It survived so long partly because Irish America financed its activities, even issuing a $100 bond carrying pictures of Emmet and Tone,[14] but largely because of its ability to penetrate other, even non-violent movements and appeal to generations of young men who in some way felt excluded. Above all it was a frame of mind, a perpetuation of romantic Young Irelandism, which helped create the 'literary nationalism' of more formidable talents like W. B. Yeats. Patrick Pearse had a point in

his claim that the baton of republicanism had come to him
and Emmet through the Young Irelanders and the Fenians. Fe
was particularly adept at utilising processions, funerals and   r
commemorations to whip up national feeling, the funerals, mock and
real, of Terence Bellew MacManus (10 November 1861), the 'Man-
chester Martyrs', first in 1867 and annually for many decades after-
wards, of John O'Mahony (4 March 1877), and Sergeant Charles
McCarthy (20 January 1878) proving the most impressive.[15]

Such funerals established St Catherine's church in Thomas Street as
one of the stopping points of nationalist demonstrations – as much in
recognition of the primacy of the execution in the legend as the absence
of a grave. The analogy with Emmet was most clear-cut in the case of the
Manchester Martyrs. The glorious dead tradition had not been reforti-
fied by new examples since Emmet. Transportation and a variety of
other punishments had been judicially applied between 1803 and the
1860s. Had the attack happened in Ireland, the executions might well
have been avoided. The fact that they took place in England, before a
hostile crowd, inflamed Irish opinion, and the emphasis placed on the
love-story of the youngest, William Allen (who was about to be mar-
ried), picked up the story line of Emmet's tragic romance and further
enhanced the picture of the young martyr.[16] That the death of police
sergeant Brett was accidental was likened to the killing of Kilwarden in
1803, as unintended by the Fenians as the latter was by Emmet.[17] In the
weeks after the executions huge mock funerals took place in various
parts of Ireland, that in Dublin mustering 30–50,000 in atrocious
weather conditions, while another estimated 50–70,000 looked on.
They showed how Irish people with little sympathy for separatism or vi-
olent means could be mobilised behind the idea of the young hero cut
down by the British. The Emmet legend became an important reference
point in grooming the Fenian hero and creating the outrage displayed in
Ireland by the execution of three of those involved. A Fenian bombing
in Clerkenwell on 13 December 1867 – killing or maiming dozens of
civilians – deflated some of the indignation. But the outpouring of

verse, song and printed works (not least the Sullivans' *Speeches from the Dock*) left an enduring legacy. T. D. Sullivan's 'God Save Ireland' (picking up one of the men's defiant call at their trials) became an unofficial national anthem. Other poems on the executions added new names to the apostolic succession of Irish martyrs:

> Upon the scaffold grim they died, the last in Erin's cause
> Upon the gallows high they swung, by England's
>   bloodstained laws;
> Like Emmet, Sheares, Fitzgerald, Tone, and hundreds
>   true and bold
> They died to make their native land a nation as of old.[18]

II

Many of the generation of 1916 learnt of Robert Emmet through the 'historical romance' approach of the writers of the period. Gaelic Leaguer Lily McManus called for more in a 1911 article, reminiscent of the Young Irelanders, 'Irish Historical Romance: Its Need To-Day'. Despite the success of A. M. Sullivan, in spreading through 'Anglo-Ireland a story of the nation's life filled with adventure and romance ... the work of vivifying our history in the popular mind still remains to be done. We have to get Irish history ... before the imagination of the people. The teaching of Irish history alone will not do it; romance must be called into aid. The task of the writer of historical stories is not to write exact history, but to colour it. The colours may be wrong, the drawing incorrect, but if he makes some scene in history present and near, flinging the charm of romance about it, while the historical characters, from being vague far-off forms, appear human and living, he will have achieved much. His art is to stimulate imagination; he is to idealise the past.' [19] She had already contributed an article to the *Leader* that prefigured Pearse's sense of the ghosts of Emmet and Sarah Curran haunting Rathfarnham.[20]

Sinn Féin activist Brian O'Higgins (1882–1949) ̄
literary influences on his childhood. He read T. D. Su
and the youth magazines beginning to be put out by t
press and sang the songs taught to him by his father, a for   ...an.
Others recorded the importance of song and ballad in their early political education, not least Moore's 'She is far from the Land'.[21] Many
of O'Higgins's generation had first learnt about Emmet from their
mothers or other female family members. Robert Emmet had a particular appeal for women writers and readers in a way that Tone never
did. It was O'Higgins's mother who introduced the illustrated magazines and weeklies into their home in Co. Meath, notably the *Shamrock*, the *Irish Fireside*, the *Irish Emerald* and the *Weekly Freeman*.[22] Nearly
all the popular writers of the day wrote for them and he remembered
a number of 'fine historical romances', including those on Emmet.
They told of the tragic love affair, the exaggerated sentimentalism
often pulled up short with gothic imagery of the prison cell, the
'clanking of chains', the tearful parting of the two lovers, or the execution and burial, graphically illustrated.[23] The dialogue is fashioned
from Moore, Whitty, Irving and Madden. They were part of that outpouring of historical fiction that Eileen Reilly has analysed in her fine
study of the 'reciprocity' of Irish history and fiction during the nineteenth century, fiction influencing the political debate, writers consciously 'synthesising' the past into a nationalist narrative.[24] Indeed,
it was the illustrations from these magazines of his youth that O'Higgins continued to use decades later in his militantly republican magazine, the *Wolfe Tone Annual*.[25]

In time all the leading newspapers produced illustrated weeklies,
with aspects of the Emmet legend figuring regularly and most of the
leading illustrators of the age tackling the subject. There is – surprisingly in a well-off family – no contemporary portrait of Emmet before his trial. Three artists – Brocas, Petrie and Comerford – drew
hasty sketches at the trial. But all were modified afterwards, usually
adding *gravitas* and retaining little of the boy revolutionary aspect that

so many commented upon. A contemporary portrait accompanying a version of the speech[26] does convey a sense of youth, as does a later portrait by Petrie (frontispiece to Madden), said to have been seen by Sarah Curran. Petrie's more famous son, George Petrie, recalled Sarah Curran having asked his father to paint a portrait from memory and then her visit to view it. As a little boy in the corner of his father's study, he saw a lady 'thickly veiled' entering when his father was out, gazing lengthily at the picture, sobbing and 'shaken with a storm of passionate grief'.[27]

And yet, although some of these would have been available, the National Portrait Committee chose to contact the son of Thomas Addis, Judge Robert Emmet of New York, when it sought one to exhibit in 1872. In response Judge Emmet told of a miniature in the family's possession, which he thought Emmet himself, while in prison, commissioned from Comerford for his elder brother, and he sent an enlarged photograph of it. In fact, the miniature was commissioned later by Robert Holmes, after seeing the rough drawing, and sent to Thomas Addis Emmet in New York. Comerford told Holmes that because he was held in some suspicion by government, he had only managed to slip into the court after dark, and 'with the poor light and in his cramped position he could do little more than get the outline of the face, lest he might be seen at work and arrested as a confederate. The head, body and style of dress were finished at home.'[28] The *Nation* duly advertised reproductions for sale on 14 September 1872.

However, as with much else to do with the Emmet legend, it was the fictional portraits that held sway over popular imagination. In 1868 the *Shamrock* claimed that Emmet's portrait and speech were displayed 'in many an Irish home'.[29] In 1903 Michael MacDonagh made much the same statement: 'In the humblest cabins of the land may be seen – with the pictures of the Blessed Virgin and St Patrick – rude portraits of Emmet, as he would wish perhaps to be remembered – in his cocked hat and feathers, his green and gold and white uniform, as Commander-in-Chief of the forces of the Irish Republic'.[30] Many of those republicans who fought in 1916–22 recalled this picture of Emmet. Constance Markievicz remembered it from her childhood and her early writings show a familiarity with the detail of the romantic legend. It was part of the familiar surroundings of Seán O'Faoláin's youth and his idea of dying for Ireland was then visualised as 'people in cocked hats with gilt tassels and plumed feathers, waving swords like Lord Edward Fitzgerald or Robert Emmet'.[31] Ernie O'Malley encountered it frequently in the cottages where he took refuge during the war of independence. It even appears as one of the props in Roddy Doyle's fictional tale of 1916–22, *A Star Called Henry*.[32] This drawing became the most widely accepted image of Robert Emmet and yet it bears no resemblance to him whatsoever. Who was the artist? Henry O'Shea, a distinguished Limerick artist, provided the answer in 1902. His article in the *Evening Telegraph* opened with the kind of hyperbole that characterised most accounts of Emmet by now. Yet, he complained, 'it is almost impossible to meet with a correct likeness of the man as he was in life'. Two 'popular' pictures were singled out for criticism. The first was that mentioned by MacDonagh: 'Emmet ... in what I would call a Bridge of Lodi attitude, waving or flourishing a plumed or cocked hat ... there is not even a pretence of a likeness to Emmet's face'. This he recalled as having first appeared in the 1850s and was the work of a young Kilkenny artist [Edmond Fitzpatrick] 'who had very probably little or no authority for the face, but ... to have made an apotheosis of the hero rather than a portrait of the man'.[33]

The second, modelled on Petrie's trial sketch, was engraved by William Read – and partly reproduced in Maxwell's *Irish Rebellion* in 1839. This, continued O'Shea, was of 'Emmet at his trial, in a pair of white inexpressibles that would have made the reputation of any melodramatic actor of the last generation, and a rather truculent-looking scowl upon his face'. Though admiring of Petrie's original rough sketch – which captures the irritation shown by Emmet at certain points of his trial – 'sadly it has been spoiled in the too frequent and unskilled elaboration of cheap copyists'. A check against the death mask might have shed some light on all this, but O'Shea doubted its authenticity and I am inclined to agree. At the sale of Petrie's effects after his death, a large number of such casts were sold. John Patten saw what he thought was Emmet's subsequently displayed in a shop-window in Liffey Street and Madden had a daguerreotype made for his 1846 series.[34] Maxwell's friend George Cruikshank illustrated his account of Emmet's rebellion in a series of hostile though brilliant scenes. That in the Thomas Street depot became the model for a succession of popular illustrations – though not before the hostile elements were airbrushed out. But it was the sympathetic portrait of Emmet that most informed the popular representations. It has been attached to the standard 'unfortunate' gentleman sketch that was the house-style of *Walker's Hibernian Magazine* at the turn of the eighteenth/nineteenth centuries.[35] And so it was that the famous image of Emmet in white breeches and Hessian boots emerged, to inform endless illustrated stories and theatrical productions. It was just as well for the development of the legend, for it is unlikely that the romance of Robert Emmet could ever have taken off quite as it did from the portrait of Petrie, which Sarah Curran had thought such an accurate representation.

There is still a strong recollection in parts of Ireland of another wall picture that also contained the full patriotic version of the speech. This was issued for the 1898 centenary, a large and lavishly produced poster retailing at 2s. 6d. The portrait bears no relation to the contemporary images of Emmet, but is characteristic of turn-of-century depictions, a cross between typical pictures of young priests and those of the young Napoleon. At the top of the poster is a frieze of national symbols, a round tower, Irish wolfhound, dolmen and Celtic cross, with an angel and pikes the central image. A brief introduction sets the scene. Emmet's request for a delay of the sentencing has been rejected. 'Robert Emmet, upon the instant, exhausted as he was by the

trial … [delivered a] speech, which may safely be pronounce
one of the most splendid and powerful effusions of impassioneo
quence and patriotic devotion which ever fell impromptu from the
lips of man.' The full speech follows and the scene closed with a description of the day of execution, taken from the many pictures of
Emmet in his cell, Sarah Curran waving from her carriage and the
other embellishments of the legend. 'Day dawns through the prison
bars. Emmet, rousing from his reverie, lifts his eyes to Heaven; and
on bended knees, whilst offering up his young life as a willing sacrifice for that country which he loves so clearly, calls down blessings
upon its martyred people.' As the aggravated sentence is carried out,
'England's vengeance' and 'brutality' are 'satiated'.[36]

III

Rising national awareness throughout the western world in the second half of the nineteenth century was reflected in the erection of
statues and other public memorials. Thomas Davis and the *Nation* had
already called for such in the 1840s. The long-overdue rise of a
Catholic middle-class in Ireland added to this impetus to celebrate
their new-found success in public sculpture, and the O'Connell monument campaign (1862–82) – enlisting the support of the Catholic
establishment, including door-to-door collections by the Catholic
Church – was phenomenally successful.[37] But this was constitutional
nationalism and, whatever its rhetoric and admiration for Emmet as a
romantic figure, such public celebration of his memory was quite another matter, particularly since such campaigns tended to be taken
over by the IRB. Suggestions for a statue to Emmet appeared in the
press as the centenary of his birth (1878) approached. It sparked off
a correspondence about whether such would be appropriate when
Emmet had called for no epitaph to be written, though generally it
was agreed that a memorial and an epitaph were two different things.
The statue would be dedicated 'to his pure and stainless memory'

and need carry no inscription. For 'the statue would tell its own story ... if posed in the attitude which the prints of his trial have made familiar to the whole Irish race' and should be erected 'on the spot where he offered up his young life as a sacrifice for the cause of his country'.[38] The 1878 St Patrick's Day issue of the *Nation* carried 'a full-page drawing' by John F. O'Hea (in reality a relatively faithful copy of the now standard breeches-and-boots portrait) of the proposed statue in front of St Catherine's church. The *Nation* opened a subscription list and set up an Emmet Monument Committee, which commissioned a plaster model from Thomas Farrell — a renowned sculptor of public statues. But nothing further appears to have happened, even though the project was taken up again in 1897 as part of the 1798 centennial celebrations.[39]

The story of the Emmet statue was not unusual. Difficulties were encountered raising the subscriptions for most of the others, not least and most famously that for Wolfe Tone.[40] Perhaps Irish people did not quite share the nationalist elite's crusade to de-anglicise the public spaces, a crusade voiced by the *Nation* during the 1878 debate over the Emmet commemoration:

> We have been told that public honours to Emmet's
> memory ought to be deferred until Ireland is a nation.
> We confess that with the single exception of the writing
> of Emmet's epitaph we do not know of any good work
> which ... should be deferred until Ireland is a nation ...
> We shall be contributing to make Ireland a nation by
> nationalising the whole life of the country, and taking the
> 'West British' tone and aspect from it in every possible
> way ... In this Irish metropolis even our street corners
> are made to speak of England by the names that are
> branded on them. A few years ago every public
> monument in the city was a monument of an Englishman
> or a Dutchman. But we are changing that state of things.

Names that England would wish forgotten we are keeping
before the public mind … by erecting public
memorials.[41]

It was also more difficult to collect subscriptions for statues in Dublin
than in the counties. Most of the statues commissioned during the
centenary of the 1798 rebellion represented local heroes. Tone,
Emmet and Lord Edward Fitzgerald were confined to relief portraits
on the pedestal of statues in counties Sligo, Wicklow and Tipperary.[42]

It would be wrong to read too much into the failure to erect statues. Emmet's iconic status was achieved without them. His birth date
was chosen to officially launch Dublin's '98 centenary preparations in
1897. In Dublin the Robert Emmet '98 Centenary Club promoted
his reputation with a missionary zeal. Its minutes record programmes
of Emmet songs and recitations, processions to St Michan's (and
other patriot graves) to lay wreaths, raffles and bazaars to raise funds
for memorial statues and correspondence with other clubs up and
down the country, including the Sarah Curran Ladies Association, the
Anne Devlin Auxiliary Committee and the Thomas Russell '98 Committee in Downpatrick. Penny editions of the 1836 pamphlet, *The
Life, Trial and Conversations of Robert Emmet, Esq.*, also reproduced
Moore's songs in an effort 'to stamp out the demoralising songs of the
London Music Hall class'.[43]

A new song on Emmet from this era was particularly influential in
defining (and narrowing) the legend as it was projected to the future.
This was 'The Last Moments of Robert Emmet', *c.*1900, better
known as 'Bold Robert Emmet'.

> The struggle is over, the boys are defeated,
>   Old Ireland is surrounded with sadness and gloom;
> We were betrayed and shamefully treated,
>   And I Robert Emmet, awaiting my doom.
> Hung, drawn and quartered, that was my sentence,

But soon I will show them no coward am I,
My crime was the love of the land I was born in,
   A hero I lived and a hero I'll die
Bold Robert Emmet, the darling of Erin,
   Bold Robert Emmet will die with a smile;
Farewell! companions both loyal and daring,
   I will lay down my life for the Emerald Isle.

Even today, people's 'memories' of the Emmet legend have been influenced by this ballad and the ideal of the hero dying with a smile would recur in the oratory of Patrick Pearse.[44]

It was in the decades building up to the centenaries that the outpouring of pictorial and popular treatment of Emmet noted earlier occurred. Madden was again serialised in the press, this time accompanied by illustrations of the highlights of the legend: Anne Devlin's 'torture', Emmet's speech from the dock, Emmet chained in his cell, Sarah Curran waving from her carriage as he passed en route to the scaffold.[45] There were calls for Madden's *Robert Emmet* to be reissued; it was, in cheap popular format, 'a people's edition' retailing at eight pence, post free from the Glasgow publisher.[46] There was another outpouring of cheaply printed pamphlets about Emmet, the speech and the songs, Moore as influential as ever. James Duffy's publishing company was well to the fore; it also advertised pictures of Emmet for framing. Indeed, it is likely that the illustrations generated by the centenary decade had more impact on replenishing the legend than anything in print, and in certain cases (notably some theatrical productions and even major works such as Joyce's *Ulysses*) it is the visual images that inform the story line. The kind of pen-drawings that accompanied the serialisation of Madden now become routine: portraits of Emmet, Sarah Curran (or rather a mistaken Romney portrait, progressively prettified), Anne Devlin, the death mask, sites of the various graves and of buildings like the Priory in Rathfarnham.[47]

IV

Apart from the addition of Dr Emmet's illustrations and guiding advice, the new batch of Emmet works simply recycled the legend for a new audience. But this is their significance, for this was a new age, the values and obsessions of which would come to redefine Irishness for the future. It was marked by a new energising of Irish nationalism in nominally cultural or sporting bodies like the Gaelic Athletic Association (1884) and the Gaelic League (1893), and a phenomenal coming together of talent in the literary revival (c.1890–1922, ending with Joyce's *Ulysses*, itself testimony to the prevalence of the Emmet legend in previous decades). At first these different strands of the revival sat easily enough together. Young Irelandism remained an inspiration, partly through the organisational talents of Charles Gavan Duffy (former editor of the *Nation*) – returned from a successful political career in Australia, and co-founder with Yeats and T. W. Rolleston of the Irish Literary Society in London – and above all Fenianism infused the whole revival. John O'Leary, former Fenian activist (though no longer a militant nationalist) was the figurehead in the centennial celebrations of both 1798 and 1803 and was very largely the inspiration behind Yeats's involvement. Yeats – and the literary revival generally – adopted Carlyle's belief about a nation's history being that of its great men, its heroes. Yeats became president of the '98 centennial committee and gave a large number of talks and addresses, all invoking the litany of those who had died for Ireland, Emmet included. Yeats delighted a group of advanced nationalists on the anniversary of Emmet's birthday by quoting the 'thrilling' speech of Robert Emmet ('the saint of Irish Nationality'), by now a set piece of Irish eloquence (particularly in America). Twenty years later another, more militant, generation was listening to a young Volunteer called Michael Collins reciting the same speech in Constance Markievicz's home.[48]

However, the new kind of cultural nationalism represented by the GAA and the Gaelic League envisaged an Ireland restored to the purity and self-reliance that it imagined to have existed before the English conquest, an Ireland in which Irish-speaking would again be the norm. Political independence was no longer enough. Irish culture had to be 'de-anglicised' and all English influences – including its literature – rejected. This the young James Joyce, attracted like many of his age group to the idea of language revival, found repellent when he encountered it in Patrick Pearse, to whom he had gone to enquire about learning Irish.[49] Though there were a number of Protestant supporters of the movement – not least the Gaelic League's president Douglas Hyde – such had been the identification of Irishness with Catholicism for at least the past three centuries (not least by England herself) that the expulsion of Protestants from nationalists' perceived Irish 'race' was predictable. They became the 'sourfaces' in the brilliant, but sarcastically destructive journalism of Irish-Ireland's flawed genius, D. P. Moran, and, along with those who aped English ways, 'West Britons', 'Shoneens' (*séoinin*, i.e. little Englishmen, toadyism) or 'Castle Catholics', a tendency to petty name-calling that characterised extreme nationalism thereafter. There was, of course, a logical explanation for this small-minded bitterness in the long-standing resentment at stage-Irishry and condescension towards Catholic-Irish culture and the sense of inferiority it had produced.[50] For Moran, upper-class Protestant patriots like Emmet had only limited relevance for Catholic Irish-Ireland. He was ambivalent about militant separatism and very critical of the kind of 'lip-rebellion' that accompanied recreational Fenianism. He paints a picture of a kind of patriotic 'snobbery' that lay behind politico-nationalism. A young man nurtured on the anti-English 'Emerald green incorruptible' nationalist papers of the day starts out with 'a great desire to be thought a hero … his day dreams were mostly woven of stricken fields, of English redcoats, triumphant pike men, defiant orations from dock and gallows tree'. As the years go by he recognises the 'blatherimskite' and repetitiveness of the nationalist periodicals. 'Each number usually consisted of an amateur essay on Robert Emmet or some '98 or '48 man which, however, taught him, nothing that he did not know before, and besides it was mostly composed of adjectives.' They all told him that all Irishmen 'were a lot of injured saints' and although he now recognised this as blarney, the only way he could progress in nationalist politics was by telling the multitude the same old story, for that is what he knew they wanted.[51]

Although, in the event, the philosophy of Irish-Irelandism did not lead to the expulsion of the likes of Emmet and Tone from militant nationalism's gallery of heroes, it did narrow the range of those deemed qualified to identify with them. Protestants, Anglo-Irish and Irish writers operating from England (which would soon exclude the leading figures of the literary revival) began to fall into its 'West Briton' category. The Emmet centenary provided plenty of ammunition, for although it refortified militant nationalism, it was also celebrated by a wide range of interests. Michael MacDonagh — an Irish journalist in London, and reporter of the Irish Parliamentary Party — was, in 1904, to produce the only original work of the centenary decade. However, an advance article in the *Cornhill Magazine*, though it was sympathetic towards Emmet and differed little from the endless romantic accounts of the previous century, nevertheless condemned the rebellion and treated Emmet as a boy dreamer. Arthur Griffith's *United Irishman* denounced this 'Briton' as 'one of the great array of Titsbitsian goosequillers whom Britain produces' and proceeded to fillet the article for every critical or condescending phrase. It headlined 'Another Briton on Emmet' the following week to discuss, or rather demolish, the admittedly rather bad novel *The Island of Sorrow* by 'George Gilbert', in reality the moderate Unionist Mary Lucy Arthur. It was the stage-Irishry of the dialogue and historical inaccuracies as much as her disapproval of the boy revolutionary that provided Griffith with the weaponry for his comprehensive demolition: 'It is sad to reflect that an intellectual people like the Irish are ruled by the countrymen of Mr George Gilbert.'[52] Yet neither Griffith nor Moran thought violence essential to achieve their all-Irish, self-reliant and independent Ireland. Indeed, Griffith was more than anything a Young Irelander, still influenced by the ideas of the eigh-teenth century.[53] But their irreverent and sarcastic language, requir-ing uncompromising adherence to the Irish-Ireland idea of a de-anglicised and regenerated nation, appealed to the young militants for whom the Emmet centenary was a call to arms. New poetry for the occasion dwelt on the themes of blood sacrifice and unfinished business. Brian O'Higgins's eighteen-stanza poem 'The Death of Emmet', published in the centenary number of the militant youth journal *St Patrick's*, lingers on the scene of the execution and puts for-ward an idea that came increasingly to the fore in 1916: that Ireland needed to redeem itself for permitting the death of Emmet.

> Go! hide your heads in guilty shame unending,
>   And see that blood-stained form before your eyes;
> Nor time, nor change, nor storms the wide earth rending,
>   Shall stifle in your hearts his anguish cries.
>   . . .
> Some day guilt receives its own red wages
>   And if *we* fail to pay back every debt;
> There's One Who rules o'er all, thro' all the ages,
>   And He remembers well – if we forget.[54]

Terence MacSwiney – who in turn would join the list of those who died for Ireland – pursued similar themes in his 'Address for the Emmet Centenary', and later in his play 'The Revolutionist' (1914).

> Hear ye that message, ringing down the years,
> Rise! sons of Eire! rise! Your sloth off-shake;
> No longer lie thus bound in slavish fears –
> Hark to that voice, cry from the tomb – awake,
> Spring to that call that pleads for Eire's sake.
> Look back across the century that's sped;
> From Emmet learn the course that ye should take,

Thus did he point the path for us to tread:
'Till Eire is unfettered let my name be dead.'
. . .
This was his dying wish – until our land
Amongst the nations takes her rightful place
His grave should be unmarked – to this command
List ye of falt'ring heart, who would retrace
The path he, fearless, trod mid the brief space
Of that young life he to his country gave.
Half-measures now, must not our cause disgrace,
His creed – o'er us no foreign flag must wave
Young hearts of Eire learn 'tis ye this land must save.[55]

It was, unsurprisingly, on the anniversary of Emmet's execution, rather than that of the rising that the centenary celebrations took place in 1903. Many towns had their own celebrations, and areas in England and Scotland with large Irish populations sent delegations, Liverpool seeing off its delegates in a torchlight procession. Trains brought contingents and their bands from various parts of the country, music accompanying each as they proceeded to the rendezvous at St Stephen's Green. It all had the air of a great and orderly carnival. The railway companies took measures to facilitate the great numbers, even permitting the country delegations who travelled through the night to remain sleeping on the trains till the time for assembly arrived. There was no interference from the authorities. Indeed, the Dublin Metropolitan Police assisted in clearing the route. When the GAA clubs assembled – the hurlers shouldering their hurling sticks – they backed all the way up Dawson Street to St Stephen's Green and Earlsfort Terrace. There were groups of Cumann na nGaedheal (which became Sinn Féin in 1906), the Gaelic League, the Catholic Literary Societies, the Daughters of Erin. Children from the Gaelic schools followed, their bannerettes 'bearing pictures of Emmet and suitable mottoes' – one seven-year-old attired in Emmet costume rode on a donkey. Among the children, one group from Dublin's poorest districts attracted particular attention: 'barefooted' and 'ragged', they carried homemade pikes and wore roughly made sashes and green hats. Their band beat tin drums and played bugles and tin whistles to Thomas Davis's 'A Nation Once Again'. The Irish National Foresters lined up behind their banner, displaying Emmet on one side and the Manchester Martyrs on the other. They had representatives also from branches in Liverpool, Manchester, Glasgow and Sheffield. Some of the women from Manchester came in 'costume', one dressed as Erin. At the head of the Foresters were the members of the Robert Emmet Costume Association, in 'full Emmet uniform' – as represented in the famous wall picture – and carrying pikes and swords.[56] Then came the various trades and labour organisations, from Dublin and elsewhere in the country, all with their banners and bands. 'An object of general interest' was the 'original' death mask of Emmet displayed on the van carrying the stonecutters' banner. A commentator to the *Derry People* who followed the procession described it as 'making a pilgrimage, as it were, from Emmet's cradle to his grave – from his birth-place at St Stephen's Green to the scene of his execution at Thomas street'. As they passed the walls of the Green Street courthouse he heard them sing 'Ingram's ballad, "The Memory of the Dead"' and he imagined the refrain: 'The fame of those who died;/And true men, like you men,/Remember them with pride', echoing through the passages of the courthouse.

As the head of the procession arrived at St Catherine's church, two men carrying Irish and American flags took up position. The rest of the procession moved forward, heads bared, playing funeral marches, until the carriage carrying the 73-year-old symbol of venerable republicanism, John O'Leary, reached the spot. He spoke a few words from the carriage, a strangely downbeat performance, given the 'stirring' addresses delivered at the many other Emmet centenary ceremonies around the country. Perhaps the reason was the dispute with the Dublin tram-drivers that broke out at this point as they tried to get through the throng.

My friends, we are here today in our thousands to show
that the memory of the hero who died for us a hundred
years ago is still green in our souls (Hear, hear). We are
not here to talk. Emmet desired that his epitaph should
not be written till his country was free – (hear, hear and
applause) – and I hold that the best way we can do
honour to his memory is to strive might and main to
bring about the time when the epitaph can be written.
(Hear, hear). I have nothing more to say, but I think you –
all of you – have very much more to do. (Loud cheers).[57]

The speech was as ambiguous as the occasion itself. Nationalists of all
hues lionised Emmet and, despite the large showing of the GAA and
an IRB-led centenary committee, the 60–100,000 said to have
processed and the thousands more who looked on, the occasion was
more of a carnival than anything else, a carnival celebrating Irish nationalism, however diverse the strands.

Not all were happy with the commemorations. Extreme nationalists thought them insufficiently solemn. Griffith's paper, the *United
Irishman* (soon to become the organ of Sinn Féin), spoke admiringly
of the role of the GAA in the Dublin procession – 'there were the
making of half-dozen fine regiments in that body of Gaels' – but
thought the rest tawdry and reminiscent of what it considered the
shoddy compromising of the constitutional Irish Parliamentary Party.
'It was not for a Land Bill* Emmet died', proclaimed its editorial on
the anniversary of the rising. 'It was not for a Legislature in College-
green, under the Union Jack he suffered a felon's death. He died for
the Irish nation … So long as a vestige of foreign rule remains in this
country, his tomb must remain uninscribed'.[58] Its columnist recalled
with contempt the cheers he had heard for the visiting King Edward

---

*Wyndham's Land Act, 1903, the cornerstone of legislation creating a peasant
proprietorship.

VII, in the very week of the rising's centenary. As the royal cortege passed near St Michan's, he imagined the martyr's 'silent' reproach to the cheering of the 'séoinini'.[59] The imitation pikes carried by the Foresters in the Dublin procession were singled out for criticism, 'Tinpikery' symbolising the 'humbug' and 'Sham' of the parliamentarians, who paid lip-service to Emmet's ideals, but little more. In an exchange with the *Enniscorthy* (Wexford) *Echo,* Moran's *Leader* pronounced them tame rebels 'masquerading with tin-pikes as "last dhrop o' me blood" rebels'. But this is not what it seems and the *Echo* in its counter-attack missed the point. The real message was in the word 'masquerading'. Since 'the Irish people are not rebels' what are they trying to achieve by 'playing the role' asked the *Leader*. If the celebrations of the previous Sunday really were an endorsement of Emmet's aims and methods, then they were 'a hideous farce', benefiting the receipts of the railways and 'Bung' (i.e. the drinks trade). Particular scorn was meted out to the 'Green Foresters ... waddling along' in the costume some had worn in a recent music-hall event. The authorities recognised this better than the 'last dhrop o' me bloods', by helping such parades rather than 'firing cannon at the lip-treason of a green people ... we never suggest that there is a short cut to success ... if Ireland is to be successful, she must work for and earn the success; and certainly one of the most loyal and tame people in Europe show themselves very stupid and incapable when they assert and believe that they are immortal rebels'.[60] The *Leader*'s argument was that the national pastime of masquerading as rebels wasted time and resources and, it could be added, allowed the real men of violence to claim that they were furthering the national cause. It was not until the Troubles in Northern Ireland at the end of the century that this was finally understood.

Predictably there was renewed debate about physical versus moral force methods, the constitutionalists claiming there was no longer any need for force. But the 'stirring' and 'thrilling' speeches were ambiguous, and those at the Emmet commemorations in the United States

17. Popular illustration by Edmond Fitzpatrick, c. 1850s: Emmet in 'a Bridge of Lodi attitude, waving or flourishing a plumed cocked hat'.

18. The execution of Robert Emmet, depicted by F. W. Byrne, 1877.

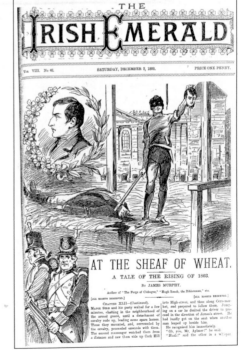

19. Robert Emmet's execution, Irish Emerald, *2 December 1899.*

20. Sarah Curran at Bully's Acre, from the Irish Fireside *colour supplement,*
12 August 1885.

21. *Statue of Robert Emmet by Jerome Connor, 1912, finally erected in St. Stephen's Green, Dublin, 1968, facing the former Emmet family home (now demolished).*

22. *After the signing of the Anglo-Irish Treaty, granting a level of Irish independence to twenty-six of the thirty-two counties of Ireland, many asked if Robert Emmet's epitaph could now be written. The new satirical magazine,* Dublin Opinion, *made this the subject of its very first cartoon, March 1922.*

NEWSPAPER REPORTER : " And now, Sir, your epitaph ? "
SHADE OF ROBERT EMMET : " NOT YET ! "

23. 1898 centennial poster.

24. St. Michan's, after railings were erected to deter souvenir collectors searching for Emmet's grave.

25. Old Glasnevin, showing Dr Madden pointing to the grave during the 1880 search. He was accompanied by Dr. T. A. Emmet.

26. Portrait of Emmet, by John Mulvany 1897, commissioned by Dr. T. A. Emmet in New York and donated to the Irish government in 1925.

27. *Brandon Tynan as Robert Emmet, in Tynan's New York play* Robert Emmet; or, the days of 1803, *staged in 1902.*

28. *Terence Burns, the author's father, as Leonard MacNally, delivering the 'Judas Kiss' to Louis Rolston as Robert Emmet in Seamus McKearney's 1957 play, staged in Belfast.*

were invariably militant. At a 1904 Emmet birthday commemoration organised in New York by the Irish-American revolutionary grouping, Clan Na Gael, there was euphoria from the 4,500-strong audience when a one-line telegraph message from Chicago arrived: 'No compromise with our common enemy England.' This was followed by a 'stirring oration' from a US judge and a staging of Emmet's trial, which had all the women weeping and all the men jumping up and shaking their fists.[61] It was at such meetings that Clan Na Gael recruited for the IRB.[62] That they usually ended with the singing of sentimental songs such as Moore's made them none the less militant. When even the constitutional politicians – who frequently visited the United States on fund-raising tours – felt the need to rattle sabres for American audiences, it is not surprising that militants (most notably Patrick Pearse, who delivered his famous Emmet speech at the same venue in 1914) were 'intoxicated' by such occasions.[63]

By then Yeats thought Pearse 'half-cracked and wanting to be hanged – has Emmet delusions same as other lunatics think they are Napoleon or God'.[64] However Yeats had likewise found himself carried away by the occasion when invited to address the 1904 New York gathering for Emmet's birthday, giving the audience what he thought it wanted to hear. He was tired at the end of his American tour and it shows. It was a rather sloppy rejigging of Moore and Madden, with standard quotes from all the time-worn sources, and the anecdotes about Emmet's last hours in prison and the sighting of Sarah Curran in her coach, much as they had appeared in the press illustrations of the centenary years. The atrocities of '98 were carried out by England to effect the Union; the idea of Emmet as a 'hare-brained' youth was English disinformation, the loss of his body a conspiracy to prevent pilgrimages to his grave. It was about this time that Yeats was beginning to question, shortly to abandon the extreme nationalism of his early years, and the speech would return to haunt him. England denied Emmet a last resting place and in so doing 'made all Ireland his tomb' (echoes here of Sullivan). 'His martyrdom has changed the whole temper of the Irish nation ... When Ireland is triumphant and free, there will yet be something in the character of her people, something lofty and strange, which shall have been put there by her years of suffering and by the memory of her many martyrs.' He concluded with the tale of Emmet's picture hanging in Irish cottages beside St Patrick and the Mother of God and reciting a 'touching' street ballad about the memory of those who have gone. When one of Ireland's literary geniuses could find so little to say about Robert Emmet beyond the stock-in-trade platitudes, then this 'legend' was having a stultifying influence on Irish thinking. Predictably, D. P. Moran, who took no hostages, recognised it: 'Irish people cannot spend all their time mourning over the grave of Emmet.'[65]

V

Unsurprisingly, the Emmet centenary also produced a new crop of plays. Maureen Hawkins has studied this in depth. She finds Robert Emmet the most represented of all Irish historical figures, with seventy-four productions devoted to him, a large number appearing in the centenary decades.[66] The earliest were melodramas of love, heroism and villainy, Sirr the villain, Quigley, or Delaney the informer. The first staged in Ireland was Gerald O'Sullivan's *Robert Emmet, The Irish Martyr* in December 1862. It preceded the time when the main elements of the legend had been established in public consciousness and the love story is entirely missing. The execution scene is staged, scaffold and all, before St Catherine's church – a piece of bad taste that would have been unthinkable once the romantic image of the noble hero had taken root. But these were different times and the drama critic W. J. Lawrence, writing in 1911, thought it a 'melodrama of the cheapest and rankest order', which, nevertheless, enjoyed great popularity for nearly a decade after its first performance. By the 1880s plays about Emmet were considered politically dangerous and a restaging of O'Sullivan's in Dublin, and another commissioned by the legendary English actor Sir Henry Irving in London, were banned.[67] Irving's was later rewritten by the Irish actor Dion Boucicault, with an ending in which Emmet is executed by firing squad, then drawn up to heaven by a figure of Ireland.[68]

In the build up to the centenary new plays deviated little from the legend, and there was increasing cross-fertilisation between Ireland and America, much as there was on the political front. Joseph Clarke's *Robert Emmet: a Tragedy of Irish History* was staged in New York in 1888 and drew on information supplied by Dr Emmet. The action encompasses the love story, the torture of Anne Devlin, the tyranny of Sirr, the treachery of Delaney, an emphasis on the chains fettering the young hero, a final meeting with Sarah Curran, and Emmet executed at sunrise (hinted at, not staged). Part of the script was reproduced in the Irish press in 1894, one of the many examples of fiction posing as fact in the continuing progress of the Emmet legend.[69] Another New York play, *Robert Emmet: Ireland's Patriot Martyr*, was even more influential, not because it was any better than those that had gone before, but because pictures of its author, Brandon Tynan, son of a Fenian and 'a graceful young romantic actor', according to Lawrence, now began to influence visual representations of Emmet. After the centenary, and in line with the 'muscular' nationalism of the age, there was some re-action against the notion that Emmet was a dreamer and 'reckless enthusiast'. This was a slander put about by 'hostile English writers' and 'thoughtless Irish panegyrists'. His was a bold, daring and well-laid plan, foiled only by treachery.[70] Tynan's robust stature was more in tune with these contemporary readings of Emmet as a man of action and dashing general than the rather weedy portraits of Petrie and Comerford.[71] He was also the model for Jerome Connor's statue of Emmet (1912). This was paid for by Irish-Americans, but only finally erected in St Stephen's Green in 1968. Two other bronzes cast from the 1912 model were erected in San Francisco in 1919 (unveiled by Eamon de Valera) and in Washington D.C. in 1966.[72]

But the play that caught the mood in 1903 was Henry Connell

Mangan's *Robert Emmet*. It was staged in Dublin, Derry and Kilkenny and proved so popular with provincial dramatic societies that it was published for circulation the following year. It was first produced by the National Players Society – a talented dissident group from Yeats's and Lady Gregory's National Theatre Company. It has been described as 'a slavish piece of historical accuracy'.[73] Rather it is entirely faithful to the legend, including the unhistorical meeting with Napoleon, the rebellion as a government plot, dialogue taken from Whitty and Madden's rendition of Anne Devlin's story. This is romantic Emmet and the play ends with the court scene and the speech. Lawrence thought Mangan's 'a fairly sound commemorative play' and despite the 'boisterousness' of some minor actors, he considered Dudley Digges's delivery of Emmet's speech – 'possibly ... the first time that the great piece of inspired oratory was ever given in its entirety in a dramatic representation' – a 'powerful' indication of the actor's future greatness. Its success lay in its competent portrayal of the now familiar plot.

Predictably the Emmet legend attracted the attention of the infant American film industry, with an eye to the Irish-American audience. Irish-Canadian Sidney Olcott sympathised with Irish republicanism, and during his 1914 shooting of *Bold Emmet, Ireland's Martyr* in Co. Kerry, he supplied the film's prop guns to the Irish Volunteers for military training. The authorities insisted on its withdrawal the following year, claiming that it was damaging recruitment for the war. Walter MacNamara had also used the Emmet legend in his 1914 film, *Ireland a Nation*, which featured the trial scene and speech. It was awarded a licence in 1916, but given the tense political climate after the Easter Rising, the censors required that several scenes be removed, including Emmet's execution and the soldiers' rough handling of Sarah Curran. When it was screened at Dublin's Rotunda in January 1917, the characters of Lord Castlereagh and Major Sirr were hissed by the audience.[74]

Emmet had by now become 'iconographically static'.[75] Audiences and readers disliked any deviation from the legend and two playwrights who attempted something new in this period had to explain themselves to the theatre-going public. *An Imaginary Conversation*, a one-act play by Norreys Connell (Conal O'Riordan) was staged by the Abbey in 1909. Though based on the story from Moore about Emmet's reaction to his playing of 'Let Erin Remember' (see p. 17), it depicts the zealot weighed down by anxiety for the cause rather than the enthusiast dreaming of heading an Irish army. This, of course, was acceptable enough to those reacting against the romantic or boy-revolutionary image. But to treat Moore as frivolous and timid, which O'Riordan does, was less acceptable and Lawrence thought this performance 'altogether too modern for remote heroic types'. When Lennox Robinson's Emmet play *The Dreamers* was staged at the Abbey in May 1915, he felt obliged to explain that it was not meant to be dismissive of Emmet. He spoke of the dream of liberty, passed on to Emmet by previous generations and 'being dreamed today, as vivid as ever'. Rather, he depicts Emmet as having failed only because he had been let down on the day by a drunken mob. The play remained very close to the legend, all the incidentals (so frequently depicted in the printed images), the hessian boots, the uniform and cocked hat, the lock of hair from Sarah Curran, being incorporated into the story. But critics and audiences did not like the emphasis on the drinking, nor the demotion of Emmet from centre stage, in favour of the artisans who had made the boots.[76] By now it was becoming more and more difficult to present Emmet in any other mode than that of the icon of legend and he increasingly becomes symbolic rather than a real figure, the ideal against which others are measured. However, the older melodramas remained popular with working-class and rural audiences and continued to be so for the next half-century. Actor Val Vousden recalled being booed by young men attending the Coffee Palace in Townshend Street, Dublin, when he played sketches from Dickens, but cheered when he played Robert Emmet. 'If you people want to know how Ireland has suffered and is suffering still,' a circus ringmaster pre-announced the arrival of his play in the west of Ireland, 'go and see Val Vousden play Robert Emmet.'[77] Irish people still preferred the Emmet of legend. 'Robert Emmet's fame might be better left to Moore's poetry and Washington Irving's prose', commented a reviewer in the Jesuit *Irish Monthly* for November 1902, and 'we prefer ... the less authentic version we are used to'.[78]

It may well have been one of these plays that Brinsley MacNamara had in mind in his novel *The Clanking of Chains*. The title refers to one of the most recurrent images of the legend: Emmet fettered in his prison cell. MacNamara (John Weldon) had toured with the Abbey Theatre as a young man. The novel is set in the rural village of Bally-cullion just before the First World War in 1913/14. On the national scene the Irish Party is confident that Home Rule is finally within reach – indeed, it has been approved by the British parliament, but suspended because of the outbreak of the war. In Ballycullion the young purist republican – shop boy Michael Dempsey – has been re-hearsing his role as Robert Emmet in the village play. He is taken over by the character and contrasts the meanness of the agrarian crime that made heroes in his day with the high nationalism and republican sacrifice of the past. He is steeped in the rhetoric of Sinn Féin and the Gaelic League and disgusted that the despicable 'Shoneen', who had played the part of Leonard MacNally and buys filthy English weeklies, should be using the proceeds from the play to create a dance hall rather than to further the republican cause. As the years go by and militant nationalism is in the ascendant, the gombeenmen (money-grabbing shopkeepers, who exploited the poor), with no ideals save that of money-making, recognise the potential of turning a penny. Michael misreads the signs and when, in another showing of the Emmet play he goes beyond the script to call for an Irish republic, he is shunned. He finds solace in the recognition of his own purity and isolation. As the village turns on him, the best insult-word they can find is 'informer' and he begins to see how his dream of dying for Ire-land has blinded him to the 'uncharitableness' of the new Irish na-tion. But, after all, failure was noble. Is that not what the Emmet play had shown? So he withdraws into himself and builds a life of republican purity and isolation, seeing in his persecution a form of heroic ecstasy.[79]

Michael Dempsey's sense of isolated republican purity would have been typical of that generation, which had grown up with the language of the Gaelic revival and the Emmet centenary. The puritanism of the new 'cultural' nationalism was evident in the call put out by the GAA to avoid fêtes and sports on 'Emmet's Day', and treat it rather as a day of national mourning.[80] Ireland was not alone in its turn-of-the-century romantic and messianic youth movements that glorified violence, and in Emmet they had the perfect model. After all, the legend told them that his character was above reproach, pure, noble, heroic, romantic, and virtuous. Even the relationship with Sarah Curran was virtuous. Nor is there ever a mention of Emmet taking a drink (the ideal republican is teetotal). A Sinn Féin manual of 1912 told Sinn Féiners to ensure that their characters were above reproach. If they all became Emmets then 'courage, and temperance, and manliness, and gentleness' would mark the Irish nation and its people would become 'a comely and heroic and self-sacrificing and loveable race'. There was, of course, the ultimate virtue of dying for Ireland 'but it is not everything'. Its moral regeneration and de-anglicanisation was also required.[81] It was no distance from such puritanism to the position of moral policemen of the nation when the generation of 1903 assumed power after independence.

VI

The gentle romantic reading of Emmet has clouded recognition of his pure zealotry, his belief that people would respond to the heroic act. The centenary literature was full of references to redemptive violence and the triumph of failure. 'In revolutionary movements, as in all struggles against great odds', wrote the republican youth journal *St Patrick's* in an article on Emmet's plan, 'boldness and seemingly insensate recklessness succeed where crabbed caution would assuredly fail.'[82] On the political front constitutional nationalism was winning its long battles for land reform and Home Rule, interrupted only by the outbreak of war in 1914, and its brand of nationalism was still dominant in Ireland.

However, the republicans in the IRB were organising under the guise of the Wolfe Tone Memorial Association and both it and the sister organisation in America, Clan Na Gael, continued to commemorate Emmet's birthday, using the occasions to rally support. 'Dublin must one day wash out in blood' its shame in having failed Emmet, Pearse had told his New York audience in 1914, and his speeches increasingly called for another act of redemptive sacrifice. The Emmet commemorations in Dublin under the IRB's aegis took on the aspect of a call to arms. In the final such programme before the Easter Rising (Mansion House, 7 March 1916) the call was made in verse by Brian O'Higgins:

> Robert Emmet! Robert Emmet!
>   In your lonely, nameless tomb,
>   Do you see the light of morning
>   Breaking through the long night's gloom?
>   Do you feel the heart of Eireann
>   Throbbing high with hope and pride –
>   That she thought was dead for ever –
>   On the dreary day you died?
>
> Robert Emmet! Robert Emmet!
>   When the tyrant struck you down
>   In the springtime of your manhood,
>   In the heart of Dublin town;
>   When she gave the dogs your life-blood,
>   When she mocked your dying moan,
>   Did she think the power of Emmet

Was for all time overthrown?

Did she think the murdered patriot
    Has no strength within the grave?
That his spirit speeds no message
    To the leal and strong and brave?
That his voice can send no slogan
    Through the dark and weary night?
That his name can rouse no memories,
    Set no vengeance fires alight?

Robert Emmet! Robert Emmet!
    Soldiers soon shall chant your name,
As they drive the power of England
    From our shores in fear and shame.
O, your eyes will glow with gladness
    On that morn so soon to be
When your epitaph is written
    In a land forever free!

Pearse discounted the traditional picture of Emmet as a youthful en-thusiast. Rather Emmet's speech and the documents prepared for his rebellion made them, with Tone's life, 'the chief texts which Irish rev-olutionaries have to study ... He [Emmet] saw clearly that one must march to freedom through bloodshed'. In this, and his speech in Belfast five days earlier, he spoke of Emmet having 'redeemed' Ireland after she had been purchased with bribes at the Union and likened it to the 'more recent treachery' of the parliamentarians.[83]

Six weeks later the Easter rising began. There was an uncanny re-semblance to Emmet's: key buildings were seized in Dublin, another proclamation by a 'Provisional Government' of Ireland invoked the name of 'the dead generations' who had summoned them once again to strike for freedom. 'In every generation the Irish people have as-

ir right to national freedom and sovereignty; six times dur-
ast three hundred years they have asserted it in arms.' Pearse
and his colleagues on the IRB supreme council led some 1,500 men
and held key buildings in Dublin for six days. Whether they had any
real expectation of success is debatable. Pearse had felt the need for
his generation to make another stand for Irish independence by taking up arms, thereby passing the 'faith' on to future generations. In
his speech at his trial he avowed this as the main achievement of the
rising. After all, look what Emmet had achieved by a 'two-hour rising'
and theirs had lasted a week. Desmond Ryan recalled Pearse's exul-
tant cry in the GPO: 'Emmet's two-hour insurrection was nothing to
this.'[84] Outside the GPO people gathered, mostly hostile, but a new
generation of young men was fired by the example. There was appalling bloodshed, some 450 killed and 2,600 injured and the majority of people in Ireland (including Arthur Griffith) were horrified.
But this was soon forgotten, for, just as in 1803, the authorities acted
with haste and lack of political judgement and rushed through the executions of the main leaders. The Liberal Chief Secretary, Augustine
Birrell, whose appeal to his government not to overreact was ignored,
felt obliged to resign – like his predecessor William Wickham a century earlier – effectively ending his career.

Those familiar with Irish nationalism's mesmerisation with the
glorious dead foresaw the consequences. 'It is absolutely impossible
to slaughter a man in this position without making him a martyr and
a hero', warned George Bernard Shaw, no sympathiser with militant
Irish nationalism, 'even though the day before the rising he may have
been only a minor poet. The shot Irishmen will now take their places
beside Emmet and the Manchester Martyrs in Ireland.'[85] And so they
did, and others too recognised Pearse's and the other executed leaders' apotheosis, most famously W. B. Yeats. He had long been out of
sympathy with Pearse's kind of nationalism, but in the summer of
1916 he changed his mind, and predicted accurately that it would in
future be 'our part/To murmur name upon name', adding the men of

1916 to the litany of fallen heroes. How, he asked, could people who sought compromise continue, 'While those dead men are loitering there/To stir the boiling pot? ('Sixteen Men Dead')? The end of Parnell's once-great party came two years later. It was the conscription crisis and the mistiming of a British general election that provided the occasion. But Pearse's belief that Irish people would rally to the example of heroic sacrifice, much as they had done with Emmet, proved well founded. Sinn Féin (which had not endorsed the rising) seized the moment, winning the bulk of the parliamentary constituencies, and following Griffith's simple but brilliant plan of keeping the MPs at home rather than sending them to the Westminster parliament, they set up Ireland's first Dáil. The Anglo-Irish war (1918–21) completed what 1916 had started. Constitutional nationalism had lost and the new Ireland was to romanticise another generation of rebels. Independence of a sort was won, minus six counties of Ulster. Perhaps it was time to write Emmet's epitaph?

That was a different country, different men,
though just as dead now, and for similar dreams.
Hung askew at one end of the rails
an iron label says half what it means,
the rest absolved by rust. Undecked by fame,
here are Robert Emmet, Wind and Rain –

. . .

Three Elementals I might say, but that
such might come near to challenging the ban.
Let No Man Write My Epitaph.

. . .

The last offence we practise on the dead
is how we summarise, for histories need
that wind and rain supply here, Emmet dead.[1]

Robin Skelton, 'At Emmet's Grave', 1962

Emmet remained an important icon to be claimed by different
(and differing) brands of Irish republicanism and nationalism.
Indeed, the luxury of independence allowed some intellectuals to introduce a challenging, even irreverent note. Others asked if his epitaph could at last be written. Most thought not and the divided island
now became the new unfinished business. Yet his legend had been so
central to the concept of an Irish nation that to challenge it was unthinkable, even among those who recoiled from the levels of violence

that it had produced. The simplicity of the Emmet legend (and of United Irishism) was part of the appeal: remove the power of England and all Ireland's problems would disappear. Few thought of the kind of Ireland that would succeed it. Seán O'Faoláin, who joined the IRA during the Anglo-Irish war as one of those 'exhilarating' things that the young men of his day were doing, recalled an English reporter's efforts to discover the practical aims of the republican movement after 1916. 'Would you at least say what exactly you yourself want?' he asked of Sinn Féin's general secretary, in some exasperation at the unsatisfactory answers he was receiving. 'Vingeance, bejasus!' was the retort.[2] And so it remained the priority of those who rejected the Anglo-Irish Treaty of 1921 and prompted the civil war in the nascent Irish Free State. By the time it ended many more Robert Emmets had been created. This time Britain could no longer be blamed. Even so, they were quietly added to the litany of those who died for Ireland and successive Irish governments continued to pay lip service to the Emmet legend in the interests of a form of stability. The romanticisation of violence had been widespread in nationalist Ireland until the civil war. Thereafter it was toned down, except by militant republicans and northern nationalists, excluded by partition from the new state. Little wonder that some thought the 'revolution' was not over, while others wondered whether it had happened at all. The dominant constitutionalism of Irish nationalism reasserted itself, and despite the violent origins of the new state, a working democracy was soon in place. It was, as Charles Townshend has judged, an impressive achievement.[3]

I

When the Anglo-Irish Treaty was signed in December 1921 and ratified by a slim Dáil majority the following month, there was some sense that Emmet's epitaph could now be written. 'Robert Emmet – Patriot – Martyr – Victor', ran a headline in the *Cork Weekly Examiner*;

'Robert Emmet's Epitaph Can Now Be Written', was the front-page headline in a Canadian paper.[4] Significantly it was the Irish Free State's newly acquired dominion status that the latter was celebrating. The treaty granted Ireland self-governing status within the British Commonwealth, but retained a level of subordination by the require-ment of an oath of allegiance to the British crown and the presence of a Governor-General. The exclusion of six counties of Ulster from the new state caused less controversy at this stage, though ultimately this would prove the main argument against the writing of Emmet's epi-taph. That it remained so talismanic for most of the twentieth cen-tury was a token of the symbolic status it had acquired in nationalist imagination prior to 1916.

Ominously, at the 1922 commemorative celebration of Emmet's birthday in the Theatre Royal, Dublin, Liam Mellows (IRA director of purchases and Sinn Féin TD for Galway) denounced the treaty. Emmet had wanted an independent Ireland, he said, faced with 'dis-senting interruptions' from the audience, not simply a repeal of the Union.[5] Mellows was born in 1892, one of that generation of young republicans who had been groomed in the Fianna and later fought in the 1916 rising. A month after delivering this speech he led the anti-treatyite takeover of the Four Courts in Dublin, the shelling of which by the provisional government under Michael Collins signalled the start of the civil war. Most historians are critical of the anti-treatyites, particularly of de Valera, who for these crucial months seemed to have lost sight of his normal pragmatism, for the majority of the Irish people were heartily sick of the violence. There was no clear thinking, little to guide us 'but those flickering lights before the golden ikons of the past', recalled O'Faoláin. Pearse (and he might have added Emmet) would have been horrified at the brutality of the Anglo-Irish war, much of it directed by Catholic Irishmen in the IRA against other Catholic Irishmen in the RIC.[6] Worse was to come during the civil war of 1922–3. The death toll of perhaps 4,000 should, as J. J. Lee reminds us, be seen in the perspective of fatalities elsewhere in

Europe at the time. But as he admits, it was the 77 executions and the 10,000 internments of anti-treatyites carried out by the new Free State government over ten months that bequeathed such a 'poisonous' atmosphere to independent Ireland and defined its politics for nearly half a century, not least in Ireland's two main political parties, Fianna Fáil and Fine Gael, which were the products of the split.[7] Mellows was among those executed and firmly believed that he would be joining Tone and Emmet and Pearse and Connolly in heaven.[8] But there would be no Emmet-like apotheosis in poetry and song for these men; 'dying for Ireland' hardly carried the same meaning when England was no longer on the scene.

It was because of the shocked recognition of the consequences of such glorification of violence (and particularly since the dissident IRA remained active) that the Irish government became rather coy about references to 'the glorious dead'. When an Irish priest in New Zealand wrote congratulating the post-1923 government for having rescued the nation from civil war and enclosing £50 to start an 'Emmett Epitaph Fund', the government returned it. In a letter that anxiously sought to avoid offence, Liam Cosgrave, President of the Executive Council (i.e. Prime Minister) spoke of Ireland's emergence from 'the dangerous transition period, which all countries newly born to freedom have to suffer through', and his hope that in peaceful conditions 'those influences which have caused troubles and difference amongst our people may lose their potency for evil'.

> I have given careful thought to your suggestion that the time is ripe to undertake the erection of a monument worthy of the heroic soul and lofty patriotism of Robert Emmett … I feel, however, and my colleagues whom I have consulted agree, that so long as a minority of our fellow-countrymen, professing in great part the faith of Emmett, are sundered from us by an unnatural partition of our common country, it would not be in accord with

Emmett's dying wish that we should proceed to write his epitaph.

We hope and fervently pray that wise administration may soften misunderstandings and obliterate differences of opinion on the part of that minority and that they will in the early future of their full accord and by their own desire join with us in a community of council and administration for the whole of Ireland. When this occurs the tribute of Emmett's memory can be offered by a united people.

... in the circumstances I have come to the conclusion that my proper course is to return you your cheque ... with the earnest wish that it will not be very long until the noble project which you and the whole of us have so much at heart can be taken up in a manner which will do honour to one of Ireland's greatest sons.'[9]

Besides the political implications of raising any memorial (now firmly associated with the 'epitaph'), there was a move away from the heroic representations of the past in favour of unromantic figures of soldiers from the war of independence – even though the rhetoric at their unveiling ceremonies still used Emmet-associated imagery of the task left unfinished.[10] Sculptor Jerome Connor suddenly found himself out of fashion and when, in 1931, Senator Oliver St John Gogarty tried to persuade the government to acquire his Emmet statue for the state, the government dragged its feet and seemed glad of the National Gallery's less-than-enthusiastic response to do nothing.[11] Besides, in the philistine culture of the first decades of Irish independence public art was not a priority, except for propaganda purposes.

However, this is only part of the story. In the 1930s extremism again threatened the new state, from the right, with Ireland's own brand of Fascism, the Blueshirts, and most of all from extreme republicanism. The IRA misread the electoral victory of de Valera in 1932, thinking its time had come and looking for revenge. De Valera had recognised that democratic politics was the only future for Ireland. In 1926–7, 'coming slowly to his normally shrewd senses',[12] de Valera resigned from Sinn Féin, set up a new party, Fianna Fáil, and re-entered the Dáil from which he had led the anti-treaty secession five years earlier. Thereafter he dominated the politics of southern Ireland. Between 1932 and 1959, he was out of power for only six years and was President 1959–73. His governments' policy towards the idea of an Emmet epitaph continued that of his predecessor and his line on his old comrades in the IRA was tougher than that of either Britain or the Northern Ireland state. De Valera moved quickly – much as Cosgrave had in 1922 – to underpin the state's legitimacy by laying claim to the heroes of the past. In 1932 he added plaques of anti-treatyites from the civil war to the treatyites already figuring on a cenotaph memorial erected by the Cosgrave government in 1922, much to the disgust of extreme republicans who now regarded him as a traitor. Three years later he and Fianna Fáil 'appropriated' 1916, Pearse and Cú Chulainn, by acquiring the famous Sheppard statue of Cú Chulainn for the GPO and mounting huge 1916 commemorative demonstrations (a year early). His homily at the unveiling of Sheppard's statue was deeply ambiguous, for it called on 'the youth of this country' to emulate 'the great deeds' and 'sacrifice' of those who had gone before – still the traditional rhetoric of the IRA which was now declared illegal.[13] This was continuing civil-war politics and while lip service was still being paid to pre-1916 republican heroes, they do not yet figure in the rush for official commemoration. It is possible that their Protestantism was a problem for a nation now largely defined by its Catholicism. Yeats had suggested as much in a controversial 1925 speech to the Irish Senate.[14] The continued outpouring of writings about Emmet in the 1930s does not quite bear this out and it is more likely that the heroes of 1916–23 had supplanted those of old, as more relevant to the new age. The only public monument to Emmet at this time was a republican plaque placed in 1938 on the bridge over which he would have walked to Harold's Cross. The occasion was the 140th anniversary celebrations for 1798, which were being used by republicans to denounce any talk of Ireland aligning with Britain in a possible war against Germany, and the procession duly routed past the place of Emmet's execution.[15]

Despite the coyness about public memorials, a large portrait of Emmet had hung in the Irish government's Council (Cabinet) chamber since 1926. It was that commissioned by Dr Emmet in 1897 from the very successful American-based Irish artist John Mulvany. Dr Emmet had supplied Mulvany with family likenesses, copies of the death mask and Comerford's and Petrie's sketches. Petrie's, which Dr Emmet thought captured Robert Emmet's 'supreme degree of contempt' for the conduct of his trial, was the dominant influence. At first Dr Emmet considered Mulvany's the only true likeness of Robert Emmet, and Michael Davitt, who saw it on one of his visits to America, pronounced it 'a picture of the real Robert Emmet as he looked, in the act of repelling the odious Norbury's brutal allegations'. It was donated to the Irish people by Dr Emmet's former librarian, Thomas P. Tuite, at a special ceremony in New York in October 1925. Tuite felt it was fulfilling Dr Emmet's words in giving it to him: 'It belongs to Ireland!' Some people might think it 'stern and forbidding, but it represents the stern, unbending spirit of an Ireland whose head was "bloody but unbowed"; it conveys, as words fail to convey, that moment during Robert Emmet's speech from the dock when, with biting scorn, he faced Judge Norbury, as he exclaimed "what farce is your justice."' The final result is nothing like the boy revolutionary of the legend, or any of the traditional representations of Emmet, and in consequence it was rejected in 1950 by Ireland's Cultural Relations Committee for its photographic exhibition.[16]

Although a commemorative stamp (using Brocas's profile) was issued in 1953 (again on the anniversary of his death), the official reticence about the legacy of Emmet continued – at least south of the border. One Fianna Fáil deputy raised a question in the Dáil about an attack on Emmet in a Dublin newspaper and proposed that government introduce legislation 'to prevent anti-national attacks such as this on Irish patriots', particularly since the paper in question had a wide circulation among the young 'and can influence wrongly the minds of people in matters of this kind'. However, such a move would most certainly have re-awakened the controversy about who owned the patriot past, as General Richard Mulcahy, former treatyite and leader of Fine Gael, mischievously hinted at in the same debate. This kind of question had been posed before in the Dáil (about Roger Casement) and the Taoiseach's office checked and reproduced the anodyne answer. 'The reputation of Robert Emmet, like that of the other patriots who gave their lives in efforts to secure the freedom of our country, is safe in the affections of the people.'[17] Nor was the claim without foundation, for extra staff were needed at the GPO to cope with the rush for the first-day issue of the commemorative stamp.[18]

The dangers associated with some aspects of the Emmet legend had been revealed two years previously in an example of Irish-America's high expectations of the Irish state. The librarian of Boston College, Helen Landreth, had used the occasion of a visit by Taoiseach John A. Costello to enlist his help in securing photocopies of relevant documents for her book *The Pursuit of Robert Emmet* (1948). The books that had continued to be published on Emmet since independence had been uncontroversial and were generally well received. However, although Landreth's was well written and undoubtedly the best researched to date, it surpassed Madden in its preoccupation with informers and traitors and the now-outmoded idea that Emmet had been the dupe of a government plot. In this she had accepted uncritically Dr Emmet's claims and they became the central theme of her book. For this she was trounced in a number of hostile reviews and articles. In her responses she repeated the charges, threatened legal action and accused many more than the traditional MacNallys of being informers in a way that the government eventually thought defamatory, for, once again, she had tried to enlist the Taoiseach on her side. The Public Record Office told the Taoiseach's office that one of the conditions required of researchers was the suppression of the names of suspected informers, to protect their descendants 'particularly those living in country districts where memories are long'. How right he was, for the emphasis on the villains of the Emmet legend would continue even after some of the more romantic elements began to fade. In the end the government thought it best not to respond to Helen Landreth's charges, in case any comment by the Taoiseach should be used publicly in the controversy.[19]

The 150th anniversary of Emmet's rebellion and death was relatively subdued. There were none of the years of preparation that had preceded the centenary. A suggestion that one of the American Emmets be invited to address the Irish people from the spot on which his ancestor had been executed received the standard evasive response by government: it was too soon to write Emmet's epitaph. With Ireland partitioned the time for such commemoration had not yet arrived. Intriguingly, it was Emmet's old *alma mater*, Trinity College, from which Dublin's Catholic students were about to be debarred by their archbishop, that organised the major exhibition of the year. Its opening was attended by Ireland's foreign minister Frank Aiken and members of the Oireachtas (Irish parliament). The Irish president, Seán T. O'Kelly, formally opened the exhibition with a toned-down version of Pearse's 1914 Emmet speech. Indeed, after independence there was a common tendency to view Emmet through Pearse's words.[20] 'The President … said there had been many changes in Ireland since Robert Emmet entered Trinity College at the age of 15 years. It was not necessary for him to dwell on the events that ended in Emmet's trial for high treason and his execution in Thomas Street on 20 September 1803. He wanted only to say that rarely did a failure, judged as the world judges failure, appear to be more complete or pathetic as

Emmet's. And yet had he not left us a memory as proud as the memory of even the most eventful episodes in our history. His attempt in fact was not a failure, but a triumph for Irish nationality. For it asserted in blood, Ireland's *opposition to the Union* [my italics].'[21] This reinterpretation of the motivation behind Emmet's rebellion – to reverse the Union rather than win independence – was to create the illusion that the 1921 Treaty was what the Emmets of the past had fought for and to distance them from the extreme republicans of the present.

But things were ordered differently in Northern Ireland, where the IRA (banned in the south since 1936) would soon concentrate its campaign and against which southern politicians could still indulge in the kind of republican rhetoric that they were reluctant to use at home. Minister Aiken, invited to address a Robert Emmet pageant in Fermanagh, delivered a lengthy attack on partitition: 'I salute here today the gallant men and women who are holding the fort in these six partitioned counties ... We of the Irish race seek the God-given rights of the Irish people ... as a duty to the men who died for Irish freedom.'[22] The anniversary was the occasion for widespread defiance of Stormont's ban on Irish flags. A week of celebrations in Belfast culminated on Sunday 20 September in a massive parade on the Falls Road, headed by the Irish tricolour, the Sunburst, the Plough and the Stars (Connolly's Citizens' Army flag), those very symbols and icons that Seán O'Faoláin recalled as having helped produced the terrible muddle and unnecessary violence of Ireland's civil war.[23] In the north, however, such symbolic defiance continued to define the identity of most of the Catholic population. It became an outpost for the pre-1916 extreme Irish-Irelandism of the Gaelic revival, the Gaelic League, Sinn Féin and the Ancient Order of Hibernians being to the fore in the 1953 celebrations. Verbal extremism disguised the non-violent nationalism of most northern Catholics, much as it had done of those in the whole island in the previous century. The popularity of a new batch of rebel songs, following the deaths of two IRA men in a bungled attack on a Fermanagh police barracks on 1 January 1957, disguised the condemnation of this new IRA campaign by the Irish government, the Catholic Church and a majority of northern Catholics. In the twentieth century Tone and Pearse had largely replaced Emmet as republicanism's main icons – though not amongst the Irish populace generally. However, it was the Emmet tradition of the heroic youth dying with a smile that continued to inspire the balladry:

> Not since the days of Padraig Pearse
> > Was there a Man like Sean,
> With Soul aligned to a Heart that pined
> > For Freedom's Blessed Dawn,
> Young Emmett's mind was his combined
> > With the Principles of Tone,
> While his Christian zeal crowned the Great Ideal
> > Of Sean from Garryowen.[24]

The most prolific composer of new rebel songs was our old friend Brian O'Higgins. O'Higgins had grown up in those pre-centenary years when the Emmet legend was most pervasive and he had remained totally unreconciled to the Anglo-Irish treaty. Now he was adding the names of IRA men executed by the Irish state to the litany of those who had died for Ireland:

> Emmet and Barry and the Manchester Martyrs
> A comrade have met in the bright halls above,
> Another young life has been laid down for Ireland,
> Another true heart full of faith and of love.
> With Barnes and McCormaic he will live in our memory
> And inspire us to fight on 'till Ireland is free;
> A friend to the faithful, a foe to the traitors –
> > Young Cathal O Ceirin,
> > > The Boy from Tralee.[25]

Of all the republican literature of the twentieth century it is O'Higgins's periodical, the *Wolfe Tone Annual*, which is the most admiring of and obsessive about Emmet. In the kind of talented and sarcastic prose of his generation of Irish-Irelanders, he continued to denounce the West Britons and former republicans who had turned on the IRA. He exposed the myth of the good/bad republican by arguing (correctly) that Tone and Emmet sought separation from Britain, not simply a reversal of the Union. He continued the early century attack on the idea of Emmet as a romantic failure and weighed in with some unlikely collaborators in the attack on Helen Landreth for her suggestion that he was simply a pawn in a British government plot. He even checked her sources in the Irish State Paper Office. While his analysis here was sound, his Irish-Irelandism got in the way, for he questioned the right of non-Irish people like Helen Landreth and Raymond Postgate (author of the best twentieth-century work on Emmet) to write on Irish subjects. O'Higgins was steeped in the Emmet legend, much of his knowledge traceable to the popular prints of his youth. Indeed, many of the illustrations of Emmet in the *Wolfe Tone Annual* are taken from the *Shamrock* of the 1880s and 1890s. Tone he considered the major inspiration in Irish nationalism, but Emmet 'is the best loved'. His criticism of post-independence Ireland involved both an attack on the way that its Catholic ethos and reservations about non-Catholic patriots had placed O'Connell above Tone and Emmet and, predictably, the way Fianna Fáil tried to promote the myth of an all-inclusive republican tradition: linking pro-treaty Michael Collins with anti-treaty Cathal Brugha (killed in the civil war), or Liam Mellows with Arthur Griffith, he argued, was like linking Lord Norbury with Robert Emmet.[26]

Like other 'irreconcilables', O'Higgins and the *Wolfe Tone Annual* were laying claim to the heroic dead of the past in order to attack 'the lapsed republicans' of the present.[27] As an earlier republican journal had stated: Emmet, Tone, Pearse and Connolly had 'died in vain for many of this generation ... let them frankly give up talking

about Ireland a Nation'.[28] Apart from the partition issue, some re-
publican intellectuals were dismayed at the narrow and oppressive
Catholic ethos of the post-independence state, denouncing it as a
conspiracy of the bishops and the bourgeoisie to keep out the people.
So the most prominent republican intellectual of the age – Peadar
O'Donnell – argued in a tribute to his friend Sean Murray, former
IRA commandant, trade unionist and first general secretary of the
Irish Communist party. In a pamphlet entitled *Not Yet Emmet*, he argued that the treatyites and the Catholic Church had simply gone
along with the rich to keep the rabble out. 'This is why such phrases
as "when we won our independence" are resented by so many people
– it is dangerously near the ultimate blasphemy – "Emmet's epitaph
may now be written".'[29]

Although the Irish Free State had secured a surprising level of democratic stability in a very short time, its 'Ourselves Alone', Irish-Ire-
lander policies had turned it, by the 1930s, into a narrow-minded
and intolerant state, which its rural young (supposedly the essence of
Irishness) were abandoning in the hundreds of thousands, and its best
writers were squeezed out by some of the severest censorship laws in
the western world. It represented, as Terence Brown has written, 'an
almost Stalinist antagonism to modernism … combined with prudery … and a deep reverence for the Irish past'.[30] As O'Faoláin and
others declaimed, these were the petit-bourgeois victors of the 'revolution', the publicans and shopkeepers so famously denounced by
Yeats. The heroic nationalism that had inspired so many writers in the
past now seemed out of place and was avoided. Poet Austin Clarke
had been one of the young men who stood outside the GPO in 1916.
He had been a student of one of its leaders and was himself a devotee
of the cultural nationalism that had inspired it. 'I wanted to be alone,'
he recalled, 'that I might think of Wolfe Tone, Robert Emmet, and
the hosts of the dead.'[31] His work would later fall foul of the Irish
Free State's censorship laws and his private life of its anti-divorce legislation. When he returned to writing in the 1950s, his thoughts

turned again to Emmet, this time in criticism of those who paid lip service to a republican ideal that they had sabotaged:

THE TRIAL OF ROBERT EMMET
to be re-enacted
at Green Street Courthouse
for An Tostal, 1956[32]

Sentence the lot and hurry them away,
The court must now be cleared, batten the spot
Swung up with rope and ladder, lighting-plot
Rehearsed. No need of drop-scene for the play
To-night: bench, box and bar in well-mixed ray
Make do. Though countless miscreants have got
A life-term here, and some, the scaffold knot,
Forget the cells our safety fills by day.
See British greed and tyranny defied
Once more by that freethinker in the dock
And sigh because his epitaph remains
Unwritten. Cheer revolution by the clock
And lastly — badge and holy medal guide
Your cars home, hooting through our dirtiest lanes.

Clarke's poem was published in the *Irish Times* before the event itself. Because of the smallness of the Green Street courthouse and the high prices of the tickets, the judiciary protested and 'after some weeks of patriotic delay' — according to Clarke's account — the Minister for Justice cancelled the project.[33]

II

If some criticised the heirs of the heroic past for betraying its spirit, others saw that spirit in itself as having contributed to the tawdry present. Whichever way, Emmet's iconic status remained undiminished; even the increasingly critical treatment of the legend testified to that. James Joyce had left Ireland in 1904 and *Ulysses* was published abroad in 1922. However, the setting was Dublin 1904 and the frequent Emmet references testify to the pervasiveness of the Emmet legend in the centenary years. The central character, the unassuming Dublin Jew Leopold Bloom, walks the streets of Dublin, the 1798 and 1803 sites of remembrance recalling to his mind snippets of Moore's melodies, more recent rebel songs, images from Madden and the weekly supplements, phrases from the press re-telling of the story during the centenary decade. Joyce by now was in revolt against the Ireland that pious nationalism has produced and his work was profoundly iconoclastic. The emphasis, unsurprisingly, is on Emmet's speech and death. Bloom attends his friend's funeral at Glasnevin and wonders if a tombstone might be that of Robert Emmet 'buried here by torchlight'. That afternoon Tom Kernan, who had also been one of the mourners at the morning funeral, walked through Thomas Street towards the quays. 'Down there Emmet was hanged, drawn and quartered,' he thought – which he was not, but 'Bold Robert Emmet' added that detail to the legend. 'Greasy black rope. Dogs licking the blood off the street when the lord lieutenant's wife drove by in her noddy [here adapting the story of Sarah Curran in her carriage] ... Is he buried in St Michan's? Or no, there was a midnight burial in Glasnevin. Corpse brought in through a secret door in the wall.' As he hums the tunes of other rebel songs, his thoughts turn to other 'gentlemen' heroes like Lord Edward Fitzgerald, villains like Sirr and the Sham Squire, and the floggings that took place in the stables behind Moira House. And then, as he reaches the quays, he curses the fact that he had just missed the splendour of the viceregal cavalcade.

Bloom too is making his way along the quays, suffering the dyspeptic after-effects of lunch. Just as Madden had discovered Emmet's death mask in the window of a shop near the Liffey, so Bloom espies a picture of Emmet in Lionel Mark's window and farts his way through the last words of the speech, the 'I have done' conveying a meaning quite subversive of the original. Later that afternoon Bloom is in Barney Kiernan's pub near Green Street (parish of St Michan's). Here he encounters the Fenian 'Citizen' – modelled on Michael Cusack, founder of the GAA – the name reminiscent of the French Revolutionary Terror's murderous thought police. The Citizen is presented as the intolerant and inflexible face of new nationalism, his talk peppered with the stock phrases of Griffith's *United Irishman* and Moran's *Leader*, denunciations of 'Shoneens' and snips from nationalist balladry about the memory of the dead, dying for your country and 'the Tommy Moore touch about Sarah Curran and she's far from the land'. Emmet's execution scene is parodied in the melodramatic language of romantic nationalism. Peels of thunder, muffled drums, cannon fire, thunder and lightning accompanied 'the ghastly scene' as the 'gentle … hero martyr … with a song [smile] on his lips' ascends the scaffold. The block – or was it a table – stood by, the executioner testing out his range of instruments, all made by 'the world-famous firm of cutlers' in Sheffield. While – in a parody of the sacrifice of the mass – the house steward of the amalgamated cats' and dogs' home waited to convey the entrails and jugs of 'the most precious blood of the most precious victim'. The final meal prepared for the hero is detailed, but 'he rose nobly to the occasion and expressed his dying wish' that the meal should be divided among members of the sick and indigent roomkeepers' association [located beside Dublin Castle]. The *'ne plus ultra'* of emotion was reached as 'the blushing bride' broke through the bystanders and flung herself upon his 'muscular bosom', he enfolding her 'willowy form in a loving embrace'. She swore always to cherish his memory and there was not a dry eye in the assemblage. Then a 'gallant young Oxonian' [Sturgeon], noted for his chivalry, steps forward and offers his hand.

This is the romance. The more gruesome details of the Emmet legend – and in particular those revealed in the press during the search for the grave – are recalled elsewhere in the book, with the discussion of the cervical vertebrae and the judgement pronounced by an eminent scientist and the physical effects of execution. Appropriately this occurs in the nightmarish scene in the brothel later that night. The Citizen reappears, damning the English who hanged 'our Irish leaders', as 'The Croppy Boy'[34] - the representative boy martyr – is hanged singing his song, holding his bowels, his tongue and penis protruding, his semen spouting over the cobblestones as the ladies move forward to mop it up with their handkerchiefs. Few Irish writers went quite so far in their irreverent treatment of the Emmet legend, but after the civil war the contrasting pieties of the Emmet legend and the realities of the nation it helped produce, inspired much of the best drama.

Seán O'Casey set the trend in looking at the impact of the blood-sacrifice origin-legend of the state through the eyes of the bystanders, the innocent victims, the poor, the excluded (including the doubly-excluded, the working-class Protestant Unionist). Emmet is a ghostly presence in the fight for Irish freedom in *The Shadow of a Gunman* (1923) and *The Plough and the Stars* (1926), both set in Dublin tenements. In the former young, pretty Minnie Powell has a hopelessly romantic notion of the idea of dying for Ireland, which she has acquired through the story of Robert Emmet. She glamorises the discovery of bombs in the tenement, thinking the two feckless anti-heroes are IRA men. But it is she who is the innocent victim of the conflict, dying in an IRA ambush.

The Plough and the Stars is set during 1915–16, culminating in the Easter Rising. Here the romantic nationalists, besotted with Moore's melodies and the fancy Emmet uniforms of the Foresters, are satirised in the figure of labourer Peter Flynn. He preens himself before the popular Emmet picture on the tenement wall, seeing the Emmet green uniform of the Foresters as some kind of affirmation of nationalistic respectability. 'The Foresthers is a gorgeous dhress!' comments Mrs Gogan, the tenement busybody. 'I don't think I've seen nicer, mind you, in a pantomime … Th' loveliest part of th' dhress, I think, is th' osthrichess plume … When yous are goin' along, an' I see them wavin' an' noddin' an' waggin', I seem to be lookin' at each of yous hangin' at th' end of a rope, your eyes bulgin', an' your legs twistin' an' jerkin', gaspin' an' gaspin' for breath while yous are thryin' to die for Ireland!' However, it was the impiety of associating Pearse's speeches and the flags of 1916 with prostitutes and drunkenness that largely prompted the riots when the play was first staged by the Abbey in 1926. O'Casey recalled in particular the 'hysterical' voices of the women (some mothers, widows and sisters of the martyrs of 1916–22 to the fore) 'squealing that Irish girls were noted over the world for their modesty, and that Ireland's name was holy; that the Republican flag had never seen the inside of a public house; that this slander of the Irish race would mean the end of the Abbey Theatre'.[35]

The classic play in this vein was Denis Johnston's *The Old Lady Says 'No!'*. O'Casey, whose working-class origins and genuine trade union-ism gave him some authority to speak for the excluded, commented on the 'well-groomed hands' of the clenched fists protesting at his Abbey production. Respectable Catholic Ireland had fashioned a holy-picture perception of its identity (as W. I. Irwin argues in a sym-pathetic analysis of the *Plough* rioters of 1926) and the Abbey nor-mally reflected it. So in 1929 when Johnston submitted his iconoclastic play about Robert Emmet to the Abbey, it was rejected, as legend would have it, with the comment (from Lady Gregory) 'The Old Lady Says "No!".' It then became the first and most popular play of the alternative Gate Theatre. It is considered Ireland's first 'ex-pressionist' play and, in Emmet, Johnston was parodying a legend consisting almost entirely (at least by now) of clichés. 'It was in-evitable,' as he recalled, 'that such a play would be written in Ireland by someone or other', particularly after 'several years of intermittent and unromantic civil war had soured us all a little towards the woes of Cathleen Ní Houlihan [mythical name for Ireland, used by Yeats and Lady Gregory as the theme of their advanced nationalist 1902 play].' Johnston explained the background to his writing of the play in his in-troduction to a 1970s edition:

One of the best-loved figures of Irish romantic literature is Robert Emmet. The story of his rebellion of 1803 has all of the elements that make for magic. It was very high-minded, and completely unsuccessful. It was picturesquely costumed and insufficiently organised. Its leader – a young Protestant university man of excellent social background – having failed to achieve anything more than an armed street riot, remained behind to bid goodbye to his forbidden sweetheart, instead of taking flight as any sensible rebel should do. In consequence of this he was captured by an ogre of melodrama called Major Sirr, and was hanged after making one of the finest speeches from the dock in the annals of the criminal courts – and we have some pretty good ones in Ireland.

So we all love Robert Emmet ... Even the hoardings along the Canal have been known to display a chalked inscription, 'UP EMMET'. We all agree that it was a pity that some of his supporters had to murder one of the most liberal judges on the bench, Lord Kilwarden, and that the only practical outcome of his affray was to confirm the Union with England for about a hundred and twenty years. Our affection is not affected by these details.

The tragedy of his love has been immortalized by Tom Moore in one of his finest ballads ['She is far from the Land'] ... Who cares that this reason for her absence from the land is the fact that she subsequently married an English officer, and ended her days happily with him elsewhere? For us, her heart will always be lying in Robert's grave [line from Moore]. And lying is the operative word.

The whole episode has got that delightful quality of storybook unreality that creates a glow of satisfaction without any particular reference to the facts of life.[36]

In this Johnston has captured perfectly the nature and impact of the legend. The humour of the play lies, as Johnston intended, in putting it 'into conflict with the facts'. Familiar lines from the nineteenth-century romantic poets (notably Moore), from rebel songs and other nationalist literature feature prominently in the dialogue, their comic effect achieved through the often-ridiculous circumstances and the incongruous context of 1920s Dublin. The plot requires intimate local knowledge and familiarity with the Emmet legend on the part of the audience and, as Johnston recognised, would have been largely unintelligible outside Ireland. 'Across the sea its intentional clichés are no longer clichés, and the various daggers concealed within its lacy sentiments find no flesh into which to probe.'[37]

The Old Lady opens with a melodramatic playlet on the arrest of Emmet. The Speaker (Emmet) is dressed as in the popular picture, green uniform, plumed hat, 'Wellington boots with gold tassels', sword by his side. He has returned to see Sarah Curran. As Sirr and the redcoats arrive to arrest him, the farce begins. The Speaker is accidentally knocked unconscious by one of the redcoat actors and Sirr calls for a doctor from the audience. The boots are removed and in response to the doctor's request for a rug to keep the concussed man warm, the dim-witted stagehand brings a gaudy pair of carpet slippers. The Speaker awakes in College Green in Dublin of the 1920s, thinking now that he really is Robert Emmet. Behind him is the statue of Grattan, an old flower-lady/Cathleen Ní Houlihan seated at its base, who wails repeatedly 'Me four bewtyful gre-in fields' — an irreverent take on the celebrated lines from the 1902 play, as spoken by Maud Gonne. He needs to return to Rathfarnham to find Sarah Curran and is told the number 17 bus will take him there, but it is full and he is left with the statue. Robert Emmet! snorts the statue – that's who all the young men claim they are when they come here. Shouting to be heard above the noise of the twentieth-century traffic, Speaker/Emmet delivers a speech consisting of a string of clichés about red graves, clanking chains, centuries of oppression and injustice, unfurling the green flag,

...ie in fire across the pages of Irish history. In response ...es the legend to talk about Kilwarden's blood staining ...rimson and he chastises the impatient 'young Messiahs' like ..., with his 'eternal play-acting' and 'strutting upon the stage'.

Various characters from 1920s Dublin pass through, emphasising how out of place Emmet is and how parochial are their concerns – very far removed from the high drama of the legend. His name conjures up the standard phrases of the legend, his 'manly bearing', 'kindness', 'spotless reputation', referred to by an 'older man'. But the 'young things' from Phibsboro think Speaker/Emmet a dirty old man in a Foresters' uniform and as he continues to declaim about the 'dead generations' and 'patriot graves', the older man suddenly notices the slippers. How can this be Emmet, where are his boots?

The second act opens in a 'fantastically respectable' drawing room at a soirée hosted by the Minister of Arts and Crafts. He talks nostalgically about his war against the British, but is now part of the new establishment, trite phrases in Irish symbolising the new order, which is nevertheless thoroughly bourgeois. Of course, there is no favouritism in the new state, though the Minister will put in a good word for the favoured, while keeping an eye on the sort of stuff released to the public (censorship): 'Clean and pure Art for clean and pure people.' Emmet's knock at the door, offstage, to enquire about the Rathfarnham bus, occasions a hilarious staccato description of his appearance, uniform, sword and slippers. A man in uniform, rants the Minister, could this be a 'Daring Outrage'? Terribly nice Lady Trimmer of 'the old regime' flaps over Emmet, anxious to 'get in touch with' contemporary trends, much like an anxious mother meeting the friend of her teenage child. Confusing him with the more recent Troubles, she wants to hear about his 'wonderful experiences in the Trouble ... You must have had such interesting times all through the fighting', causing panic in Speaker/Emmet and reminders from his ghosts that he is 'beaten'. The old flower woman now contributes to Speaker/

Emmet's confusion: 'Ay, mister, have ye e'r an old hempen rope for a neck-cloth?' she taunts. Grattan's statue has been invited: 'We always have a few of the nicest statues in on Sunday evening.' But Emmet's is not among them, the Minister making lame excuses to his wife's plea 'you really must get a proper statue of Mr Emmet', and making equally evasive comments when a song is called for. 'Nothing political ... Or calculated to excite you-know-what.' 'She is far from the Land' is acceptable and unthreatening. In a cacophony of voices, blood and thunder republican songs mingle with the apparently gentler Moore, until the two merge at the end. 'Their graves are red. O make her a maddening mingling glorious morrow' to Moore's 'When they promise a glorious morrow'. And all through it, the one note of sanity is the innocent and recurring question of the child: 'Mammy ... Why ith that man wearing hith thlipperth in the dwawing woom?'

The final scene has Speaker/Emmet increasingly confronted with the Ireland he has died for. Only — since the fictional play has not yet reached that part — he does not yet know that he has died for Ireland. Of course you have, says (or rather sings) the Blind Man, as 'Bold Robert Emmet' told us so. But the Dublin he had fought for was now a 'small ... rather provincial' place, that used to be fun, but now 'seems more serious, somehow ... so damned depressing'. Never mind that the young prefer the mailboat to England, that the winds are cold, the beds hard, the sewers stinking, 'when they can see a bit of a rag floating in the wild wind, and they dancing their bloody Ceilidhes'. But the Blind Man appreciates the reality behind the appearances: 'the will-o'-the-wisps and the ghosts of the dead and the half dead and them that will never die while they can find lazy, idle hearts ready to keep their venom warm ... In every dusty corner lurks the living word of some dead poet, and it waiting for to trap and to snare them ... this land belongs not to them that are on it, but to them that are under it.'

Speaker/Emmet has by now progressed through the romantic phase of his legend to nationalism's reinvention in the Gaelic revival, and is hailing Sarah as his Deirdre and Queen. The scene switches to an O'Casey tenement, where the young boastful republican is strong on the 'Up the Republic' kind of rhetoric and impatient with the men of the past, including Emmet. As another young man slowly dies from gunshot wounds (accidentally inflicted by Emmet himself), his passing becomes a metaphor for both the end of the struggle and Emmet's own death. 'A word-spinner dying gracefully, with a cliché on his lips ... He passed on magnificently. He knew how to do that.' The child, at the piano, still worried about the slippers, thumps out the opening lines from 'Bold Robert Emmet', 'The struggle is over.' The Minister arrives with a funeral offering and the usual platitudes. And Speaker/Emmet finally delivers his speech to plaudits and rhetorical republicanism made to sound ridiculous: 'Up Emmet! Up Rathfarnham! Up the Up that won't be Down.' Emmet has now arrived on a hill overlooking Dublin, reminiscent of Anne Devlin's description of him sitting forlornly and defeated in the Wicklow Hills. Yet this is play-acting and Speaker/Emmet does not recognise his defeat. He finally gets to deliver his speech, a mock eulogy of Dublin as 'Strumpet City' ending with the lines: 'There now. Let my Epitaph be written.'

Johnston was warned that the play would be seen as anti-national, but in the event he was not subjected to the same assault as that on O'Casey. True, 'nearly every night indignant women' walked out during the last act, though it seems from prudery rather than political objections. For he had treated Dublin as a whore and offended the Irish-Irelanders by calling Ireland's children 'bastard brats' of mixed ancestry.[38] Why he escaped so lightly puzzled him. Perhaps it was the absence of an O'Casey-like attack on the 1916/Pearse origin-myth. Perhaps it was the satire of the treatyite state that would not have displeased the republicans. There would be many more plays in this critical vein, though never such a devastating attack as Johnston's on the Emmet legend and the kind of Ireland it had helped produce.

Was this the end of Emmet's popular appeal? The answer is not at all. This was simply another level; a token of how representative Emmet was of the rebel myth. Otherwise the traditional legend continued to dominate representations of Emmet into the 1960s. In the plays of the south Pearse is often depicted as having completed Emmet's work. The one such play to come out of the north was Seamus McKearney's *Robert Emmet*, first staged in St Mary's Hall, Belfast, in 1957 and then toured round nationalist venues elsewhere in Northern Ireland. This is the stereotypical legend. It is Emmet betrayed by his own, the drunken rabble in Dublin, the informers and villains, Sirr and above all MacNally and the finale is the 'Judas' kiss of the latter. It must surely have been this play that Bishop Edward Daly recalls being staged in Tyrone, the 'villains' of the trial scene being so hissed and booed that the intimidated actors of the jury returned a verdict of not guilty, thereby excising the highlight of the production, the speech.[39]

III

The Gate Theatre was founded by Micheál MacLiammóir and his life-long partner Hilton Edwards. MacLiammóir was to become independent Ireland's most legendary actor, known to thousands outside the narrower confines of the Gate through his many radio broadcasts and recordings. He was cast as Emmet in *The Old Lady* and Nicholas Grene thinks it would have been a perfect vehicle for his characteristic histrionics and flamboyance.[40] Yet the Emmet that became most associated with his name was the traditional one of the legend. It was from MacLiammóir's recording of the speech that Bernadette Devlin and many others learnt to recite it at various festivals and school events.[41] In the same year that *The Old Lady* was staged, MacLiammóir wrote a traditional Emmet pageant (*The Ford of the Hurdles*). The legend was well suited to the real-life Michael Dempseys and the explosion of amateur dramatics in the 1940s and 1950s. Irish audiences for the most part wanted the familiar story of Robert Emmet: the romance, the noble sacrifice, the villains and betrayers. After all the famous picture of Emmet, his plumed hat held aloft, was still displayed into the fifties, and possibly longer. Like rural societies generally, Ireland's did not alter its interior decor frequently.

The persistent influence of this picture and the ballad 'Bold Robert Emmet' on popular perceptions of Robert Emmet is remarkable. My mother recalls both in her recollections of childhood in Co. Kerry in the 1930s. A celebrated account of the memories of Malachi Horan of Co. Dublin, first published in 1943, likewise testifies to the impact of these two aids to popular memory. Pointing to a house where Emmet stopped after the rising and recalling a Protestant farmer who was said to have betrayed him, Horan's recollections become interspersed with lines from the ballad. 'Ay, poor Mr Bob Emmet – the darlin' of Erin. May God be good to him.' And later in the conversation: 'You want to hear about Emmet again, sir? But, sure, it is little enough I know; except what is in the ballad.' He recalled the 'shocking dressing-down' he received from Anne Devlin after the defeat. 'And a handsome figure he must have been that day, what with his green coat, white breeches and cocked hat; his sword hanging from his hip. Ah, bold Robert Emmet!'[42] Unsurprisingly, the Robert Emmet Benefit Society, when established in Dublin in 1930, chose as jacket illustration for its rulebook this popular picture of Emmet, flanked by an Irish wolfhound, round tower and Celtic cross.[43]

The nineteenth-century-created Emmet legend has continued to hold pride of place in what the *Irish News* termed 'the romantic drama of Irish history',[44] defying the overall rethinking of Irish history since the 1930s, and, more surprisingly the Northern Ireland Troubles. Reviews of every work on Emmet were respectful of the man, even if the work being reviewed was criticised. The trend for female writers to be particularly impressed by the Emmet legend also continued, although the effusiveness of Catriona MacLeod's 1935 *Robert Emmet* gave way to some rather good works by women in the later decades of the century. The belated recognition of the maleness of 'the romantic drama of Irish history' has begun to privilege the Anne Devlin legend above that of Emmet, and he appears as a weak, if noble, creature in Pat Murphy's film of 1984. Why not Sarah Curran, whose letters reveal a much stronger personality than the wistful creation of Moore? Was it because her marriage to an English army officer rather destroyed that image as Irish heroine? Why in the 1950s did Major MacMullan fail to find a publisher for his edition of Sarah Curran's letters, which would have shown that she had a perfectly loving marriage with Sturgeon?[45]

As I was drawing this book to its conclusion, I asked a number of Irish people (in ages ranging from twenty-one to eighty-eight) when and what they had first heard about Robert Emmet. The continuing traces of the legend in living memory, even among the younger, are astonishing. Dubliners still associate Emmet and Sarah Curran with Rathfarnham, Harold's Cross, St Catherine's church, as do the local guidebooks.[46] Outside Dublin most people consulted recalled what they had been taught (or heard) in primary school. A number remembered the speech being recited on much the same kind of occasion as that described by Bernadette Devlin. From Donegal came the recollection of a cartoon strip about Emmet in an Irish-language magazine. A particularly strong impression was made by a Co. Clare teacher in a national school of the early 1970s: 'We were told that he was a young man who laid down his life for Ireland and that he was a true patriot. We were also told about the wonderful speech he made on the scaffold before he was hung, drawn and quartered [as in 'Bold Robert Emmet' — indeed, this aggravated punishment was mentioned by a number of those consulted]; that his girlfriend Anne Devlin had been tortured by the British rather than reveal his hideout, that although the rising had no chance of succeeding, he was one of the very few patriots with guts enough to oppose the Union and was perceived as braver than Tone, meeting his death rather than committing suicide.'

Although Tone was by now the most influential of the patriot dead, distaste for his suicide was common in post-independence Ireland. This informant had a very good recall of the schoolbook used, which contained black and white sketches of Anne Devlin's torture and Emmet delivering his speech. Those with grandparents and families that had been divided by the civil war recall Emmet being more revered by the anti-treatyites, which partly explains the reluctance of successive governments to make much of Emmet thereafter. Those with hazier recollections still knew about his speech, his execution in Thomas Street, the loss of the body, and, undoubtedly as a result of Pat Murphy's film, the details of Anne Devlin's story.

Emmet is largely absent from the litany of dead heroes cited by northern republicans, although he is still there in the background as a representative icon that good republicans are expected to know about. Indeed, nearly all of the later ballads that mention Emmet come from the North, not least one written by Bobby Sands, the first IRA republican hunger striker to die in 1981.[47] There is also a continuing interest in the villains and informers of the legend in the republican press[48] while, at the height of the Troubles, songs about Emmet still had the power to fire the imaginations of other young men like himself. Henry Glassie's magnificent study of a community on the Fermanagh–Cavan border tells of such an occasion, in the late 1970s/early 1980s, when songs linking Tone and Emmet to the ongoing 'fight our fathers fought' visibly moved a young IRA man. The singer had memorised Emmet's speech from the dock and sneered at 'coward and tyrant' as he went through the litany of the martyred dead.[49]

The Northern Ireland Troubles caused a similar rethink about traditions of violence as that which had occurred after 1923. By now the Irish Republic had joined the EEC and was rapidly emerging from its past isolationism, laying the basis for the 'Celtic Tiger' of the 1990s.

There was an ongoing debate about the kind of nation.
Emmet and his like represented and considerable unease at re.
of the unfinished business of the North. There was little made
bicentennial of Emmet's birth in 1978, besides some revival of interest in the lost grave. Even Dr Emmet's great-grandson now found it
necessary to re-interpret the message of the famous speech. 'The only
interpretation I can put on freedom is peace. Not peace among politicians, but peace among people; that Ireland will be free when we can
live together in peace. So I don't think Emmet's epitaph can be written, no. The time is not yet right.'[50] Anthony Cronin — one of the
most influential literary critics of the last century — wrote one of the
more informed reflections during the 1978 bicentennial. He opens in
dismissive mode, referring to those popular *aide-mémoires* to the legend, the ballad 'Bold Robert Emmet', the popular illustration, 'when
he hung in his green cut-away coat and white pantaloons on every
cottage wall'. But 'heroism', 'romanticism' and 'martyrdom' were not
topics to be applauded in this the most vicious decade of the Northern Ireland Troubles, and Cronin thought that few really wanted to
hear much about this apparently most incompetent of conspirators.
Then he contrasted Emmet's public statements with those of the
careerist lawyers and the bought press of 1803 and wondered if the
heroic legend did justice to the man. Three years earlier, in a postgraduate thesis, I had asked the same question. Legends distort and
are usually far removed from the reality. However, if I have shown anything in this book, it is the power of the simple image to sustain an entire tradition of blood sacrifice, the ease with which young men could
be inspired to follow in Emmet's footsteps, given the right climate,
and the overlap of the romantic and the militant. Irish nationality has
consisted disproportionately of the celebration of heroic sacrifice and
legends like that of Robert Emmet. Is it perhaps fear of what would be
left that deters many from questioning such legends?

Today Ireland is reinventing itself as a modern-world nation and
has come through a lengthy reconsideration of its past in the process.

Yet no one to my knowledge has questioned the Emmet legend. The bicentennial celebrations planned for 2003 show that it is as strong as ever and the sources cited are still those recycling the likes of Moore and Whitty. Dying stoically is not the same as heroic sacrifice. The former is real; the latter is legend. Poet Eavan Boland (b.1944) recalls how, as an intense teenager, she had been captivated by the Emmet legend. Largely raised outside Ireland because of her diplomat father's postings, she had imagined the Irish nation, rather than directly experienced it. The imagined nation was disproportionately defined by the songs of Thomas Moore and the images of gibbets on the skyline. Emmet had been 'the exemplary hero'. At the age of sixteen, when she returned to Dublin, she found the 'city marked with buildings, corners, alleyways where a hero had died; a point had been proved'. But, as she reflected outside St Catherine's church on the grim detail of the execution scene, she began to realise how much had been invention.

> And this is where, outside St Catherine's church, before
> my eyes and the eyes of that teenager, Robert Emmet
> disappears. He vanishes into soft words, garbled accounts
> of his speech from the dock. He becomes legend and
> excuse. He drifts in a slow haze of half-truths, into
> memories that are neither clear nor accurate. He
> becomes romantic fable and nationalist invention. And so
> in doing, he describes the typical trajectory of the
> nationalist hero: from action to image. From event to
> invention ... Tom Moore has turned him into a soft
> option ... Emmet became a fiction. Into that fiction were
> subsumed all the awkwardness, all the untidy events of
> conspiracy ... a dark violence blurred by Victorian
> sentiment.[51]

Notes

List of abbreviations and short forms

Short titles for books and abbreviations for journals and manuscripts are used in the notes. Please refer to the Bibliography for full references to the books and the following list for journals and MS sources.

AAE	Archives des Affaires Étrangères, Paris
AN	Archives Nationales, Paris
BCL	Belfast Central Library
BL	British Library, London
BNL	*Belfast News Letter*
CPA	Correspondance Politique: Angleterre, AAE
DEP	*Dublin Evening Post*
Hants	Hampshire Record Office
IFC	Irish Folklore Commission, University College, Dublin
IHS	*Irish Historical Studies*
NAI	National Archives of Ireland, Dublin
NLI	National Library of Ireland
PRO	Public Record Office, London
PRONI	Public Record Office of Northern Ireland, Belfast
RIA	Royal Irish Academy, Dublin
SHAT	Service Historique de l'Armée des Terre, Vincennes
SOC	State of the Country Papers, NAI
TCD	Trinity College, Dublin

Introduction

1. Madden, *The United Irishmen*, 3rd ser., iii, 300, 'Arbour Hill', named after the place in Dublin where a number of the executions took place in 1798.

2. The literature is voluminous and often unhelpfully jargonistic. Paul Connerton's *How Societies Remember* (Cambridge, 1989) provides an overview and there is an impressive and readable array of studies by scholars working on Ireland, not least McBride, ed., *History and Memory in Modern Ireland*, Leerssen, *Remembrance and Imagination*, and Foster, *The Story of Ireland*.
3. Ernest Renan, *Qu'est-ce qu'une nation?*, in *Oeuvres Complètes*, i, 892.
4. *Irish News*, 31 December 1948.
5. 'The United Irishmen and France, 1793–1806' (Oxford Univ. D.Phil thesis, 1975); Elliott, *Partners in Revolution*.
6. Ó Súilleabháin, *A Handbook of Irish Folklore*, xxix, 521.
7. [Whitty], 'Robert Emmet and his Contemporaries'.
8. Carlyle, *On Heroes, Hero-Worship and the Heroic in History*, 154,165.
9. George Dangerfield, *The Strange Death of Liberal England*, 2nd edition (London, 1966) 62–3 – I owe all of this to the acute observations of Owen Dudley Edwards.
10. Very popular 1878 ballad composed by John Boyle O'Reilly, Fenian and editor of the *Boston Pilot*.

Chapter 1

1. *Memoirs of the Life and Times of the Rt. Hon. Henry Grattan*, iv, 356–9.
2. Walsh, *Ireland Sixty Years Ago*, 158–9.
3. PRO, HO 100/75/130–34, information enclosed in Lord Lieutenant Camden to Home Secretary Portland, 26 February 1798, and HO 100/71–4, showing that Fitzgibbon alone of the Irish 'cabinet' was given access to the secret intelligence from France.
4. PRO, HO 100/75/213–14, Camden to Portland, enclosing the list of those arrested, 12 March 1798.
5. Taken from a masterly biography by Kavanaugh, *John Fitzgibbon, Earl of Clare*, 170.
6. Walsh, *Ireland Sixty Years Ago*, 159.
7. For Egan see TCD, Mun V/23/4/117, Entrance Books, 1769–1825; also Burtchaell and Sadleir, eds., *Alumni Dublinenses*, 260 – neither says whether Egan was a Catholic.
8. His journal is extracted in Maxwell, *A History of Trinity College Dublin, 1591–1892*, 257–80.

9. Walsh, *Ireland Sixty Years Ago*, 167–8; *Memoirs, Journal, and Correspondence of Thomas Moore*, i, 61–6.

10. Agnew, ed., *The Drennan–McTier Letters*, i, 306.

11. Whitelaw, *An Essay on the Population of Dublin*, 50–56 : Maxwell, *Dublin under the Georges*, Chap. V; Elliott, *Wolfe Tone*, 17–18; Hill, *From Patriots to Unionists*, 197–200; Smyth, *The Men of No Property*, 122–4.

12. Emmet, *Memoir of Thomas Addis Emmet and Robert Emmet*, i, 181–2; *Drennan–McTier Letters*, i, 520.

13. Budd and Hinds, *The Hist and Edmund Burke's Club*, 20–21.

14. She never married and died *c*.1827, Madden, *The United Irishmen*, 2nd ser., ii, 3; TCD, MS 873/562, notice of Christopher Temple Emmet.

15. *Memoirs of the Life and Times of the Rt. Hon. Henry Grattan*, iv, 356–7; 'Dr. Madden's Life of Emmet', *Dublin University Magazine*, xxviii (December 1846), 682–4.

16. *Drennan–McTier Letters*, i, 349.

17. TCD, Mun V/25/3/192–215 and 4/2; Keane, Phair, and Sadleir, eds., *King's Inns Admission Papers, 1607–1867*, ix, 153.

18. Madden, *United Irishmen*, 3rd. ser., iii, 4–5.

19. Landreth, *The Pursuit of Robert Emmet*, 111; PRO, HO 100/86/301–2, Information given by Thomas Wright, enclosed in Castlereagh to Wickham, 1 May 1799.

20. Moore, *Memoirs*, i, 62–3.

21. McDowell and Webb, *Trinity College Dublin 1592–1952*, 75–6; Elliott, *Wolfe Tone*, 19–21.

22. Emmet, *Memoir*, ii, facing p. 3.

23. Dagg, *The College Historical Society*, 72; Maxwell, *History of Trinity College Dublin*, 143–6; Budd and Hinds, *The Hist and Edmund Burke's Club*, 30–35.

24. Moore, *The Life and Death of Lord Edward Fitzgerald*, 189.

25. Moore, *Irish Melodies*, vii.

26. NAI, 620/11/129/16, information of John Doyle who identified Emmet in Kilmainham as the man they called General; Madden, *United Irishmen*, 3rd. ser., 2nd edn, iii (1860), 336–7.

27. Emmet, *Memoir*, ii, 8–9.

28. Moore, *Memoirs*, i, 58.

29. The relevant registers are TCD, Mun V/5/5, Registers of the Board; see Mun V/27/2, Michaelmas term, 1781, Tone censured for non-attendance at lectures, and Mun V/5/3, May 1781, Emmet censured for absence without leave; Mun V/5/4, Censures – there is no mention of Robert Emmet.

30. Madden, *United Irishmen*, 3rd. ser., iii, 6–7. The emphasis is Madden's. On Lefroy, see Maxwell, *Trinity College,* Dublin, 143–4.

31. Moore, *Lord Edward Fitzgerald*, 189–90.

32. Sadleir, ed., *An Irish Peer on the Continent, 1801–1803,* 54.

33. Account of the 1798 visitation taken from TCD, MSS 1203, 3363 and 3373; Maxwell, 'Sources in Trinity College Library Dublin, for researching the 1798 Rebellion', 3–22; *DEP*, 24–28 April 1798; Strong, *The Minstrel Boy*, 52–4; Moore, *Memoirs*, i, 61–6; Walsh, *Ireland Sixty Years Ago,* 157–73.

34. NAI, 620/11/130/60, Marsden to Flint, 30 November 1803.

35. *DEP*, 17–26 May 1798.

36. Fitzpatrick, '*The Sham* Squire'. His *Secret Service Under Pitt*, is more restrained: 58, n.2, 'There were informers from the first, but not to the extent suggested … it was not until 1798, when ropes were round their necks' that some turned.

37. Elliott, *Partners in Revolution*, 64, 73; NAI, 620/10/121/1–161, his information, 1794–1802; Phair and Sadleir, *King's Inns Admissions*, 316.

38. *Memoirs and Correspondence of Viscount Castlereagh*, i, 336 also 329–30, 347–72. For the prisoners' accounts, see Teeling, *Sequel to the History of the Irish Rebellion of 1798*, 352–76; MacNeven, *Pieces of Irish History*, 142–73. Some of the prisoners felt the execution of Byrne on 26 July should have stopped their negotiations. Cornwallis had been overruled in wanting to delay the execution. But it brought the remaining prisoners (including O'Connor) to endorse the negotiations in return for a respite of Bond's execution. For the continuing dispute between Emmet and O'Connor, see BL, Add. MS 33,106/79–84, TCD, MS 873/557, Madden, *United Irishmen*, 2nd ser., i, 154–60, 164–5, and ii, 100–106; and PRO, PC1/44/A.161, for John Chamber's disillusionment.

39. *Castlereagh Corr.*, i, 350–51.

40. MacNeven, *Pieces of Irish History*, i–ix, 235–48.

41. *Castlereagh Corr.*, i, 414.

42. MacNeven, *Pieces of Irish History*, 243; Madden, *United Irishmen*, 2nd. ser., ii, 77–113.

Chapter 2

1. PRONI, D.1748, Robert Tennent to Margaret Tennent, 24 April 1800.

2. NAI, 620/3/32/19, Pollock's information, 29 December 1798.

3. Madden, *United Irishmen*, 3rd ser., iii, 300–301.

4. Fitzpatrick, *The Sham Squire*, 149–50; *Castlereagh Corr.*, i, 217–20, 255, 261; NAI, 620/3/32/13 and 620/18A/11 pt.2, early information from McGucken; PRONI, D.607/G, for MacNally's new ineffectiveness.

5. NAI, 620/8/72/2, 'Booklet containing causes for UI failure 1798, and new organisation drawn from the lessons of that 1799'.

6. AAE, CPA, 592/386–7, memorandum presented to the Directory by Hugh O'Hanlon, 15 July 1799; copy in AAE, Mem. et Doc., 53/266–73.

7. PRO, HO 100/86/195–6, Castlereagh to Wickham, 26 March 1799.

8. Information about the new organisation from NAI, 620/7/74/1–22, 620/8/72/2, 620/47/100, PRO, HO 100/86/301–2 and AAE, CPA, op.cit.

9. Landreth, *Pursuit of Robert Emmet*, 115.

10. PRO, PC 1/44/A.161, correspondence concerning Fort George, particularly that of Thomas Addis Emmet, September–October 1799.

11. NAI, 620/49/38, J. King to Marsden, 29 August 1800.

12. PRO, HO 100/87/5–7, Castlereagh to Portland, 3 June 1799.

13. Elliott, *Partners in Revolution*, 258, 269.

14. NAI, 620/49/38, J. King to Marsden, 29 August 1800.

15. NAI, 620/11/130/26, secret information, 31 August 1803.

16. NAI, 620/11/130/20, secret information, 31 August 1803.

17. AAE, CPA 594/150, Talleyrand to the First Consul, 6 January 1801.

18. NAI, 620/10/118/17, McGucken to Cooke, 14 October 1801.

19. *Cornwallis Corr.*, iii, 390.

20. Emmet, *Memoir*, ii, 27.

21. Madden, *United Irishmen*, 3rd ser., iii, 25.

22. Emmet, *Memoir*, ii, 27.

23. Baronness d'Haussonville, *Robert Emmet*.

24. Wilmot, *Irish Peer on the Continent,* 54; NAI, 620/130/43, secret information, 2 October 1803, Emmet 'lived very privately at Paris'.

25. NAI, 620/12/146/30, Emmet to Patten, 7 August 1802.

26. Emmet, *Memoir*, ii.

27. SHAT, MR 1420/42, Humbert to the Minister for War, 23 October 1800.

28. NAI, 620/12/146, Patten's papers seized in August 1803, 'Remittances made to Robert Emmet'.

29. MacDonagh, *The Viceroy's Postbag*, 259–60.

30. TCD, MS, 873/557, documents on the dispute, supplied by John Sweetman; NAI, 620/12/143, correspondence between O'Connor and MacNeven, June 1802.

31. NAI 620/12/146/30, Emmet to Patten, 7 August 1802.

32. Emmet *Memoir*, i, 331–4; Madden, *United Irishmen*, 3rd. ser., iii, 21–7.

33. AAE, CPA 601/54, MacNeven to [Bonaparte], 11 January 1803; Elliott, *Partners in Revolution*, 299–300.

34. TCD, MS 873/638, Russell to John Templeton, 5 June 1802.

35. Information enclosed in PRO, HO 100/114/113, Wickham to King, 24 October 1803.

36. There is a very interesting garbled account 620/64/147, from William Corbet, who had been in Kilmainham (not the ex-TCD student), that money had been offered by France, that if their object could be obtained without invasion that Ireland would be independent, but in the event of invasion Ireland and France would be connected. I am fairly sure this is picking up on what is being said.

Chapter 3

1. Iremonger, 'Wrap up my green jacket', 26. This play was produced by Louis MacNeice for BBC radio, 3 February 1947.

2. Howell, *State Trials*, xxviii, 1177. See also Hope's statement to this effect in Madden, *United Irishmen*, 3rd ser., iii, 99. PRO, HO 100/113/143, examination of John Russell, 17 September 1803.

3. For Thomas Emmet's plans to go to America, see BL, Add. MS 33,110/209–10, Emmet to Dr Curry (Guy's Hospital London), 5 December 1802; Emmet, *Memoir*, ii, 26–7.

4. *Drennan–McTier letters*, iii, 87, also p.124.

5. Various on Long in NAI, 620/11/130/152, 620/11/138/3, 620/14/187/11; Elliott, *Partners in Revolution*, 278–9.

6. PRO, HO 100/114/179–84, examination of Michael Quigley (enclosed in Hardwicke's letter of 15 November 1803).

7. PRO, HO 100/122/220, Marsden to J. King, 16 May 1804; and for Hamilton's financial difficulties in France, AN, F[15] 3511, correspondence between Hamilton, Lewins and the French Ministers for Foreign Affairs and the Interior, November 1799 – October 1801; NAI, 620/14/195, Notes on William Henry Hamilton, 1803.

8. Elliott, *Partners in Revolution*, 175–6; *Castlereagh Corr.*, i, 409.

9. For Allen see NAI, 620/36/56; PRO, TS 11/122/33; Elliott, *Partners in Revolution*, 182, 185, 289, 319.

10. For Dowdall see NAI, 620/11/138/3, examination of Ross McCann, 11 August 1803; 620/36/227, 'J.W.' (MacNally), to Cooke, 17 October 1797; PRO, HO 100/112/158–72, his papers taken in August 1803, including his correspondence with Grattan; *Memoirs of the Life and Times of the Rt. Hon. Henry Grattan*, iv, 407–26.

11. Elliott, *Partners in Revolution*, 282–97; Elliott, 'The "Despard Conspiracy" reconsidered', *Past and Present*, 75 (1977), 46–61.

12. AN, F⁷ 7459, Hamilton, President of UI refugees to the Minister of Police, 5 July 1800; AAE, CPA 592/409, Central committee of UI in Paris to the Minister of Foreign Affairs, 13 September 1799; Woods, *Journals and Memoirs of Thomas Russell, 1791–95*, 130–32, 142, 144.

13. PRONI, D.272/39, Marsden to General Nugent, 21 August 1798.

14. *Castlereagh Corr.*, i, 397–9; also PRONI, D.3030/302, 'Secret information relative to Ireland'.

15. 100/113/103, Note on J. Farrell August 1802 and 100/114/113, information on Hamilton, in Wickham to King, 24 October 1803.

16. For the disturbances see NAI, SOC, 1025/29 and 620/50/1; PRO, HO 100/112/13–18; also *Castlereagh Corr.*, iv, 325; NAI 620/12/155, the Manifesto of the Provisional Government shows how much store they placed on these disturbances, Madden,*United Irishmen*, 3rd. ser., iii, 307.

17. PRO, HO 100/114/61, Hamilton to King, 6 November 1803 and HO 100/115/175–92, draft report on Emmet's Rebellion.

18. SHAT, B¹⁴/5, War Ministry correspondence January–June 1803, shows something of a phony war taking place at this time and considerable military movements around the French coasts – CPA 600/266, Talleyrand to Whitworth, 25 March 1803, very angry letter about the landing of brigands on French territory and the story circulating in the London papers about sinking of several ships carrying 100,000 stand of arms for Ireland and flying the UI flag.

19. NAI, 620/11/135 and PRO, HO 100/114/179–84, Michael Quigley's statements, November 1803; 100/114/199–200, Kiernan's examination; also on Hamilton, 620/13/168/1, and 620/14/194–5.

20. NAI, 620/11/130/44, statement of Thomas Frayne, October 1803.

21. Madden, *Antrim and Down in '98*, 142–3; Elliott, *Partners in Revolution*, 249; Byrne, *Notes of an Irish Exile*, 251, 260–62.

22. Howell, *State Trials*, xxviii 1178–84.

23. Byrne, *Notes of an Irish Exile*, 257–8, 268–9; and Madden, *United Irishmen*, 3rd ser., iii, 127–35.

24. PRO, FO 27/70, secret intelligence from France, 20 August 1803.

25. BL, Add. MS 35,708/127–8, Hardwicke to Wickham, 11 March 1803; Hants 38M49/5/31, Marsden's correspondence with Wickham, March 1803.

26. Byrne, *Notes of an Irish Exile*, 264–5.

27. For his mission see AN, AF IV 1672/2/202, NAI, 620/11/130/67–8 and Hants 38M39/5/29.

28. Howell, *State Trials*, xxviii, 1223–5, testimony of Edward Wilson.

29. NAI, 620/11/129/16, information of John Doyle, 31 August 1803; Howell, *State Trials,* xxviii, 1122, 1139–41, 1148; Quinn, *Soul on Fire*, 176; *BNL*, 25 October 1803.

30. PRO, HO 100/114/19, Wickham to R. Pole Carew, 5 October 1803.

31. Madden, *United Irishmen*, 3rd. ser., iii, 303–17; NAI, 620/12/155, papers found at the Thomas Street depot; and Hope (TCD, MS 7256/10) on the property issue.

32. Howell, *State Trials*, xxviii, 1285–7; *The Diary and Correspondence of Charles Abbot, Lord Colchester*, i, 450; NAI, 620/11/138/11, Farrell's information 3 September 1803; PRO, HO 100/113/181–3, Wickham to Pole Carew, 25 September 1803, on the doubts among the Wexford men.

33. *Castlereagh Corr.* iv, 333–4; NAI, 620/11/138/11, Farrell's information; Howell, *State Trials*, xxviii, 711–14, evidence of Edward Wilson, magistrate and chief peace-officer in the workhouse division.

34. NAI, 620/11/135 and 620/11/138/11, statements of Quigley and Farrell.

35. Howell, *State Trials*, xxviii, 720, evidence of Wheeler Coultman of the 9th regiment.

36. Howell, *State Trials*, xxviii,1136.

37. TCD, MS 873/583, narrative of John Fisher, 10 April 1854.

38. NAI, 620/11/129/17, information of Sylvester Costigan, 1 September 1803.

39. NAI, 620/11/129/14, information of Richard Wornall, 30 August 1803; 620/11/138/45, Stafford's account, 4 December 1803.

40. Madden, *United Irishmen*, 3rd. ser., iii, 127–34 and Howell, *State Trials*, xxviii, 1183, and *Life of Curran*, 515–22.

41. Howell, *State Trials*, xxviii, 720–23, testimony of the officers who entered the depot; *DEP*, 27 August 1803; Landreth, *Pursuit of Robert Emmet*, 209–11.

42. *The Life and Correspondence of the Rt. Hon. Henry Addington, First Visc. Sidmouth*, i, 209.

43. MacDonagh, *Viceroy's Postbag*, 337.

44. Geoghegan, *The Irish Act of Union*, 205–6.

45. NAI, 620/67/63, Sirr to Marsden, 15 July 1803; Madden, *United Irishmen*, 3rd. ser., iii, 116, says they were seditious, one opposite Redmond's house on Coal Quay, another in Kevin St.

46. MacDonagh, *Viceroy's Postbag*, 292–3; see letter of John Croker, surveyor-general of the port of Dublin on the various commands and confusion among the defending forces that night, *Colchester Diary*, i, 434–6; Hants 38M49/5/27 and 30, for the panic in Wickham's letters August–September, also PRO, HO 100/113/149–50, little sense of relief that they had got off so lightly, rather this just the tip of the iceberg and a belief the French about to come quite unsustained by the French evidence.

47. TCD, MS 873/640, Russell to Frank McCracken, misdated 15 July 1803.

48. Quinn, 'In pursuit of the millennium: the career of Thomas Russell, 1790–1803' (NUI D.Phil thesis), 205.

49. NAI, SOC, 1023/3 and 35; NLI, MS 9553: Townley Hall Papers, 'Memorandums of the year 1803', entries for 23–27 July.

50. NAI, 620/11/129/5–7 and 620/11/130/5, for events outside Dublin, also SOC 1025/71, Denis Browne's report that the midlands quiet, whatever the wild rumours circulating.

51. See e.g. PRONI, T.2627/1/7, J. Pollock to Lord Hobart, 17 September 1803.

52. *Most Rev. Doctor Troy's Exhortation, addressed to the lower order of Roman Catholics of the Archdiocese of Dublin*, 24 July 1803.

53. Material on the 'violent Protestant feeling' about Emmet's rebellion is voluminous; for a representative selection see: *Cornwallis Corr.*, iii, 498–9, 505–7; PRONI, Redesdale Papers, T.3030/2–5; *Castlereagh Corr.*, iv, 298–313; *Colchester Diary*, i, 436–7; and BL, Add. MS 34,456/21 seq., correspondence between Redesdale and the Catholic Lord Fingall – and their exchange was printed, see RIA, Haliday Coll., vol. iii, pamphlets 871/1–17; *Dropmore MSS,* vii, 188; MacDonagh, *Viceroy's Postbag*, 306–26; PRONI, T.3030/2–3 and 7, Redesdale's correspondence. For Cornwallis's return see Hants 38M49/1/45, Wickham to Addington, 22 August 1803; PRO, HO 113/57–64, examination of Troy about confession.

Chapter 4

1. See, e.g., Madden, *United Irishmen*, 3rd ser., iii, 95; Emmet, *The Emmet Family*, 143; Landreth, *Pursuit of Robert Emmet*, vii–ix. But the accusation is made in most of the popular accounts.

2. *Colchester Diary,* i, 443.

3. *Dropmore MSS*, vii, 180.

4. *Parliamentary Debates*, i, 750, this was Castlereagh, but in private he was furious. *Colchester Diary*, i, 463, 487–91, showing attack on government continued into 1804.

5. *Parliamentary Debates*, i, 1690. French propaganda was saying much the same: *The Argus: or the London Review in Paris*, nos. 122–129 (August 1803).

6. Byrne, *Notes of an Irish Exile,* 284; Madden, *United Irishmen*, 3rd ser., iii, 177–8; and Finegan, *Anne Devlin*, 54–5.

7. Howell, *State Trials*, xxviii, 1137 and 1151; NAI, 620/11/129/16, information of John Doyle, of Ballinameece, Co. Dublin, 31 August 1803.

8. Madden, *United Irishmen*, 3rd ser., iii, 176ff.

9. NLI, Ir. 92.E43, ii: 'Emmet's Betrothed. Some Passages, in the Life Story of Sarah Curran. By One Who Knew Her', cutting from the *Irish Emerald*. Madden, *United Irishmen*, 3rd. ser., 2nd edn, iii, 529.

10. Hants 38M49/5/35/6–9, exchange of letters between Emmet and Wickham, 3–9 September 1803.

11. MacDonagh, *Viceroy's Postbag*, 358–9.

12. PRO, HO 100/113/237–8, Wickham to Pole Carew, 28 September 1803.

13. Hants 38/M49/5/29; MacDonagh, *Viceroy's Postbag*, 359.

14. TCD, MS 869/2/31–2, Wickham to Sirr, 2.00 p.m. Friday [9 September]. There was some controversy over whether any letters were taken by Sirr, see Sirr, *Sarah Curran's and Robert Emmet's Letters*, MacDonagh, in *Notes and Queries*, 10th. ser., iii, iv, Madden, *United Irishmen*, 3rd. ser., iii, 257–8.

15. *Life of Curran*, ii, 204–9.

16. MacDonagh, *Viceroy's Postbag*, 371–2; Howell, *State Trials*, xxviii, 775–806; *Life of Curran*, ii, 209–220.

17. PRO, HO 100/113/129, in Wickham to Pole Carew 14 September.

18. Hants 38M49/5/40/12, the Attorney General to Wickham, 18 September; 38M49/5/34/64, frantic note of Richard Curran, morning of 19 September, asking to see Wickham; Howell, *State Trials*, xxviii, 1124–5, her letters.

19. Hants 38M49/113/131–2, Wickham to Pole Carew, 15 September

20. Hants 38M49/5/35/7, Emmet to Wickham, 7 September 1803.

21. Howell, *State Trials*, xxviii, 1276–9, and Byrne, *Notes of an Irish Exile*, 271–2, 276–8, 282–3.

22. MacDonagh, *Viceroy's Postbag*, 402.

23. Moore, *Memoirs*, vi, 133–4.

24. *Colchester Diary*, i, 455, Wickham to Abbot, 22 September 1803.
25. Vance, 'Text and tradition: Robert Emmet's speech from the dock'; Madden, *United Irishmen*, 3rd. ser., 2nd edn, iii (1860), 556–63; speculation on a manuscript of the speech said to be in Emmet's handwriting, Dr Emmet in his 1915 *Memoir*, ii, 221–2, thought this implausible.
26. NLI, MS 4597, copy of a letter of R. Rainey.
27. RIA, Haliday 851/5c: *The Speech of Robert Emmet, Esq., at the Sessions-House, Green-Street, September, 1803* – this cheaply produced pamphlet has the version taken up by Plowden in 1806 and most nationalist versions thereafter.
28. Moore, *Memoirs*, vi, 172.
29. BL, Add. MS 34,456/32, Lees to Auckland, 19 September 1803.
30. *DEP*, 22 September 1803.
31. PRO, HO 100/113/171, Hardwicke to Charles Yorke, 20 September 1803.
32. Schwoerer, 'William Lord Russell: the making of a martyr, 1682–1983', 41–71.
33. Madden, *United Irishmen*, 3rd ser., iii, 273–5.
34. PRO, HO 100/113/171, op.cit; NAI, 620/11/133, Gamble to Marsden, 20 September; MacDonagh, *Viceroy's Postbag*, 404–6; Hammond, 'The Emmet Insurrection', 92–3.
35. See NLI, LO 1,047, for the commentary, NAI, 620/12/155, for the poem.
36. I am grateful to Dr. C. J. Woods for this latter observation; *DEP*, 22 and 24 September; NLI, MS 4597, the yeomanry was ordered to patrol the lanes around the court that night, suggesting that a rescue attempt was expected.
37. The original is in PRO, HO 100/113/203–6; there are also many copies, e.g. Hants MS 38M49/5/42, *Life of Curran*, ii, 521–2 (Curran's son says a 'friend' gave it to him … I think this MacNally); Howell, *State Trials*, xxviii, 1178–84.
38. Hants 38M49/5/29, Wickham to J. P. Curran, 21 September 1803. Copy of full letter in Hants 38M49/5/42, and HO 100/113/177, and BL, Add. MS 35,742/197. The original was sold at Sotheby's on 9 November 1954, lot 437.
39. Hants 38M49/5/34/65, Curran to Wickham, 21 September 1803.
40. 'Some passages in the history of Sarah Curran', in *The Literary Souvenir*, edited by Alaric A. Watts (London, 1831), 331–6. NLI, Ir 92. E.43, i, undated cutting, 'Emmet's Bethrothed. Some passages in the life story of Sarah Curran. By one who knew her'; this was endorsed by a later informant of Madden, *United Irishmen*, 3rd ser., 2nd edn (1860), 521 and 530.

41. Though most accounts argue her continued love for Emmet and a marriage in name only, see e.g. the *Nation*, 12 June 1858.

42. *The Literary Souvenir*, op cit., 342; MacMullen, *The Voice of Sarah Curran*.

43. PRO HO 100/114/5, Wickham to Pole Carew, 2 October 1803; also his private letter to Abbot, 22 September, immediately on receiving Curran's, on how he had worked himself to the bone to ensure all this, and his satisfaction that government critics had been silenced, *Colchester Diary*, i, 456.

44. PRO, HO 100/113/237–8, 'Secret', Wickham to Pole Carew, 28 September 1803.

45. *Life of Curran*, ii, 236–8.

46. PRO, HO 100/115/15–18, 'Most Secret', Wickham to King, 5 December 1803, also 100/113/199–200, 'Most Secret and Confidential', Wickham to Pole Carew, 14 September 1803.

47. Hammond, 'The Emmet Insurrection', 91–3.

48. BL, Add. MS 35, 742/196, Emmet to [Wickham], 20 September.

49. BL, Add. MS 34,456/33, Lees to Auckland, 20 September.

50. *DEP*, 22 September; broadside 'The Trial and Dying Behaviour of Mr R. Emmet', reproduced in Emmet, *Memoir*, ii, 217.

51. Madden, *United Irishmen*, 3rd ser., iii, 281; *Hibernian Jnl.*, 21 September; also NLI MS 4597, Rainey to his brother, 20 September

52. PRO, HO 100/113/171, Hardwicke to Yorke, 20 September

53. TCD, MS 873/583, narrative of John Fisher, 10 April 1854; Madden, *United Irishmen*, 3rd. ser., iii, 283.

54. *Drennan–McTier Letters*, iii, 198, 332–3. Mary Anne died 9 March 1805 after a lengthy illness.

55. Hants 38M/49/1/55–6, Wickham's correspondence, also letter to Armstrong, 20 November 1835, enclosing a copy of Emmet's last letter.

56. Madden, *United Irishmen*, 3rd ser., ii, 261–5; Quinn, 'In pursuit of the millennium', 192–205. *DEP*, 25 October, *BNL*, 28 October and 1 November 1803.

57. *Argus*, 6 August 1803.

58. *Argus*, 11 January 1804; AN, AF IV 1092/67–8, T. A. Emmet to General Berthier, 25 December 1803, and Berthier to the First Consul, 2 January 1804; Tissot, *Les Trois Conjurés Irlandais; ou L'Ombre d'Emmet*.

59. NLI, MS 33,565/3/11, O'Connell to his wife, 28 August 1803.

Chapter 5

1. Elliott, *Catholics of Ulster*, 139; Elliott, *Partners in Revolution*, 343; Ó hOgain, *The Hero in Irish Folk History*, 310; Zimmermann, *Songs of Irish Rebellion*, 175.

2. 'Dr Madden's Life of Emmet', *Dublin University Magazine*, xxviii, (December 1846), 681–702.

3. NAI, SOC 1030/92, 16 Feb 1804, report from Westmeath, that people had turned against the French because of Emmet's speech. Phillips, *Curran and his Contemporaries*, 3rd edn, 112.

4. See RIA, Haliday Coll., vol. 3, 840/4, 844/1–5, 845/4, 849/1–2, 850/1, 851/5–8, for a sample of the outpouring of pamphlet literature on the rebellion, trial and speech; BCL, 'The Trial and Dying Behaviour of Mr R. Emmett', contemporary handbill issued by the government.

5. Dowling, *The Hedge Schools of Ireland*, ch. viii; Adams, *Printed Word*, 12–20.

6. Hants 38M49/5/34, enclosed in W. Corbet to Wickham, 7 December 1803.

7. *Drennan–McTier Letters*, iii, 156–7, also 153 and 224–5.

8. Gamble, *Sketches of History, Politics and Manners in the North of Ireland in the Summer and Autumn of 1810*; Deane, ed., *The Field Day Anthology of Irish Writing*, i, 1108; MacNeven, *Pieces of Irish History*, 162; Madden, *United Irishmen*, 3rd ser., iii, 249–55; Cox's *Irish Magazine*, v (1812), 87–8.

9. Phillips, *Curran and his Contemporaries* (1850 edition), 311–14, 395–7 (also the 1822 edition, 235); Madden, *United Irishmen*, 3rd ser., iii, 249–55; Hoey, ed., *Speeches at the Bar and in the Senate, by the Right Honourable Wm. Conyngham, Lord Plunket*, is also critical, though otherwise laudatory, xiv–xv, 'that merciless speech for the Crown, in the case of Robert Emmet' was to 'cloud in an unaccountable hour his character as an Irish patriot'; Davis, ed., *The Speeches of the Rt. Hon. John Philpot Curran*, 424–5, 456–7; Cobbet's *Political Register*, 10 December 1803; *Irish Book Lover*, i (1909), 20, ii (1910), 195, iii (1911), 13 on Plunket's 'serpent' speech and belief that he did say it.

10. Phillips, *Recollections of Curran*, 234 – this edition also gives a very laudatory account of Emmet's trial and speech.

11. Curran, *The Life of the Right Honourable John Philpot Curran*, ii, 218–19.

12. NAI, 620/13/181/19, correspondence between Marsden and Bernard, May 1804; PRONI, T.3030/5/40, Hardwicke to Redesdale, 4 April 1805; and RIA, Haliday, vol. 3, 845/4, Fox, 879/1–7, 880/1–3, case of Judge Johnson.

13. *Parliamentary Debates,* v, 641, 793; also RIA, Haliday Coll., vol 3, 844/12,

849/6, 865/3, various pamphlets on the case of Todd Jones, detained 1803–5.

14. *Parliamentary Debates*, xx, 750, xxiii, 774–6; *British Sessional Papers,* 1805 (90), 471–98, Memorials of the State Prisoners confined in Kilmainham Gaol [June–July 1804]; Madden, *United Irishmen*, 3rd ser., iii, 200–224; NAI, Private Official Correspondence, VIII^A/1/4/92–3, Dublin's answers to queries from London concerning Mason; [Mason], *Pedro Zendono.Inquisitor of Kilmainham*, 2nd edn (Dublin, 1807); *Memoir of the Case of St John Mason, Esq., Barrister at Law*; also *Pedro Redivivus. Prison Abuses in Ireland, exemplified by documents, setting forth the oppressions and atrocities of Doctor Trevor, and his associates, as practised upon the State Prisoners of Kilmainham* ... selected by St John Mason, Esq.

15. Madden, *United Irishmen,* 3rd ser., iii, 176–87; NLI, MS 9761: 'The Life, imprisonment, sufferings and death of Anne Devlin the faithful House Keeper of Robert Emmet ...'; Finegan, *Anne Devlin.*

16. Cox's *Irish Magazine*, i (1808), 511–14, ii (1809), 44–5, 164–5, 188–9, v (1812), 86–8; Fitzpatrick, *Sham Squire*, 258–63; Inglis, *Freedom of the Press*, 123–5, 143–4; Curtin, *United Irishmen*, 225–7; *The Milesian Magazine*, 123–5, 143–4. I am inclined to Inglis's opinion that in his intermittent career as government informant he played them along, rarely giving information of any importance, see e.g. NAI, 620/3/32/28 (1798) and PRO, HO 100/136/38 (1806). Against Plunket Cox also cited MacNeven, *Pieces of Irish History*, 162: 'Plunket had been the bosom intimate of Emmet, the companion of his childhood and the friend of his youth'; RIA, Haliday Coll., vol. 3, 865/5, Cox's 1804 pamphlet.

17. See my discussion of this in *Catholics of Ulster*, 125ff.

18. Nairn, *The Break-up of Britain*, 340.

19. See e.g. Deane, ed., *Field Day Anthology*, ii, 4.

20. Sullivan, *Evergreen Volume of Irish Verses*, 46: 'Tom Moore' (written after reading some captious criticism of his poetry). Also Sullivan, *A Selection from the Songs and Poems of T. D. Sullivan*, 198–202, long poem on Moore, written at the request of the Tom Moore Literary Club of San Francisco for the Moore Centenary 28 May 1879, quite a powerful defence of how Moore praised people like Emmet and Lord Edward, when others were silent.

21. *Shamrock*, 21 March 1868, also issues 28 March, 4 April, 21 November, 19 December 1868.

22. Moore, *Memoirs*, vi, 228.

23. However, see Leerssen, *Remembrance and Imagination*, 80–87; Tom Dunne,

'One of the Tests of National Character: Britishness and Irishness in the Paintings of Maclise and Barry', in Stewart, ed., *Hearts and Minds*, 281–2.

24. Moore, *Memoirs*, iii, 207.

25. Irving, *The Sketch Book*, 123–8.

26. John Swanton, see AN, F^7 3751 and 7348.

27. Berlioz, *Memoirs*, 59.

28. John Crabbe, *Hector Berlioz. Rational Romantic* (London, 1980), 113–28. I am grateful to John Crabbe for drawing his study to my attention. I owe much of the above to the generosity of Ian Kemp in providing me with the typescript of his study of Berlioz's *Neuf Mélodies*. Cairns, *Berlioz*, vol. i, 344–9.

29. Vance, *Irish Literature*, 106.

30. Moore, *Memoirs*, iii, 275.

31. McCormack, *Sheridan Le Fanu*, 11.

32. *The Poetical Works of Robert Southey*, ii, 245–7, poem headed 'Written immediately after reading the speech of Robert Emmet, on his trial and conviction for high treason, Sept. 1803'; Storey, *Robert Southey*, 162–3.

33. Storey, *Robert Southey*, 146.

34. Warter, ed., *Selections from the Letters of Robert Southey*, i, 234; also *Dublin University Magazine*, xxviii, (December 1846), 681, on Southey and Emmet.

35. BCL, Bigger Coll. Z141 (1), cutting from a sale catalogue, A. L. S. to Mrs Smith, Stroud, Keswick, 2 February 1804.

36. Quoted by Timothy Webb, 'Coleridge and Robert Emmet: Reading the Text of Irish Revolution', *Irish Studies Review*, vol. 8, no. 3 (2000), 312.

37. Griggs, ed., *Coleridge, Collected Letters*, ii, 999, 1002.

38. Rogers, ed., *The Complete Poetical Works of Percy Bysshe Shelley*, i, 1802–1813: 98–9. Also his poem 'The Tombs', 114.

39. Holmes, *Shelley, The Pursuit*, 117–32.

40. Cameron, ed., *Shelley and his Circle 1773–1822*, iii, 110.

41. Jones, ed., *The Letters of Percy Bysshe Shelley*, i, 259; Holmes, *Pursuit*, 157.

42. Emmet, *Memoir*, i, 192–4; Paulin, *The Day-Star of Liberty*, 2.

43. [M. J. W.], *Robert Emmet*, iv–v; *Dublin and London Magazine*, i, 1825 (March, 71–9, May, 116–23, June, 167–73, July, 199–205, August, 257–63, September, 315–19, November, 414–19, December, 433–6). Apart from Madden, those works which I have identified as drawing directly on Whitty are Baronness d'Haussonville, *Robert Emmet*, John P. Leonard (her translator); *The Life, Trial and Conversations of Robert Emmet, Esq.*; *The Life and Actions of Robert Emmet, leader of the Insurrection of 1803* – essentially a reprint of the foregoing; Wakeman, *Graves and Monuments of Illustrious Irishmen*,

20–21. On Whitty see [D. J. O'Donohue], 'The Dublin and London Magazine', *The Irish Booklover*, viii, 53–5.

44. Bourke, 'The Rebellion of 1803. An Essay in Bibliography', 12; Adams, *The Printed Word and the Common Man*, 196.

45. Thackeray, *The Irish Sketchbook*, 24, 14.

46. Zimmermann, *Songs of Irish Rebellion*, 40–41, 75–8, 175–5; *Life, Trial and Conversations of Robert Emmet*, 61.

47. Dudley, *Emmett. The Irish Patriot; and other poems*, xxx, claiming to have authenticated the anecdotes.

48. Welch, ed., *The Oxford Companion to Irish Literature*, 161; *The Life and Actions of Robert Emmet, Leader of the Insurrection of 1803*.

49. I am grateful to Dr C. J. Woods for kindly making available to me his forthcoming article, 'R. R. Madden, historian of the United Irishmen'.

50. Moore, *Memoirs*, vii, 107– 8.

51. TCD MS 873/425, Moore to Madden, 4 January 1842.

52. RIA, MS 24.G.33, A Collection of Rare and Valuable pamphlets on Irish Affairs; Woods, 'R. R. Madden, historian of the United Irishmen'.

53. Falkiner, *Essays Relating to Ireland*, 119.

54. Madden, *United Irishmen*, 3rd ser., iii, 8, 98, 195–7, 288; Postgate, *Robert Emmet*, 254; Landreth, *The Pursuit of Robert Emmet*, 361–2; Emmet, *Memoir*, ii, 113–16, says Madden later changed his mind, and the search continued. Among other story lines taken by Madden from Whitty is Emmet's meeting Dwyer afterwards and dissuading the Wicklow men from attacking the towns, p. 192 – Anne Devlin (Finegan, p. 55) states specifically that Emmet refused to meet Dwyer after the failure; she also denies the accusations against Delaney, ibid. p. 39.

55. TCD, MS 873/277: obituary notice from the *Nation*, 27 September, 1851; MS 873/601, acknowledgement of receipt of ten shillings to Anne 'Devliny', 5 February 1847. Finegan, *Anne Devlin*, 134–9.

56. Madden, *United Irishmen*, 3rd ser., iii, 267–9; Madden, *Literary Remains of the United Irishmen*, 250–51.

57. Hammond, 'The Rev. Thomas Gamble and Robert Emmet', 100.

58. Madden, *United Irishmen*, 3rd ser., 2nd edn, iii (1860), 257–8.

59. Madden's *United Irishmen* (along with Moore's *Lord Edward Fitzgerald*) was listed as among the most popular reading matter borrowed from the Catholic Young Men's Society reading room in the 1880s – see Foster, *Paddy and Mr Punch*, 312, n.59.

60. Duffy, *Short Life of Thomas Davis*, 79.

61. Deane, ed., *Field Day Anthology*, i, 1279.
62. Quoted Leerssen, *Remembrance and Imagination*, 150.
63. NLI, MS 1791/1; Woods, 'R. R. Madden, historian of the United Irishmen'.
64. *Dublin University Magazine*, xxix (Jan. 1847), 82.
65. *Nation*, 18 July 1846.
66. Elliott, *Partners in Revolution*, 367–8.
67. Zimmermann, *Songs of Irish Rebellion*, 226–7.
68. See the masterly discussion of Ingram: Peatling, 'Who fears to speak of politics? John Kells Ingram and hypothetical nationalism', 202–21.
69. Baronness d'Haussonville, *Robert Emmet*, 1–8. It was translated by John Leonard. This latter was serialised in the *Shamrock*, nos. 1–26, October 1866 – March 1867; reviewed in the *Nation*, 6 February 1858; *Irish Book Lover*, xi, no. 8 (March 1920), 85. This went through twelve editions, including a chapbook version retailing at a shilling. It was typical of almost everything written about Emmet in being a compilation of Moore, Madden, Irving and Whitty.

Chapter 6

1. 'Madden, *United Irishmen*, 3rd ser., iii, 299–300, 'Arbour Hill'.
2. *Life and Actions of Robert Emmet*, 6.
3. *Irish People*, 19 September 1903.
4. Gilbert [Mary Lucy Arthur], *The Island of Sorrow. An Historical Novell 1797–1808*, 6–7; Reilly, 'Fictional histories', (D.Phil thesis, 1997), 90–91.
5. Wheeler, *Death and the Future Life in Victorian Literature and Theology*.
6. *Shamrock*, 7 March 1868 ; *Irish Fireside*, 12 August 1885; and an earlier version in Dudley, *Emmett, the Irish Patriot*.
7. *United Ireland*, 19 September 1903; NLI, MS 5181: Centenary Scrapbook, also Ir 92 E43, ii, undated newspaper cutting 'Robert Emmet, Robert Holmes, Sarah Curran and Anne Devlin'.
8. *Irish People*, 22 August 1903.
9. *Irish Weekly and Ulster Examiner*, 19 September 1903.
10. Evans, *Rituals of Retribution*, 273; Gatrell, *The Hanging Tree*, 316–21; *Parliamentary Debates*, 5 April 1813.
11. See e.g. *Nation*, 2 March 1878.
12. Gatrell, *The Hanging Tree*, 46.

13. Madden, *United Irishmen*, 3rd ser., iii, 282–3, and 2nd edn, iii (1860), 466–9.

14. Evans, *Ritual and Retribution*, 90–94.

15. Madden, *United Irishmen,* 2nd edn, iii (1860), 469.

16. My thanks to Tom Desmond of the National Library of Ireland for this.

17. BL, Add. MS 34, 456/33, Edward Lees to Auckland, 20 September 1803; *DEP*, 22 and 24 September 1803.

18. Emmet, *Memoir*, ii, 239.

19. Evans, *Ritual and Retribution*, 904.

20. The serialised story was the work of a number of authors, not all named. Male authors named are: John Augustus O'Shea, James G. Meagher, Lieut.-Col. W. Linam and Victor O'D. Power.

21. *Weekly Freeman*, 17 October 1891; M. MacDonagh, 'The Tragedy of Robert Emmet', *The Cornhill Magazine*, no. 87 (September 1903), 380–401.

22. NLI, Ir 92 E43, ii, 1902 newspaper cuttings concerning protests against the siting of an electric transformer.

23. Wheeler, *Death and the Future,* 343–8.

24. *Irish News*, 23 July 1903; it was serialised in the *Irish Weekly and Ulster Examiner,* 3 October–19 December 1903.

25. McCormack, ed., 'Irish Gothic and After (1820–1945)', in Deane, ed., *Field Day Anthology*, ii, 831; McCormack, *Sheridan Le Fanu and Victorian Ireland*, 60–75.

26. NLI, Ir 92 E43, ii, news cutting for May 1898; similar wording, Hand, *Robert Emmet*, 24; Sherlock, *Robert Emmet: the Story of his Life and Death* (price 3 pence), 27.

27. Bodkin, *True Man and Traitor: or the Rising of Emmet*, 10 – all the anecdotes taken from Madden.

28. *Wolfe Tone Memorial Association. Emmet Anniversary Celebration. Round Room, Mansion House, Tuesday, 7 March 1916*, 3.

29. See in particular Edwards, *Patrick Pearse: the Triumph of Failure*, 52–4, 126–8.

30. Moran, *Patrick Pearse and the Politics of Redemption*, 124.

31. 'How Does She Stand? Robert Emmet and the Ireland of Today', in *The Collected Works of Padraic H. Pearse. Political Writings and Speeches*, 64–87; *Wolfe Tone Annual*, 1941, 106; Pearse, ed., *The Home Life of Pádraig Pearse, as told by Himself, his Family and his Friends*, 7, 39 – this was first published in the Christian Brothers' youth magazine, *Our Boys,* 1926–7.

32. Pearse, *Collected Works,* 'How Does She Stand?', 70–71.

33. Ibid, 82.

34. *Wolfe Tone Annual*, 1941, 116.

35. *Leader*, 4 October and 27 December 1902; *Notes and Queries*, 9th ser., iii (1899), 349 and 472; *Cork Examiner*, 16 April 1856; *Irish Times*, 5 February 1912; TCD MS 873/611, 'statement … on the burial and tombstone of Sarah Sturgeon'.

36. 'Anne Devlin. A reminiscence of 1803', *The Celt*, no. 15, vol. I, Saturday 7 November 1857, 225–7.

37. Pearse, *Collected Works*, 'How Does She Stand?', 83–4.

38. *Weekly Freeman* Christmas number, 12 December 1903, by W. C. Mills; also pen drawings in *Weekly Independent*, 16 March 1895 onwards; Hester Piatt, 'Anne Devlin: an outline of her story', *Catholic Bulletin*, vii (August 1917), 498–503.

39. 'Anne Devlin's lament for Robert Emmet', by northern nationalist writer Anna Johnston (Ethna Carbery), *Shan Van Vocht,* 5 April 1897, 66.

40. *Wolfe Tone Annual*, 1941, 38–9.

41. Cox's *Irish Magazine*, ii (1809), 189; *The Emmet Song Book. Specially compiled for the Irish Patriot's Centenary*, 32.

42. *Evening Telegraph*, 3 September 1910; Reynolds, *Footprints of Emmet,* 96–97.

43. MacDonagh, 'The Tragedy of Robert Emmet', 399; *Irish Emerald*, 2 December 1899.

44. Sullivan, *Speeches from the Dock*, had also gone for the butcher's block, rather than the table.

45. *DEP*, 26 February 1802.

46. *DEP*, 3, 6, 8 and 10 September 1803; for Despard's and other executions for high treason, see *DEP*, 26 February 1803; the *Sun*, 20 February 1803, Gattrell, *Hanging Tree*, 298–321; Elliott, *Partners in Revolution*, 295–7.

47. A later informant of Madden's (1860 edn, 469) identified him, though no observer of the execution would have been able to do so. *Freeman's Journal*, 22 August 1878.

48. *Freeman's Journal*, 17 August 1878; *Ulster Examiner*, 13 August 1878.

49. *Nation*, 27 November 1858, Poet's Corner. 'The Grave in St Michan's'.

50. See e.g. *Shamrock or Hibernian Chronicle*, 15 December 1810, 16 February, 16 March, 3 August 1811; Wilson, *United Irishmen, United States*, 79; O hAodha, 'A List of Plays about Robert Emmet', *The Irish Book*, 53.

51. Moore, *Memoirs*, v (1828), 293.

52. On the former United Irishmen in the United States, see Madden, *United Irishmen*, 3rd ser., 2nd edn, iii (1860) 177– 213; TCD MS 873/521a, 560–68, 573.

53. BL, Add. MS 35,724/35, Marsden to Hardwicke, 20 September, asking if

he wanted to see them – 'they now wait at your door'; and 35,742/192–4, Hardwicke to Yorke, 20 September, on their report.

54. Hammond, 'Emmet Insurrection', 91–5; Madden, *United Irishmen*, 3rd ser., iii (1846), 284–6; and ibid, 2nd edn, iii (1860), 472–4.

55. TCD, MS 873/325, Robert Holmes to Madden, 22 November 1842.

56. *Drennan–McTier Letters*, iii, 333, also 769 for Drennan's contacts with the Holmeses during this period.

57. Madden, *United Irishmen*, 3rd ser., iii (1846), 284–5, and 2nd edn (1860), 471–6; Hammond, 'The Emmet Insurrection', 94–5; Emmet, *Ireland under English Rule*, i, 384–93; Sullivan, *Evergreen Volume of Irish Verses*, 189: 'the stone was much venerated' by Dubliners.

58. [W.Gregory], *The Picture of Dublin*, 175; also repeated in Warburton, Whitelaw and Walsh, *A History of the City of Dublin*, ii, 1049.

59. NLI, MS 24,267, 'Misc. items relating to the burial place of Robert Emmet' – though nothing here of another tradition of Emmet's head in TCD's medical school.

60. A. M. E. McCabe, 'The Medical Connections of Robert Emmet', *Irish Journal of Medical Science*, 6th ser. (April, 1963), 178–84; Emmet, *Memoir*, ii.

61. TCD, MS 6727/18 and 27, MS 6844/87, Emmet's correspondence with John Dillon.

62. *Irish Book Lover*, ii (1910), 92.

63. NAI, Dept. of the Taoiseach, S.2462; RIA, MS 23.K.62, correspondence Dr Emmet and J. F. Fuller; 'Emmet Note', *Cork Hist. and Arch. Soc. Jnl.*, 2nd ser. xxviii (1922), 111; *Thomas Addis Emmet, M. D. A Personal Tribute by the Revd John Cavanagh*, 16–18.

64. BCL, Bigger Coll., MS EM2/5, Emmet to David A. Quaid, 23 April 1903.

65. Emmet, *Ireland Under English Rule*, i, 293.

66. *National Hibernian*, 15 May 1913.

67. Fitzpatrick, *Sham Squire*, 298–301; NLI, MS 8077, Memorandum of Edward Lawlor, 1892.

68. Emmet, *Incidents of My Life*, 269.

69. *Weekly Independent*, 22 April and 13 May 1893; *United Irishman*, 8 and 22 April 1893.

70. BCL, Bigger Coll., Z140(3), Dr Emmet to Bigger, undated.

71. BCL, Bigger Coll., EM2/5: Emmet to Quaid, 23 April 1903 and EM2/6, for the travel arrangements.

72. Emmet, *Memoir*, ii, 287; RIA, MS 23.K.62/18, Mahaffy to Fuller, 12 October 1908.

73. *Irish Weekly and Ulster Examiner*, 26 September 1903; Dr Emmet's report on the findings had been published in the press the previous week, see *Irish People* and *Irish Weekly and Ulster Examiner*, both on 19 September 1903.

74. *Irish People,* 15 August 1903.

75. *Irish People*, 15 August 1903; Sullivan, *Evergreen Volume of Irish Verses*, 4–5, 189–90.

76. Barry, *The Mystery of Robert Emmet's Grave*, 58–63.

77. Reynolds, *In the Footprints of Emmet*, 86–106 (also his Banba art.); BCL., Bigger MSS, FUI/4–6, EM2/4 and RIA, MS 23.K.62/A(i)/9–15, 23; *Dublin Evening Mail*, 11 July 1905.

78. BCL, EM2/15, Dr Emmet to Bigger, 11 November 1912.

79. BCL, LE6 (1), Shane Leslie to Bigger, 5 March 1919.

80. BCL, LE9, Levins to Bigger, 29 January 1921, and LE6(1), Leslie to Bigger, 5 March 1919.

81. *Irish Times*, 25 July 1978; and correspondence it inspired, ibid, 28 July and 7 August 1978.

82. *Weekly Independent*, 13, May 1893.

83. Ó Broin, *The Unfortunate Robert Emmet*, 177–8. Also Robin Skelton's poem 'At Emmet's Grave', *Poetry Ireland* (Autumn, 1962), 20–21

84. Emmet, *Memoir*, ii, 260.

85. Emmet, *Incidents of My Life*, 269; Madden, *United Irishmen*, 3rd ser., iii, 298–9; Reynolds, *Footprints of Emmet,* 95; *Evening Telegraph*, 17 November 1906: 'Death masks of Irish Patriots'. Along with masks of Tone, Mitchell, O'Connell, it was displayed at an exhibition in the Gallery in November 1906.

86. *Derry People*, 26 September 1903; RIA, MS 23.K.62/A(i)/10, Quaid to Fuller, 12 August 1905 and MS 23.K.62/A(i)/8, 'W.A.' to Fuller claiming that the father of Dr Willis had taken the head.

87. *Irish Weekly and Ulster Examiner*, 19 September 1903.

88. *United Ireland*, 19 September 1903.

Chapter 7

1. *Shamrock*, 23 May 1868.

2. *Nation*, 2 March 1878.

3. *Irish Weekly Independent*, 2 March 1895.

4. NLI, Ir 92 E43, ii, cutting from the *Evening Telegraph* for 1902.

5. Fr Yorke's oration on Emmet in San Francisco, 2 June 1900 (NLI, Ir 92 E43, i, cutting from the *Weekly Freeman*); Lysaght, 'Norbury, "The Hanging Judge" (1745–1831)', 58–65.

6. I am grateful to Dr Daithí Ó hOgain for this information.

7. MacDonagh, 'The tragedy of Robert Emmet', 394–5.

8. *Evening Telegraph,* 3 September 1910; Sirr, *Sarah Curran's and Robert Emmet's Letters.*

9. J. Pope Hennessy, 'What do the Irish read', *The Nineteenth Century*, June 1884, 920; Foster, *The Irish Story*, 6–8

10. *Nation*, 21 December 1867, cited in Gary Owens, 'Constructing the martyrs: the Manchester executions and the nationalist imagination', in McBride, ed., *Images, Icons and the Irish Nationalist Imagination*, 23ff.

11. See Goldring, *Pleasant the Scholar's Life*, on this point, 43–56.

12. Sullivan, *Robert Emmet; Speeches from the Dock*, 31–49.

13. O'Leary, *Recollections of Fenians and Fenianism*, i, 80.

14. Blaazer, 'Sterling Identities', 16.

15. NLI, Ir 92 E43, untitled news cutting, 28 February 1878; Comerford, *Fenians in Context*, 74–9, though pointing out popular love of public display and turn-outs for a large number of occasions, including royal ones. Hill, *Irish Public Sculpture*, 265, n.181.

16. Owens, 'Constructing the martyrs', 18–36; Comerford, *Fenians in Context,* 147–50. NLI, Ir 92 E43, ii, untitled news cutting, October 1869, 'able and manly lecture on the Life and Times of Emmet' by Mr Kirk to the Drogheda Young Men's Society, goes into the clouds with angry high-flown rhetoric against tyranny, aristocracy, etc.

17. *Shamrock*, 21 March 1868.

18. *Nation,* 21 December 1867, Gary Owens, 'Constructing the martyrs', 23.

19. Lily McManus, 'Irish Historical Romance', *The Catholic Bulletin* (January 1911), 24–6.

20. 'The Nameless Grave', *Leader*, 4 October 1902.

21. Costello, *Enduring the Most*, 21–2; O'Malley, *On Another Man's Wound*, 21–2, 43–4.

22. *Wolfe Tone Annual,* 1949, 17–25

23. See e.g. 'Heroines of Irish History', *Irish Fireside,* 12 August 1885; NLI, Ir 92 E.43, ii, Stella Garvey (Doheny), 'Romance of Robert Emmet and Sarah Curran'; 'Robert Emmet and Sarah Curran. A Sketch for the Times', *Shamrock*, Christmas Number, 1903; 'Her Young Hero. Concerning Robert Emmet's Love for Sarah Curran', *The Lady of the House*, 15 October 1803;

Ada Peter, 'An Immortal Romance', *Weekly Freeman*, 10 December 1910 (this rather better). 'Sarah Curran at Bully's Acre', *Irish Fireside*, 12 August 1885, descriptive words from the text. Sherlock, *Robert Emmet: the Story of his Life and Death.*

24. Reilly, 'Fictional Histories' (D.Phil thesis, 1997), 10–20.
25. *Wolfe Tone Annual,* 1948.
26. *The Speech of Robert Emmet, Esq., who was tried for High Treason.*
27. Stokes, *The Life and Labours in Art and Archaeology of George Petrie,* 389.
28. Emmet, *Memoir*, ii, 257, and 253.
29. *Shamrock* , 23 May 1868.
30. MacDonagh, *Viceroy's Post Bag*, 454; *Evening Telegraph,* 3 September 1910.
31. O'Faoláin, *Vive Moi! An Autobiography*, 90.
32. O'Malley, *On Another Man's Wound*, 200–201; English, *Ernie O'Malley. IRA Intellectual*, 75; Haverty, *Constance Markievicz. Irish Revolutionary*, 66.
33. NLI, Ir 92 E43, ii; O'Shea, 'Robert Emmet. Materials for a True Portrait of the Patriot'; also *Nation*, 4 March 1865, advertisement for picture of Emmet in his general's uniform.
34. Madden, *United Irishmen*, 3rd ser., iii, 299.
35. *Walker's Hibernian Magazine*, September 1803, 'The Unfortunate Mr. Robt. Emmet'; ibid., October 1798, 'The Unfortunate Theobald Wolfe Tone Esq'.
36. NLI, Prints and drawings, HP (1803) 6: 1898 centenary graphic, Robert Emmet's speech.
37. Hill, *Irish Public Sculpture*, 84–97.
38. *Nation,* 12 January 1878, also 18 February 1878; *Irish Builder*, 15 February 1878.
39. NLI, MS 5181, 1798 Centenary Record, fos. 107–9; *Leader*, 16 March 1907.
40. Kinsella, 'The Nineteenth-century Interpretation of 1798', (M.Litt. thesis, 1992), 117–18.
41. NLI, Ir 92 E43, i, 1878 newspaper cutting.
42. Hill, *Irish Public Sculpture*, 126–7; Kinsella, 'Nineteenth-century interpretation of 1798', 53–76, 116–17.
43. *Memoir of Robert Emmet* (Dublin: '98 Centenary Committee Pubs, no. 2, nd); NLI, MS 5181: '98 Centenary Album.
44. Zimmermann, *Songs of Irish Rebellion*, 292, 'The Last Moments of Robert Emmet'; O Lochlainn, *Irish Street Ballads.*
45. *Irish Weekly Independent*, 16 March – 7 September 1895.
46. Madden, *The Life and Times of Robert Emmet, Esq.*; the eightpence edition was

published by Cameron, Ferguson and Co., Glasgow. See NLI, Ir 92 E43, 'Robert Emmet in Poetry' – a scrapbook containing a very wide range of press and journal cuttings on Emmet, particularly in this period, though the origin and publication dates are often omitted.

47. See e.g. *Weekly Freeman*, 17 October 1891, *Irish Weekly Independent*, 16 March – 7 September 1895, *Evening Telegraph*, 9 March 1895.

48. Norman, *Terrible Beauty. A Life of Constance Markievicz, 1898–1927*, 122; Foster, *W. B. Yeats: A Life. i. The Apprentice Mage:1865–1914*, 127, 193, 220; *United Ireland*, 11 March 1893.

49. Thompson, *The Imagination of an Insurrection*, 115.

50. Garvin, *Nationalist Revolutionaries in Ireland 1858–1928*, 88, makes this point.

51. Moran, *The Philosophy of Irish Ireland*, 57–61, also 36–7; Foster, *Paddy and Mr Punch*, 276–8.

52. *The United Irishman*, 26 and 19 September 1903; Reilly, 'Fictional Histories', 90.

53. Maume, *The Long Gestation. Irish Nationalist Life, 1891–1918*, 62–3.

54. 'The Death of Emmet', *St Patrick's*, 19 September 1903 – note the picture is that of Emmet at the arms depot; *Wolfe Tone Annual*, 1953; *Irish People*, 19 September 1903.

55. UCD, Archives Dept., MacSwiney Coll., P48b/301, 'Address for the Emmet Centenary, 1903'.

56. This tradition in the Foresters had started in 1878, with the uniforms then costing 10 guineas apiece. Thereafter they met as 'the Robert Emmet Costume Association', see *Evening Telegraph*, 20 September 1902.

57. *Derry People*, 26 September 1903; *Irish News*, 19, 21 and 22 September 1903; *Evening Herald*, 21 September 1903; *Freeman's Journal*, 21 September 1903.

58. *United Irishman*, 25 July 1903.

59. ibid, 3 October 1903.

60. *Leader,* 26 September 1903.

61. NLI, Ir 92 E43, i, 'Emmet's Birthday Celebrated with Big Demonstration in Academy', March 1904, also report of meeting March 1900 at the Cooper's Union, New York.

62. Martin, ed., 'Extracts from the Papers of the late Dr Patrick McCartan', 30–45 – McCartan was one of the young men enthused by the centenaries of 1798 and 1803; *Shan Van Vocht*, 3 April 1896, reports of various Emmet celebrations in the USA; Kenny, *The American-Irish. A History*, 192–3.

63. Moran, *Patrick Pearse,* 143.

64. Quoted in Foster, *Story of Ireland*, 62.

65. *Leader*, 15 December 1906; Frayne and Johnson, eds., *Uncollected Prose by W.B. Yeats*, ii, 310–27; *Honesty*, 28 September 1929; Foster, *Yeats*, i, 312–14.

66. Hawkins, 'Heroic Kings and Romantic Rebels', (Ph.D thesis, 1992), ii, 180, 218.

67. W. J. Lawrence, 'Robert Emmet on the Stage', *Evening Telegraph*, 4 March 1911.

68. 'Robert Emmet', in *Selected Plays of Dion Boucicault,* edited by Andrew Parkin. O hAodha, 'A list of plays about Robert Emmet', 53–7.

69. BCL, Bigger Coll. R.95, newspaper cutting 1894, 'The Last Interview between Robert Emmet and Sarah Curran'.

70. See e.g., *St Patrick's,* 14 July 1900, *Freeman's Journal*, 12 January 1905, Yeats' 1904 speech mentioned above.

71. George Moorehead, *Robert Emmet, the Irish Patriot*, with illustrations from the play.

72. Hill, *Irish Public Sculpture: A History*, 172–3; Dixon, 'Dublin Portrait Statues', 62.

73. Ferrar, 'Robert Emmet in Irish Drama', 21.

74. Kevin Rockett, Luke Gibbons and John Hill, *Cinema and Ireland* (Syracuse UP, 1988), 9–14.

75. Hawkins, 'Heroic Kings and Romantic Rebels', 231.

76. Ibid, 252–6; Hogan, Burnham and Poteet, *The Modern Irish Drama, a documentary history*, 375–7.

77. *Val Vousden's Caravan*, 30–31.

78. *Irish Monthly*, xxx (November 1902), 56: review of O'Donoghue, *Life of Robert Emmet.*

79. MacNamara (John Weldon), *The Clanking of Chains.*

80. *United Irishman,* 19 September 1903.

81. Floinn (Robert Lynd) *The Ethics of Sinn Fein.*

82. *St Patrick's*, 14 July 1900.

83. *Wolfe Tone Memorial Association.* (programme); ibid, similar programmes for the 1914 and 1915 Emmet birthday celebrations; *Wolfe Tone Annual,* 1941, 114.

84. Ryan, *The Man Called Pearse*, 4.

85. Bernard Shaw, *The Matter with Ireland* (London, 1962), 112.

Chapter 8

1. *Poetry Ireland*, i (1962), 20–21.

2. O'Faoláin, *Vive Moi!*, 145–6.

3. Charles Townshend, *Ireland. The 20th Century* (London, 1998).

4. NLI, Ir 92 E43, i: *The Saskatoon Daily Star*, 17 January 1922; *Cork Weekly Examiner,* 18 March 1922.

5. NLI, Ir 92 E43, i, news cutting, 6 March 1922.

6. O'Faoláin, *Vive Moi!,* 147–51.

7. Lee, *Ireland, 1912–1985*, 66–9.

8. Greaves, *Liam Mellows and the Irish Revolution*, 386.

9. NAI, Dept. Taois., S.1639, Cosgrave to Revd T. J. Cahill, 16 February 1923, also Cahill's letter of 12 November 1923; a similar response was made to another offer in 1939, Dept. Taois., S.2460A.

10. Hill, *Irish Public Sculpture*, 168–70.

11. NAI, Dept. Taois., S.2460A.

12. O'Faoláin, *Vive Moi!*, 170.

13. Breathnach-Lynch, 'Commemorating the hero in newly independent Ireland', in McBride, ed., *Images*, 156–7; idem, '"Executed"', 51–60.

14. Yeats, *Senate Speeches*, 99; see also Elliott, *Wolfe Tone*, 417–18 and 475–6.

15. Breathnach-Lynch, '"Executed"', 57.

16. NAI, Dept. Taois., S.2462, S.4745 and S.6539.

17. NAI, Dept. Taois., S.15467; *Dáil Éireann*, vol. 137, 1.

18. *Irish Press*, 19 and 22 September 1953.

19. NAI, Dept. Taois., S.5019D and S.15467 for the exchange of letters, 1949–50; O'Hegarty, 'The Truth about Robert Emmet', 40–45 and Landreth's reply, ibid., xxvi (1951), 44–8. See also *The Irish Ecclesiastical Rec.*, 5th ser., lxxii (1949), 561–2. For her exchange with Francis Finegan, S.J., concerning his article 'Was John Keogh an informer?', see *Studies. An Irish Quarterly Review*, xxxix (1950), 75–86, 325–8, 338–40.

20. See e.g. Ó Broin, *The Unfortunate Mr Robert Emmet*, 191.

21. *Irish Press*, 5 November 1953; also a concert, *Irish Press*, 21 September 1953.

22. *Irish News,* 20 July 1953, also 17 July, 12–21 September 1953; *Irish Press,* 21 September 195.

23. O'Faoláin, *Vive Moi!*, 148.

24. *Songs of the Irish Republic* (Cork, 1965), 20, 'Sean from Garryowen'.

25. Ibid, 33, 'The Boy from Tralee'; Barry (18-year-old medical student, executed 1920, subject of one of the most popular of rebel songs), Peter

Barnes and James McCormack were hanged 7 February 1940, convicted of planting an IRA bomb in Coventry, which killed five and wounded seventy. Others by O'Higgins in this collection in a similar vein, 96, 'England's Gallows Tree', 92, 'A Ballad of Brave Men', 78, 'Maurice O'Neill'. This booklet also contains 'She is far from the Land' and 'Bold Robert Emmet'.

26. *Wolfe Tone Annual*, 1948, 134.

27. Idem, 1957, 48.

28. *Honesty,* 29 June 1929.

29. *Not Yet Emmet. A Wreath on the Grave of Sean Murray* (Dublin, *c.* 1985).

30. Brown, *Ireland*, 147.

31. Deane, ed., *The Field Day Anthology of Irish Writing,* iii, 501 (from *A Penny in the Clouds*).

32. Community theatre festival, inaugurated 1953.

33. McCormack, ed., *Austin Clarke. Selected Poems*, 71 and 224; the poem was first published in the *Irish Times*, 7 April 1956.

34. The most popular of all the contemporary 1798 ballads. The best-known version was printed in the *Nation*, 4 January 1845. See Zimmermann, *Songs of Irish Rebellion*, 228–9.

35. Thompson, *Imagination of an Insurrection*, 203–4; *The Shadow of a Gunman* (1923) and *The Plough and the Stars* (1926).

36. *The Dramatic Works of Denis Johnston*, i, 15.

37. Ibid, i, 17.

38. Grene, *The Politics of Irish Drama*, 156.

39. Daly, *Mister, Are You a Priest?*, 86.

40. Grene, *Politics of Irish Drama*, 156.

41. Devlin, *The Price of my Soul*, 159–60.

42. Little, *Malachi Horan Remembers*, 104–6; idem, 'A link with Robert Emmet, as related by Malachi Horan', *Dub. Hist. Rec.*, v, no. 2 (1942–3), 69–72. See also IFC, Schools Coll. Ms 291/479–80, Co. Cork schoolgirl citing 'Bold Robert Emmet' as a local poem; also Catriona MacLeod, *Robert Emmet* (Dublin, 1935), 139, ending her short biography by pointing to the Irish people cherishing the picture and ballad 'Bold Robert Emmet'; Ó Broin, *Unfortunate Robert Emmet,* entitled his concluding chapter 'The Darlin' of Erin'.

43. IFC, pamphlet 37055: *The Robert Emmet Benefit Society. General Rules* (Dublin, 1930).

44. *Irish News*, 31 December 1948.

45. IFC, 37065, this is F. S. Bourke's copy of MacMullen's book, inside of

which are a number of letters on MacMullen's publishing plans, plus reviews.

46. See e.g. *Rathfarnham, Gateway to the Hills*, 26, 31–5; Nolan, *Rathfarnham and Terenure*, 20–22; Boylan, 'Robert Emmet's House at Rathfarnham', 55–8.

47. Morrison, *Then the Walls Came Down*, 104–5 – I am grateful to Richard English for drawing this to my attention; English, *Armed Struggle. The History of the IRA 1916–2002*. In all it is Pearse and 1916 that dominate. Sinn Féin also regularly reprinted Emmet's speech; the copy in my possession was issued in 1953 and reprinted some time after 1971. I am grateful to Frank Harte for drawing Bobby Sands's ballad 'Back Home in Derry' to my attention. This too talks of 'the Bold Robert'.

48. See e.g. *An Phoblacht,* 15 March 1978, 10 February 1983; IFC, Schools Coll. Mss 310/240, 314/131 and 794/427.

49. Glassie, *Passing the Time in Ballymenone*, 83–5.

50. *Irish Times*, 25 July 1978; *Irish Press*, 15 July 1978.

51. Boland, *Object Lessons*, 60–61.

Bibliography

Manuscript sources

Archives des Affaires Étrangères, Paris
Mémoires et Documents Angleterre 53
Fonds, France 1744
Correspondance Politique: Angleterre 592–601

Archives Nationales, Paris
AF IV 1101, 1672 and AF IV* 204: executive power, Consulate
F^7 7459: police générale, Irish refugees

Belfast Central Library
Bigger Collection
R95: Robert Emmet, His Life and Times (scrapbook of newspaper cuttings)

British Library, London
Add. MSS 33,106–9: Pelham Papers
Add. MSS 35,707–14, 35,740–42, 35,770–72, 35,775, 35,777: Hardwicke
    Papers
Add. MS 34,456: Auckland Papers

Hampshire Record Office (Hants)
MS 38M49: Wickham Papers

Irish Folklore Commission, University College, Dublin
Schools Collection

National Archives of Ireland
Rebellion Papers
Official Papers (CSO, Chief Secretary's Office)
State of the Country Papers (SOC)
Department of the Taoiseach Papers

National Library of Ireland
MS 1791: Notes by Thomas Davis for a History of the United Irishmen
MS 4597: Typescript copy of a letter by R. Rainey, 18–19 September 1803
MS 5181: 1798 Centenary Record
MS 5973: Crown Circuit Book, 1798–1803
MS 8077: Memorandum by Edward Lawlor on the final resting place of Robert Emmet
MS 8079 and 8235: Copies of Emmet's speech
MSS 8326–7: Sarah Curran Letters
MSS 9553–4: Townley Hall Papers
MS 9761: Luke Cullen papers, manuscript of his 'The Life, Imprisonment, Sufferings and Death of Anne Devlin'
MS 9807: F. S. Bourke Song Collection
MS 10,425: 1850 news cuttings on Emmet's rebellion
MS 18,143: John Devoy Papers
MS 18,328: Copy of reputed eyewitness account of the execution of Robert Emmet
MS 22,703–4: W. G. Fallon Papers
MS 24,120: Sheehy–Skeffington Papers
MS 24,267: Le Brocquy Papers
MS 27,947: Ó Broin MSS
MS 33,565: papers of Daniel O'Connell
Ir 92 E43: Scrapbook of news cuttings – 'Robert Emmet in Poetry'

National University of Ireland
P48b/301: MacSwiney Collection

Public Record Office, London (redesignated National Archives)
FO 27/70
HO 100/71–136
PC 1/44/A.161
TS 11/121

Public Record Office of Northern Ireland
D.272: McCance Collection
D.607: Downshire MSS
D.1748: Tennent Letters
D.3030: Castlereagh Papers

T.808/4409–4484: Emmet Family Notes
T.2627: Hobart Papers
T.3030: Redesdale Papers

Royal Irish Academy
MS 12.L.32: Journal of Kitty Wilmot, 1801–3
MS 23.K.62/A: Correspondence between Dr T. A. Emmet and J. F. Fuller
MS 23.K.53: Burrowes MSS
Haliday and Madden Pamphlet Collections

Trinity College, Dublin
Mun V/5/4–5: Trinity College registers (minute books) of the Board
Mun V/23/4: Trinity College Entrance Book, 1769–1825
Mun V/25 and 27: Trinity College examinations 1771–1798
MS V/35/5: Attendance on terms
Mun V/86/8: Trinity College chamber lettings
Mun Soc/Hist 12: College Historical Society Journal 1796–8
MSS 868-9: Sirr Papers
MS 873: Madden Papers
MSS 1203, 3363, 3373: Various accounts of the College Visitation, April 1798
MSS 1472: Madden (Luke Cullen Papers)
MSS 6727–8: 6844–7: Dillon Papers
MSS 7253–6: Hope MSS

Newspapers/magazines

Annual Register
An Phoblacht. Republican News
Argus
Belfast Monthly Magazine
Belfast News Letter
Cork Examiner
Derry People
Dublin and London Magazine,
Dublin Evening Post
Dublin Opinion
Dublin University Magazine

Evening Telegraph
Freeman's Journal
Irish Book Lover
Irish Emerald
Irish Magazine
Irish People
Irish Press
Irish Times
Irish Weekly and Ulster Examiner
Irish Weekly Independent
Leader
Milesian Magazine
Nation
Northern Star
Notes and Queries
Our Boys
St Patrick's
Shamrock
Shamrock or Hibernian Chronicle
Shan Van Vocht
Sunday Press
Ulster Examiner
United Ireland
United Irishman
Walker's Hibernian Magazine
Weekly Freeman
Wolfe Tone Annual

Printed primary

(including texts contributing to the Emmet legend)

Jean Agnew, ed., *The Drennan–McTier Letters,* 3 vols. (Dublin, 1998–9)
Henry Playsted Archer, *Emmet, the Irish Patriot: and other poems* (Canterbury, 1832)
The Birthday Dinner to Thomas Addis Emmet given by his Professional Friends at Delmonico's, New York, May 29 1905 (New York, 1905)
M. McD. Bodkin, *True Man and Traitor: or the Rising of Emmet* (Dublin, 1921)

Eavan Boland, *Object Lessons. The Life of the Woman and the Poet in Our Time* (London, 1995)

'A brief narrative of the circumstances which led to the discovery and discomfiture of Emmet's insurrection', *Dublin University Magazine*, i (1833), 541–7; 'Recollections of 1803', ibid., 671–8

John W. Burke, *Life of Robert Emmett, the celebrated Irish Patriot and Martyr*, 2nd edition (Charleston, S.C., 1852)

Cornelius. G. Buttimer, 'A Gaelic Reaction to Robert Emmet's Rebellion', *Cork Hist. and Arch. Soc. Jn.*, 97 (1992), 26–53

Miles Byrne, *Some Notes of an Irish Exile of 1798. Being the Chapters from the Memoirs of Miles Byrne Relating to Ireland* (Dublin, nd)

Catalogue of the Library of R. R. Madden ... to be sold by Charles Sharpe ... 13 Jan 1847 (Dublin, 1846), another sold by John F. Jones, 1865

H. B. C[ode], *The Insurrection of Twenty-third July, 1803* (Dublin, [1803])

The Collected Works of Padraic H. Pearse. Political Writings and Speeches (Dublin and London, 1922)

Correspondence of Charles, First Marquis Cornwallis, edited by Charles Ross, Esq., 3 vols. (London, 1859)

The Criminal Recorder: or, Biographical Sketches of Notorious Public characters ... by a Student of the Inner Temple, i (London, 1804)

Dáil Éireann. Parliamentary Debates [Dáil Debates]

Edward Daly, *Mister, Are you a Priest?* (Dublin, 2000)

Seamus Deane, ed., *The Field Day Anthology of Irish Writing*, 3 vols. (Derry, 1991)

'Anne Devlin. A Reminiscence of 1803', *The Celt*, i, no. 15 (7 November 1857), 225–7

Bernadette Devlin, *The Price of My Soul*, (London, 1969)

The Diary and Correspondence of Charles Abbot, Lord Colchester, edited by his son, 3 vols. (London, 1861)

'Dr. Madden's Life of Emmet', *Dublin University Magazine*, xxviii (1846), 681–702

Dropmore MSS. The Manuscripts of J. B. Fortescue Esq., preserved at Dropmore. HMC 13th Report. Append. pt. 3, and 14th Report. Append. pt. 5, 10 vols. (London, 1892–4)

M. E. Dudley, *Emmett. The Irish Patriot; and other poems* (London, 1836)

John Patrick Dunne, ed., *98 Club Notes ... to which is added a list of Patriot Graves*, (Dublin, 1898)

Thomas Addis Emmet, *The Emmet Family. With Some Incidents Relating to Irish History* (New York, 1898)

— *Ireland Under English Rule or a Plea for the Plaintiff,* 2 vols, 2nd edition (New York, 1909)

— *Incidents of My Life* (New York and London, 1910)

— *Memoir of Thomas Addis and Robert Emmet,* 2 vols. (New York, 1915)

Emmet Anniversary Celebration, Round Room Rotunda, Monday 5 March 1906 [programme]

The Emmet Songbook. Specially compiled for the Irish Patriot's Centenary (Dublin, [1903])

Riobárd Ua Floinn [Robert Lynd] *The Ethics of Sinn Fein* (Limerick, 1912)

John P. Frayne and Colton Johnson, eds., *Uncollected Prose by W. B. Yeats,* vol. ii (London, 1975)

John Gamble, *Sketches of History, Politics and Manners in the North of Ireland in the Summer and Autumn of 1810* (Dublin, 1811)

The Genuine Speech of Robert Emmett … carefully taken in shorthand by a professional gentleman, printed at the request of his friends (nd, but a q. from Moore's songs)

George Gilbert [Mary Lucy Arthur], *The Island of Sorrow. An Historical Novell 1797–1808* (London, 1903)

[W. Gregory], *The Picture of Dublin* (Dublin, 1811)

Earl Leslie Griggs, ed., *Coleridge, Collected Letters,* 6 vols. (Oxford, 1956–71)

Stephen Gwynn, *Robert Emmet: A Historical Romance* (London, 1909)

Joseph Hamilton, *An Impartial Enquiry respecting the Betrayal of Lord Edward Fitzgerald, and Robert Emmet* (Dublin, 1832)

John Hand, *Robert Emmet* (London, 1902)

Baronness d'Haussonville, *Robert Emmet* (Paris, 1858)

John Cashel Hoey, ed., *Speeches at the Bar and in the Senate, by the Right Honourable Wm. Conyngham, Lord Plunket* (Dublin, 1865)

T. B. and T. J. Howell, eds., *A Complete Collection of State Trials* (London, 1809–28)

Valentin Iremonger, 'Wrap up my green jacket', *The Bell,* xiv, no. 4 (July 1947)

Irish Eloquence. The Speeches of the Celebrated Irish Orators … to which is added the Powerful Appeal of Robert Emmett, at the Close of his Trial for High Treason. Selected by a Member of the Bar (Philadelphia, 1836)

Washington Irving, *The Sketch Book,* new edition., 2 vols. (London, 1823)

F. L. Jones, ed., *The Letters of Percy Bysshe Shelley,* 2 vols. (Oxford, 1964)

Revd John Kavanaugh, *Thomas Addis Emmet, M. D. A Personal Tribute* (New York, [1919])

A Letter from a Roman Catholic Farmer, to his Brother Farmers, and other industrious members of the Community (Dublin, 1803)

The Letters of Thomas Moore, edited by Wilfred S. Dowden, 2 vols. (Oxford, 1964)

The Life and Actions of Robert Emmet, leader of the Insurrection of 1803 (Dublin, 1840)

The Life and Correspondence of the Rt. Hon. Henry Addington, First Visc. Sidmouth, edited by the Hon. G. Pellew, 3 vols. (London, 1847)

The Life and Times of Robert Emmet. The Irish Library, no. 1 (London, 1908–9)

The Life of the Right Honourable John Philpot Curran, by his son William Henry Curran, 2 vols. (London, 1819)

The Life, Trial and Conversations of Robert Emmet, Esq., (Manchester, 1836)

George A. Little, *Malachi Horan Remembers* (Dublin and Cork, 1976, first published 1943)

John F. McArdle, *Catechism of Irish History* (Liverpool, 1873)

W. J. McCormack, ed., *Austin Clarke. Selected Poems* (London, 1991)

Michael MacDonagh *The Viceroy's Postbag* (London, 1904)

Major General H. T. MacMullen, *The Voice of Sarah Curran. Unpublished Letters together with the full story of her life told for the first time* (Dublin, 1955)

Brinsley MacNamara [John Weldon], *The Clanking of Chains* (Dublin and London, 1920)

W. J. MacNeven, *Pieces of Irish History* (New York, 1807)
— *Emmet Monument* (New York, 1833)
— *Address to the People of England* (New York, 1834)

R. R. Madden, *The United Irishmen. Their Lives and Times*, 3 ser., 7 vols. (London, 1843–5 and Dublin, 1846), and 2nd edition, 4 vols. (Dublin, 1857–60)
— *Antrim and Down in '98* (Glasgow, nd)
— *The Life and Times of Robert Emmet, Esq.* (Glasgow, 1903)
— *Literary Remains of the United Irishmen* (Dublin, 1887)

Henry Connell Mangan, *Robert Emmet. A History Play in Three Acts* (Dublin, 1904)

Charles Robert Maturin, *The Milesian Chief*, 4 vols. (New York, 1979)

F. X. Martin, ed., 'Extracts from the Papers of the late Dr. Patrick McCartan', *Clogher Record*, v (1963–5), 30–45

W. H. Maxwell, *History of the Irish Rebellion in 1798; with Memoirs of the Union, and Emmett's Insurrection in 1803*, 6th edition (London, 1864)
— *Erin Go Bragh, or Irish Life Pictures* (New York and London, 1979, reprint of 1859 edition)

Meeting of Irishmen in New York. To the People of Ireland (New York, 1825)

Memoir of Robert Emmet, '98 Centenary Committee Pubs, no. 2 (Dublin, 1903)

Memoir of the Case of St. John Mason, Esq., Barrister at Law (Dublin, 1807)

Memoirs and Correspondence of Viscount Castlereagh, edited by his brother, Charles Vane, 3rd Marquess of Londonderry, 12 vols. (London, 1848–54)

Memoirs, Journal, and Correspondence of Thomas Moore, edited by Lord John Russell, 8 vols. (London, 1853–6)

Memoirs of the Life and Times of the Rt. Hon. Henry Grattan, by his son, Henry Grattan, 5 vols. (London, 1839–42)

Thomas Moore, *The Life and Death of Lord Edward Fitzgerald* (Paris, 1831)
— *Irish Melodies* (London, 1854)

George Moorehead, *Robert Emmet, the Irish Patriot. The Romance of his Life* (New York, 1902)

D. P. Moran, *The Philosophy of Irish Ireland*, 2nd edition (Dublin, 1900)

Most Rev. Doctor Troy's Exhortation, addressed to the lower order of Roman Catholics of the Archdiocese of Dublin, 24 July 1803.

A. Newman [Herbert Moore Pim], *What Emmet Means in 1915: a Tract for the Times* (Dublin, [1915])

Leon Ó Broin, *A Lecture on Robert Emmet* [programme announcing his lecture, Gresham Hotel, Sunday 31 January 1954]

Sylvester O'Halloran and A. M. Sullivan, *The Pictorial History of Ireland* (Boston, 1884)

John O'Leary, *Recollections of Fenians and Fenianism*, 2 vols. (Shannon, reprint of 1896 edition, 1969)

Ernie O'Malley, *On Another Man's Wound* (Dublin, 1979)

The Opinion of an Impartial Observer, Concerning the Late Transactions in Ireland (Dublin, 1803)

Colm O Lochlainn, *Irish Street Ballads* (Dublin, 1939)

Paddy's Resource or the Harp of Erin (Dublin, nd [1830])

The Parliamentary History of England, 36 vols. (London, 1806–20), continued as *The Parliamentary Debates*, 41 vols. (London, 1812–20)

Mary Brigid Pearse, ed., *The Home Life of Pádraig Pearse, as told by Himself, his Family and his Friends* (Dublin, 1934)

Pedro Redivivus. Prison Abuses in Ireland, exemplified by documents, setting forth the oppressions and atrocities of Doctor Trevor, and his associates, as practised upon the State Prisoners of Kilmainham ... selected by St John Mason, Esq., ... (dedicated to Sheridan), (London, 1810)

The Poetical Works of Robert Southey, collected by himself, 10 vols. (London, 1859)

'Recollections of 1803', *Dublin University Magazine*, i (June, 1833), 671–8

Report of a Trial at the Bar of the Hon. Mr. Justice Johnson ... for a libel ... 23 Nov. 1805 (London, 1806)

William Ridgeway, *A Report of the Proceedings in Cases of High Treason*, 2 vols. (Dublin, 1803)

Robert Emmet. A Commemorative Booklet (Dublin, 1921)

Robert Emmet's Speech from the Dock 1803 (Dublin, [c.1953], also post-1971 edition)

Lennox Robinson, *The Dreamers. A Play in Three Acts* (Dublin, 1915)

Neville Rogers, ed., *The Complete Poetical Works of Percy Bysshe Shelley,* 4 vols. (Oxford, 1972)

'The Roscommon Militia and the Burial of Robert Emmet', *The Irish Sword*, iv, no. 14 (1959), 72–3

Thomas U. Sadleir, ed., *An Irish Peer on the Continent, 1801–1803, being a Narrative of the Tour of Stephen, 2nd Earl Mount Cashell, through France, Italy, etc, as related* by Catherine Wilmot (London, 1924)

Selected Plays of Dion Boucicault, edited by Andrew Parkin (Gerards Cross, 1987)

A Selection of Irish Melodies with symphonies and accompaniements by Sir John Stevenson Mus. Doc. and Characteristic words by Thomas Moore Esq., 1st number, 1st vol. (London, [1807–24]), also 2nd number, 2nd vol., which appears to be 1812

Shelley and his Circle 1773–1822, ed. Kenneth Neill Cameron, 4 vols. (Cambridge, Mass., 1961–70)

Thomas Sherlock, *Robert Emmet: the Story of his Life and Death* (Dublin, 1878)

The Speech of Robert Emmet, Esq., as delivered at the Sessions House, Dublin (London, 1832) – first printed in *The Poor Man's Guardian*, no.25

The Speech of Robert Emmet, Esq. at the Sessions-House, Green-Street, September, 1803 [cheaply produced pamphlet, the most widely used version, in RIA Haliday 851/5c]

Speech of Robert Emmet, Esq., Leader of the Irish Insurrection of 1803, Delivered by that Lamented Patriot, at the Close of His Trial, for High Treason (Manchester, [1840])

The Speech of Robert Emmet, Esq., who was tried for High Treason on the 19th day of September, 1803 (Dublin, 1803)

The Speeches of the Rt. Hon. John Philpot Curran, edited by Thomas Davis (2nd edition, Dublin, 1853)

A. M. Sullivan, *The Story of Ireland* (Dublin, 1867)

T. D. Sullivan, *A Selection from the Songs and Poems of T. D. Sullivan* (Dublin, 1899)

—— *Evergreen Volume of Irish Verses* (Dublin, 1907)

—— *Robert Emmet* (Dublin, 1868))

—— A. M. and D. B. Sullivan, *Speeches from the Dock* (Dublin, 1968)

C. H. Teeling, *Sequel to the History of the Irish Rebellion of 1798: A Personal Narrative*, reprint of 1876 edition (Shannon, 1972)

W. M. Thackeray, *The Irish Sketchbook* (Glos, 1990)

P. F. Tissot, *Les Trois Conjurés Irlandais; ou L'Ombre d'Emmet* (Paris, 1804)

The Trial of Robert Emmet, Esq., for High Treason … taken in shorthand by a professional gentleman (Dublin, 1803)

Val Vousden's Caravan (Dublin, nd)

John Edward Walsh, *Sketches of Ireland Sixty Years Ago* (Dublin, 1847)

John Warburton, James Whitelaw and Robert Walsh, *A History of the City of Dublin*, 2 vols. (London, 1818)

John Wood Warter, ed., *Selections from the Letters of Robert Southey,* 4 vols. (London, 1856)

Revd James Whitelaw, *An Essay on the Population of Dublin* (Dublin, 1905)

M. J. W. [Michael James Whitty], *Robert Emmet* (London, Dublin, Liverpool: 1870)

— 'Robert Emmet and his Contemporaries', *The Dublin and London Magazine* (March–December 1825)

Wolfe Tone Memorial Association. Emmet Anniversary Celebration, Round Room, Mansion House. Tuesday 17 March 1916 [programme]

C. J. Woods, *Journals and Memoirs of Thomas Russell, 1791–95* (Dublin, 1991)

W. B. Yeats, *The Senate Speeches of W. B. Yeats*, edited by Donald R. Pearce (Bloomington, Indiana, 1960)

Georges-Denis Zimmermann, *Songs of Irish Rebellion. Political Street Ballads and Rebel Songs 1780–1900* (Dublin, 1967)

Secondary

Gerry Adams, *Free Ireland: Towards a Lasting Peace* (Dingle, 1986)

— *An Irish Voice. The Quest for Peace* (Dingle, 1997)

J. R. R. Adams, *The Printed Word and the Common Man. Popular Culture in Ulster 1700–1900* (Belfast, 1987)

Michael Barry, *The Mystery of Robert Emmet's Grave* (Fermoy, 1991)

Thomas Bartlett, 'The Life and Opinions of Leonard MacNally (1752–1820): Playwright, Barrister, United Irishman, and Informer', in Hiram Morgan, ed., *Information, Media and Power Through the Ages* (Dublin, 2001), 113–136.

David Blaazer, 'Sterling Identities', *History Today,* 52(1) (January 2002), 12–18

F. S. Bourke, 'The Rebellion of 1803. An Essay in Bibliography', *The Bibliographical Society of Ireland*, v (1933), 1–16

Lena Boylan, 'Robert Emmet's House at Rathfarnham', *Dub. Hist. Rec.*, xxxi (1977–8), 55–8

Síghle Breathnach-Lynch, 'Commemorating the hero in newly independent Ireland', in McBride, ed., *Images*, 156–7

— '"Executed": the political commissions of Albert G. Power', *Eire-Ireland*, xxix, no. 1 (1994), 44–60

Stephen J. Brown, *Ireland in Fiction. A Guide to Irish Novels, Tales, Romances, and Folk-Lore* (Dublin and London, 1919)

Terence Brown, *Ireland. A Social and Cultural History 1922–1985* (London, 1990)

Declan Budd and Ross Hinds, *The Hist and Edmund Burke's Club. An Anthology of the College Historical Society, the Student Debating Society of Trinity College Dublin, from its Origins in Edmund Burke's Club 1747–1997* (Dublin, 1997)

O. J. Burke, *History of the Lord Chancellors of Ireland* (Dublin, 1879)

David Cairns, *Berlioz. i: The Making of An Artist 1803–1832*, and ii: *Servitude of Greatness, 1832–1869* (London, 2000)

Kenneth Neill Cameron, ed., *Shelley and His Circle 1773–1822*, 4 vols. (Cambridge, Mass.: 1961–70)

Julia Carlson, ed., *Banned in Ireland: Censorship and the Irish Writer* (Athens, 1990)

Padraic Colm, 'It is not wisdom to be only wise', *The Dublin Magazine*, viii, no. 4 (October–December 1933), 24–9

R. V. Comerford, *Charles J. Kickham. A Study in Irish nationalism and Literature* (Portmarnock, [1979])

—— *The Fenians in Context. Irish Politics and Society 1848–82* (Dublin, 1985)

Francis J. Costello, *Enduring the Most. The Life and Death of Terence MacSwiney* (Dingle, 1995)

Seán Cronin, *Frank Ryan. The Search for the Republic* (Dublin, 1980)

Geoffrey Cubitt and Allen Warren, eds., *Heroic Reputations and Exemplary Lives* (Manchester, 2000)

T. S. C. Dagg, *The College Historical Society. A History (1770–1920),* (Dublin, 1969)

Máirin Ni Dhonnchadha and Theo Dorgan, eds, *Revising the Rising* (Derry, 1991)

F. E. Dixon, 'Dublin Portrait Statues', *Dublin Historical Record*, xxxi (1977–8), 60–69

T. P. Dolan, 'Irish Oratory from Emmet to Casement', *Irish University Review*, 6, no. 2 (1976), 151–63

P. J. Dowling, *The Hedge Schools of Ireland* (Dublin, 1935)

The Dramatic Works of Denis Johnston, 2 vols. (Gerards Cross, 1977)

Charles Gavan Duffy, *Short Life of Thomas Davis, 1840–1846* (London, 1895)

Ruth Dudley Edwards, *Patrick Pearse: The Triumph of Failure* (London, 1977)

Marianne Elliott, *Partners in Revolution. The United Irishmen and France* (London and New Haven, 1982)

—— *Wolfe Tone. Prophet of Irish Independence* (London and New Haven, 1989)

—— *The Catholics of Ulster. A History* (London, 2000)

Richard English, *Ernie O'Malley. IRA Intellectual* (Oxford, 1999)

—— *Armed Struggle. The History of the IRA 1916–2002* (London, 2003).

Richard J. Evans, *Rituals of Retribution, Capital Punishment in Germany 1600–1987* (Oxford, 1996)

C. Litton Falkiner, *Essays Relating to Ireland* (Washington, 1970)

Harold Ferrar, 'Robert Emmet in Irish Drama', *Eire-Ireland*, i (1966), 19–28

John Finegan, *Anne Devlin. Patriot and Heroine* (Dublin, 1992)

Garret FitzGerald, *Towards a New Ireland* (London, 1972)

W. J. Fitzpatrick, *'The Sham Squire'; and the Informers of 1798,* new edition (Dublin, 1895)

— *Secret Service Under Pitt* (London, 1892)

R. F. Foster, *Paddy and Mr. Punch. Connections in Irish and English History* (London, 1993)

— *W. B. Yeats: A Life. i. The Apprentice Mage: 1865–1914* (Oxford, 1997)

— *The Irish Story. Telling Tales and Making It Up in Ireland* (London, 2001)

Tom Garvin, *Nationalist Revolutionaries in Ireland 1858–1928* (Oxford, 1987)

V. A. C. Gatrell, *The Hanging Tree. Execution and the English People 1770–1868* (Oxford, 1996)

Patrick M. Geoghegan, *The Irish Act of Union* (Dublin, 1999)

— *Robert Emmet. A Life* (Dublin, 2002)

Luke Gibbons, *Transformations in Irish Culture* (Cork, 1996)

Henry Glassie, *Passing the Time in Ballymenone* (Bloomington, 1995)

Maurice Goldring, *Pleasant the Scholar's Life. Irish Intellectuals and the Construction of the Nation State* (London, 1993)

C. Desmond Greaves, *Liam Mellows and the Irish Revolution* (London, 1971)

Nicholas Grene, *The Politics of Irish Drama. Plays in Context from Boucicault to Friel* (Cambridge, 1999)

Louise Imogen Guiney, *Robert Emmet* (London, 1904)

Joseph W. Hammond, 'Behind the scenes of the Emmet Insurrection', *Dublin Historical Record*, vi (1944), 91–106, 153–4.

— 'The Emmet Insurrection', ibid., ix (1946–7), 22–8, 59–68, 84–95

— 'The Rev. Thomas Gamble and Robert Emmet', ibid., xiv (March 1956 – May 1958), 98–101

William Domville Handcock, *The History and Antiquities of Tallaght*, 2nd edition (Dublin, 1991)

Richard Haslem, '"A Race Bashed in the Face": Imagining Ireland as a Damaged Child', *Jouvert: A Journal of Postcolonial Studies*, 4, no.1 (Fall, 1999)

Anne Haverty, *Constance Markievicz. Irish Revolutionary* (London, 1988)

Maureen S. G. Hawkins, 'The dramatic treatment of Robert Emmet and Sarah Curran', in S. F. Gallagher, ed., *Women in Irish Legend, Life and Literature* (Gerards Cross, 1983)

John Hennig, 'Robert Emmet's Military Studies', *Irish Sword,* i, no 2 (1951–2), 148–50

Brian Henry, *Dublin Hanged. Crime, Law Enforcement and Punishment in Late Eighteenth-century Dublin* (Dublin, 1994)

Jacqueline Hill, *From Patriots to Unionists. Dublin Civic Politics and Irish Protestant Patriotism 1660–1840* (Oxford, 1997)

Judith Hill, *Irish Public Sculpture: A History* (Dublin, 1998)

Robert Hogan, Richard Burnham and Daniel P. Poteet, *The Modern Irish Drama, a documentary history.* IV: *The Rise of the Realists 1910–1915* (New Jersey, USA, 1979)

Richard Holmes, *Shelley, The Pursuit* (London, 1976)

Anne C. Kavanaugh, *John Fitzgibbon, Earl of Clare. Protestant Reaction and English Authority in Late Eighteenth-Century Ireland* (Dublin, 1997)

Kevin Kenny, *The American-Irish. A History* (New York, 2000)

Richard von Krafft-Ebing, *Psycopathia Sexualis* (Brooklyn, New York, 1936)

Helen Landreth, *The Pursuit of Robert Emmet* (New York, 1948)

J. J. Lee, *Ireland, 1912–1985. Politics and Society* (Cambridge, 1989)

Joep Leerssen, *Remembrance and Imagination. Patterns in the Historical and Literary Representation of Ireland in the Nineteenth Century* (Cork, 1996)

George A. Little, *Malachi Horan Remembers* (Dublin and Cork, 1986. 1st pub. 1946)

Moira Lysaght, 'Norbury, "The Hanging Judge" (1745–1831)', *Dub. Hist. Rec.,* xxx, no. 2 (March 1977), 58–65

Ian McBride, *History and Memory in Modern Ireland* (Cambridge, 2001)

Lawrence W. McBride, ed., *Images, Icons and the Irish Nationalist Imagination* (Dublin, 1999)

Catriona MacLeod, *Robert Emmet* (Dublin, 1935)

W. J. McCormack, *Sheridan Le Fanu and Victorian Ireland* (Oxford, 1980)

Oliver MacDonagh, W. F. Mandle and Pauric Travers, *Irish Culture and Nationalism, 1750–1950* (London, 1983 and 1985)

R. B. McDowell and D. A. Webb, *Trinity College Dublin 1592–1952: An Academic History* (Cambridge, 1952)

T. H. McGuffie, 'Robert Emmet's Insurrection', *Irish Sword,* I, no. 4 (1952–3), 322–3

Michael MacDonagh, 'The Tragedy of Robert Emmet', *The Cornhill Magazine,* xv, no. 87 (September 1903), 380–401

Samuel McSkimin, 'Secret History of the Irish Insurrection of 1803', *Fraser's Magazine,* xiv (November 1836), 546–67

Nellie Maher, *Robert Emmet. His Two Loves* (Dublin, 1975)

Patrick Maume, *The Long Gestation. Irish Nationalist Life, 1891–1918* (New York, 1999)

Constantia Maxwell, *A History of Trinity College Dublin, 1591–1892* (Dublin, 1946)

—— *Dublin under the Georges* (Dublin, 1946)

Jane Maxwell, 'Sources in Trinity College Library Dublin, for researching the 1798 Rebellion', *Irish Archives. Journal of the Irish Society for Archives*, vol. 5, no. 1 (1998), 3–22

John C. Molony, *Ireland's Tragic Comedians* (Edinburgh, 1934)

G. M. Moore, 'The story of Sarah Curran', *Cork Hist. and Arch. Society*, xxvii (1921), 60–65

Séan Farrell Moran, *Patrick Pearse and the Politics of Redemption. The Mind of the Easter Rising, 1916* (Washington, D.C., 1994)

Danny Morrison, *Then the Walls Came Down. A Prison Journal* (Cork, 1999)

Tom Nairn, *The Break-up of Britain: Crisis and Neo-nationalism* (London, 1977)

J. Nolan, *Rathfarnham and Terenure* (Dublin, n.d. [1980s])

Diana Norman, *Terrible Beauty. A Life of Constance Markievicz, 1898–1927* (London, 1987)

Leon Ó Broin, *The Unfortunate Mr Robert Emmet* (Dublin, 1958)

D. J. O'Donoghue, *Life of Robert Emmet* (Dublin, 1908)

Seán O'Faolain, *Vive Moi! An Autobiography* (London, 1965)

J. R. O'Flanagan, *The Lives of the Lord Chancellors and Keepers of the Great Seal of Ireland*, 2 vols. (London, 1870)

Michael O hAodha, 'A List of Plays about Robert Emmet, *The Irish Book* (Spring, 1963), 53–7

P. S. O'Hegarty, 'The truth about Robert Emmet', [review of Landreth], *The Dublin Magazine*, xxv, no. 3 (July–September 1950), 40–45 and Helen Landreth's reply, ibid, xxvi, no. 1 (January–March 1951)

D. Ó hOgain, *The Hero in Irish Folk History* (Dublin, 1985)

Seán Ó Súilleabháin, *A Handbook of Irish Folklore*, (Detroit, 1970)

Senia Paseta, '1798 in 1898: The Politics of Commemoration', *Irish Review*, no. 22 (Summer, 1998), 46–53

Tom Paulin, *Minotaur. Poetry and the Nation State* (London, 1992)

—— *The Day-Star of Liberty. William Hazlitt's Radical Style* (London, 1998)

G. K. Peatling, 'Who fears to speak of politics? John Kells Ingram and hypothetical nationalism', *IHS*, xxxi (1998), 202–21

Charles Phillips, *Recollections of Curran and some of his Contemporaries*, 2nd edition (London, 1822)

— *Curran and his Contemporaries* (Edinburgh and London, 1850), extensively re-written

P. J. C., 'Review of Helen Landreth', *The Irish Ecclesiastical Record*, 5th. ser., lxxii (1949), 561–2

Raymond W. Postgate, *Robert Emmet* (London, 1931)

David A. Quaid, *Robert Emmet: his birth-place and burial* (Dublin, 1902)

James Quinn, *Soul on Fire. A Life of Thomas Russell* (Dublin, 2002)

Rathfarnham, Gateway to the Hills, 3rd reprint (Dublin, 1991)

Ernest Renan, *Qu'est-ce qu'une nation?* in *Oeuvres Complètes* (Paris, 1947–61), i, 887–906

J. J. Reynolds, *In theFootprints of Emmet* (Dublin, 1903)

Kevin Rockett, Luke Gibbons and John Hill, *Cinema and Ireland* (Syracuse, 1988)

Desmond Ryan, *The Man Called Pearse* (Dublin, 1919)

L. G. Schwoerer, 'William Lord Russell: the making of a martyr, 1682–1983', *Journal of British Studies*, xxiv (1985), 41–71

David Sharrock and Mark Devenport, *Man of War, Man of Peace? The Unauthorised Biography of Gerry Adams* (London, 1997)

Harry Sirr, *Sarah Curran's and Robert Emmet's Letters* (Dublin, 1910)

Jim Smyth, *The Men of No Property. Irish Radicals and Popular Politics in the Late Eighteenth Century* (London, 1992)

— ed., *Revolution, Counter-Revolution and Union. Ireland in the 1790s* (Cambridge, 2000)

Elizabeth Sparrow, 'The Alien Office, 1792–1806', *The Historical Journal*, xxxiii, no. 2 (1990) 361–84

Michael Steinman, *Yeats's Heroic Figures. Wilde, Parnell, Swift, Casement* (London, 1983)

Bruce Stewart, ed., *Hearts and Minds: Irish Culture and Society under the Act of Union* (Princess Grace Irish Library, Gerards Cross, 2002)

William Stokes, *The Life and Labours in Art and Archaeology of George Petrie, LLD., MRIA* (London, 1868)

Mark Storey, *Robert Southey. A Life* (Oxford, 1997)

L. A. G. Strong, *The Minstrel Boy. A Portrait of Tom Moore* (London, 1937)

William Irwin Thompson, *The Imagination of an Insurrection. Dublin, Easter 1916. A Study of an Ideological Movement* (West Stockbridge, 1982)

Mary Helen Thuente, *The Harp Re-Strung. The United Irishmen and the Rise of Irish Literary Nationalism* (New York, 1994)

R. N. C. Vance, 'Text and tradition: Robert Emmet's speech from the dock', *Studies: an Irish Quarterly Review* (Summer, 1982), no. 282, 185–191

— *Irish Literature: a Social History of Irish Literature. Tradition, Identity and Difference* (Oxford, 1990)

W. F. Wakeman, *Graves and Monuments of Illustrious Irishmen* (Dublin, 1886)

Brian Walker, *Past and Present. History, Identity and Politics in Ireland* (Belfast, 2000)

G.J. Watson, *Irish Identity and the Literary Revival* (London, 1979)

— 'The Politics of Ulysses', in Robert D. Newman and Weldon Thornton, eds., *Joyce's Ulysses. The Larger Perspective* (New Jersey, 1987), 39–58

Timothy Webb, 'Coleridge and Robert Emmet: Reading the Text of Irish Revolution', *Irish Studies Review*, vol. 8, no. 3 (2000), 303–23

Michael Wheeler, *Death and the Future Life in Victorian Literature and Theology* (Cambridge: Cambridge UP, 1990)

David A. Wilson, *United Irishmen, United States. Immigrant Radicals in the Early Republic* (Dublin, 1998)

Dictionaries, indexes, guides

G. D. Burtchaell and T. U. Sadleir, eds., *Alumni Dublinenses: a Register of Students, Graduates, Professors, and Provosts of Trinity College, in the University of Dublin* (London, 1924)

S. J. Connolly, ed., *The Oxford Companion to Irish History* (Oxford, 1998)

Edward Keane, P. Beryl Phair and T. U. Sadleir, eds., *King's Inns Admission Papers, 1607–1867* (Dublin, 1982)

Iain McCalmain, ed., *An Oxford Companion to the Romantic Age. British Culture 1776–1832* (Oxford, 1999)

Robert Welch, ed., *The Oxford Companion to Irish Literature* (Oxford, 1996)

Theses

Maureen S. G. Hawkins, 'Heroic Kings and Romantic Rebels: the Dramatic Treatment of Brian Boru and Robert Emmet as Irish National Heroes' (Univ. of Toronto Ph.D thesis, 1992)

Anna Kinsella, 'The Nineteenth-century interpretation of 1798' (Univ. of Dublin M.Litt. thesis, 1992)

James Quinn, 'In pursuit of the millennium: the career of Thomas Russell, 1790–1803' (NUI D.Phil thesis, 1995)

Eileen Reilly, 'Fictional histories, an examination of Irish historical and political novels 1880–1914' (Oxford Univ. D.Phil thesis, 1997)

Index